Cross and Covenant
Interpreting the Atonement for 21st Century Mission

R. Larry Shelton

DATE DUE

Paternoster:
thinking faith

Paternoster is an imprint of Authentic Media
We welcome your questions and comments
In the USA:
PO Box 444, 285 Lynnwood Ave, Tyrone, GA, 30290 USA
authentic@stl.org or www.authenticbooks.com

In the UK:
9 Holdom Avenue, Bletchley, Milton Keynes, Bucks, MK1 1QR, UK
www.authenticmedia.co.uk

Cross and Covenant
ISBN-10: 1-932805-67-2
ISBN-13: 978-1-932805-67-3

10 09 08 07 06 / 6 5 4 3 2 1

Unless otherwise indicated, Scripture is taken from the HOLY BIBLE, NEW INTERNATIONAL VERSION®. NIV®. Copyright © 1973, 1978, 1984 by International Bible Society. Used by permission of Zondervan. All rights reserved.

Scripture marked NAU is taken from the New American Standard Bible®, Copyright © 1995 (with Codes) by The Lockman Foundation. Used by permission.

Scripture marked NRSV is taken from the New Revised Standard Version of the Bible, copyright 1989, Division of Christian Education of the National Council of the Churches of Christ in the United States of America. Used by permission. All rights reserved.

Scripture marked RSV is taken from the Revised Standard Version of the Bible, copyright 1952 [2nd edition, 1971] by the Division of Christian Education of the National Council of the Churches of Christ in the United States of America. Used by permission. All rights reserved.

Scripture marked KJV is taken from the King James Version of the Bible.

Library of Congress Cataloging-in-Publication Data

Shelton, R. Larry.
  Cross and covenant : interpreting the atonement for 21st century mission / R. Larry Shelton.
     p. cm.
  Includes bibliographical references and index.
  ISBN-13: 978-1-932805-67-3 (pbk.)
  1. Atonement. I. Title.
  BT265.3.S54 2006
  232'.3--dc22
                              2006013995

Cover design: James Kessell, Scratch the Sky
Editorial team: Andy Sloan, KJ Larson, Betsy Weinrich

Printed in the United States of America

To my covenant partner, my wife, Evangeline

Contents

Foreword

Leonard Sweet

Three of the most distinctive doctrines of Christianity are the Trinity, the Incarnation, and the Atonement. The early church councils spelled out with as much clarity as they could muster the church's position on the first two. This left the doctrine of the atonement to fend for itself, and to be dealt with and debated by the church's best minds ever since.

With this book R. Larry Shelton makes as significant a contribution to the contemporary literature on the atonement as the widely heralded work of Colin Gunton and Richard Swinburne, not to mention the less well known resurrection of an intriguing medieval atonement theory by the Benedictine theologian Herbert McCabe.

Whether or not the church can hear the cadences of Shelton's covenant-renewal emphasis over the drone of the current cross-fire is another matter. But the loss to the church will be substantial if the din of the "atonement battles" between the armies of ransom, satisfaction, and exemplar warriors drowns out this lone drummer.

What the church needs for Shelton to be heard is a good dose of "Bulls & Bears," the Saturday morning Fox News round-table on financial news hosted by Brenda Buttner. Whenever I watch this show, I imagine I am listening in on the closest thing to a traditional Talmud study in a yeshiva or synagogue. In the words of an old Jewish saying about the noise of Scripture study: "two Jews, three opinions."

In fact, in my New Jersey office I have a 19th century oil painting of such study. It is a quite common genre of Judaica art: the painting portrays five study partners in an animated debate about the interpretation of the Scriptures. In the middle of a candle-studded table is an opened Talmud, with what appears to be a few frail lines of text swimming in a sea of commentary, the margins of the page crowded with contrasting and sometimes opposing interpretations by the greatest rabbinical minds in Judaism. British novelist and playwright Gabriel Josipovici tells the story of a distinguished rabbi, still alive and in England today, who was thrown out of his yeshiva for being found with the kind of commentariless text common to Protestantism.[1] It was this Protestant mentality that led Peter Bales to produce a Bible the size of a walnut in the 16th century, or King James to forbid any glosses in his version of the Bible, since no voices and no traditions should stand between the reader and the Word.

In the painting in my office, the body language of the study partners gathered around the open book (one never studies the Scriptures alone) mirrors what is on its pages. One scholar is on his knees, making his case with all the passion his mind and body can convey. Another is standing in dismissive denial of the point being made. Another is slouched over the table with his head in his hands, frustrated at the fight to keep up in such noisy company. Another is shaking his head vigorously in approval. Another is laughing at the ludicrous nature of the debate. The atmosphere is charged with such excitement and energy the painting almost vibrates on the wall.

What is most apparent to the observer, however, is that these five scholars are all friends and colleagues who are building community through learning together. Hence the Aramaic name for this mode of study, *havruta* or "fellowship," which turns the silent text into oral conversation and diverse learners into a cohesive community. In fact, when a Jewish community invites you into fellowship, it often takes the form of the offer to "Let's learn together." Thus the life of inquiry and the life of community-building are made one.

The closet thing to this *havruta* today, I am convinced, is Brenda Buttner's "Bulls & Bears." Although the five or six "experts" mock each other's predictions, kid each other mercilessly, and tell each other in no uncertain terms how wrong they are, there is a respect and affection for one another that draws the viewer into the screen like catnip. When Fox News does something silly, or makes them look ridiculous, they tell the truth: "We are a shameful network, aren't we?" When someone doesn't seem prepared with their investment ideas, they tell each other to "Do your homework, then come back and you'll see how stupid that comment is." When someone picks a stock that doesn't seem to make any sense, the response is apt to be: "You're crazy for picking that company; chasing those rabbits is why you made so little money last year."

What unites these diverse "experts" into a smiling fellowship of friends and colleagues is a couple of things. First, they are united in their commitment to helping the average investor become smarter and more savvy in their financial life. They share a common passion for helping others.

Second, they all know that they don't know all. The Market is exceedingly complex, fundamentally mysterious, and beyond one person's control or comprehension.

Third, they all celebrate diversity of views as a prerequisite for growth and creativity. In the words of Frederick Nietzsche, "I know that it is not my way, but I can bless it, accept it as it is, study it, and—now that I know this—leave it, wiser, I hope, and freer." Or in the words that brought together the Puritans for multi-day theological debates, "the sparks are beaten forth by the flints striking together." Or (one more) as the Scots came to say, they had a "good crack (sounds like craic) at it"—which means a good, sharp, brisk conversation filled with fierce and fiery debate.

And finally, there is a genuine nervousness among Fox's freewheeling panelists when they start to agree too much with one another. Interestingly, the most recent research has found that the more people of like minds converse with one another, the more likely they are to end up with extreme versions of the views with which they began.[2] Much like in the scientific world, where scientists end up signing papers for colleagues with whom they disagree to "advance the field,"[3] since as Werner Heisenberg said in his memoirs "science is rooted in conversations" where people feel free to disagree, the worst state of mind is one which upholsters arguments with passive padding, so that one can sit more comfortably in one's own prejudices and preconceptions.

In the early 20th century the story circulated of two men brought before the courts for street fighting: "As the evidence against one of them was not conclusive, the order was given for his release, and the magistrate was about to inflict a fine on the other, when the man who had been liberated addressed the magistrate thus: 'Shure we were not fighting when the Polis tuk us.' 'What were you doing then?' asked the magistrate. 'We were just trying to separate one another.'"[4]

Is it too much to ask for a *havruta* on the atonement? Maybe so. My hope is that Dr. Shelton's book will generate the kind of give-and-take whereby friends who disagree can embrace one another by seriously wrestling with the nature of "divine expectations" and the divine-human relationship.

Leonard Sweet

Foreword

Todd Hunter

In Larry Shelton's work, the reality of the atonement is not in question. To the contrary, he radically grounds his analysis of the work of Christ in the biblical theology of God's covenant relationship with humanity. Jesus—not merely something he said or did, but the whole of his life: birth, ministry, teaching, death, burial, resurrection, ascension, and present ministry of intercession—is the basis for atonement. Shelton is forthright in this claim. Jesus is set forth as the one who seeks to bring the whole of humanity—not just the people of Israel—to covenantal reconciliation with their Creator and reunion with their responsibility on the earth and their future role in the renewed cosmos (Rev. 22:5).

The various theories of the atonement need to be discussed and debated. In fact, the current poor state of discipleship in the church requires that Christian leaders and thinkers find an articulation of the atonement that, when understood and accepted by seekers, leads naturally and easily to Christian discipleship and to an understanding of our participation in the gospel. It should lead to a missional attitude toward the world as ambassadors of the kingdom.[1] Shelton makes a unique contribution toward this goal by engaging in work similar to the Old Testament prophets: energizing readers with both criticism of the present state of things and painting a picture of an alternate reality.[2]

Some explanations of the atonement lead naturally to "follower-ship of Jesus" (i.e., discipleship and spiritual formation). While certainly not the intention of Calvin, Anselm, and other responsible theologians, the popular evangelical reductionisms, often rooted exclusively in penal substitutionary thinking, often imply, "Say this prayer so that when you die you can go to heaven"—with nothing else in view, thus leaving one with no imagination of, or conceptual basis for, a transformational and eternal kind of quality of life in this world. The standard tract gives readers the sense that salvation takes care of one's sins with reference to death and going to heaven, but it does not give them any concrete idea regarding living the Christian life from day to day. On the contrary, Charles Wesley's classic hymn, "O for a Thousand Tongues to Sing," sets forth a vision of salvation/atonement that includes forgiveness but envisions freedom to actually *be* the covenant people of God:

> He breaks the power of canceled sin,
> *he sets the prisoner free* (emphasis added);
> his blood can make the foulest clean;
> his blood availed for me.[3]

This is the "deep change"[4] anticipated in followers of Jesus. It is the kind of personal revolution that leads to change in the various environments of our everyday lives. No other kind of change will do. Every believer is invited by the Spirit into "a journey inward"—spiritual transformation into Christlikeness—and a "journey outward"—to love neighbor as self.[5] The covenant renewal understanding of the atonement certainly provides the foundation not only for justification and forgiveness of sins but also for the reconciliation and transformation of spirit through participation in faith-union with Jesus Christ and empowerment by the Holy Spirit that is necessary for empowering discipleship.

On the contrary, the standard sound bite of "Christ paid for our sins" is tragic because, in the New Testament, eternal life is the result of Christ's work and it is not thought of as spatial (out there somewhere beyond the stars), nor is it seen as chronological (out there somewhere in time after we die). Rather, eternal life is qualitative. The biblical writers set forth eternal life as a different kind of life: a covenantal life derived from and lived in the kingdom of God by the power of the Holy Spirit. Eternal life is to know God experientially and his Son, Jesus, in the life-giving communion of the Spirit (John 17:1–3; Rom. 8:1–16) in a partnership wherein Christians announce, embody, and demonstrate the gospel of the kingdom.

Has Shelton erred in his desire to contextualize the doctrine of the atonement for postmodern culture? Not to my mind. To me, he is firmly in step with church history, missiological theory, and the history of missions. No theologizing is done in a vacuum; all theology arises and is communicated in concrete spaces and in specific times. This was true for the early fathers, the Reformers, the Wesleys, and so forth. Different times evoke different questions; it is existing people with whom we want to talk, not their ancestors. Sure, one does this with knowledge of and respect for traditions. But we build on tradition; we use it. It doesn't use us and make us a slave to it. Some have reacted excessively in rejecting our evangelical Christian heritage altogether. However, I do not believe Shelton is falling into this ditch. He is asserting something very mainstream in Christian theology. It just sounds strange to many contemporary evangelicals who are used to hearing the gospel abridged to "going to heaven when you die."

God is not against culture. As the designer and force behind a diverse creation, he may rightly be viewed as the maker of culture. Thus, using correct and appropriate missiological principles,[6] Shelton argues that the postmodern context is important, something to which any theologian seeking to engage culture in conversation must pay attention. Having done so, he rightly says that the covenant story is highly valued, in contrast to mere propositions, and that abstract expressions of theology are suspect. It is his concern for a holistic understanding of the atoning work of Christ that drives his examination of the dynamics of the work of Christ. Exactly what is it that happens in the ministry of Christ that effectively accomplishes the reconciliation of God and humanity? A set of propositions, orthodox as they may be, does not convey the depth of meaning in what occurs between humanity and God in the life, death, and resurrection of Jesus Christ. Shelton's point is that the wholeness of that meaning is best conveyed through the central biblical narrative of covenant relationship between a Trinitarian God and humanity—not simply in the various aspects of salvation theology, whether they contain legal, cosmic deliverance, ransom, or moral example emphases.

The most important issue I have in mind with the use of the covenant story is to make sure that we are not giving reductionisms, "contextless" snippets about "how to get to heaven when you die," versus the gospel according to Jesus (Mark 1:14–15), the gospel of the kingdom. Jesus' story, rooted in the covenant, is large and all encompassing. It holds the potential to become the organizing principle and force for someone's life. The idea of inclusive substitution, as Shelton points out, maintains the objective emphasis of God's own response to Christ's sacrificial gift and brings the believer into intimate spiritual relationship with Christ, as well. This brings together the assurance of "going to heaven when we die" *and* participation in the transformational life in the Spirit for discipleship.

Shelton's covenantal explanation of the atonement leads one to see that on the cross Jesus is the Lamb, dealing with the sins of the whole world, providing the way back into covenant righteousness for any who would put their trust in Jesus and follow him. This augments, rather than diminishes, Jesus' salvation work, since we see him as also model and teacher for the servants of God. He is humanity (Adam and Eve), Israel, and the church as God intended it. For all the last thousand or so years of trying to nail down a theory of the atonement, and rightly seeing the centrality of the cross, we often missed that *Jesus himself*—virgin birth, life, ministry, teachings, crucifixion, burial, resurrection, ascension, and present-day ministry at the right hand of the Father—is the atonement, not merely one thing he said or did.

This, I think, is the way forward: by retelling the Big Covenantal Story, pouring new—not novel, but rather old-truth-filled-but-sounds-new—meaning into living as, in John Wesley's words, "a real Christian." If I am right, our evangelistic question should change from, "If you knew for sure you would die tonight, do you know where you would go?" to questions such as, "If you knew for sure that you were going to live tomorrow and live for a long, long time after that, what story would you live in? Around what would you organize the various aspects of this life? Do you want to become a full-time student of Jesus and trust him to show you the way in this covenantal story?"

These questions put the matter in a fresh perspective; the kind of relational, covenantal framework suggested by Shelton's covenant renewal emphasis forms a holistic basis for atonement. It includes not only eternal salvation but the fullness of "eternal life" here and now in covenant relationship with God's intimate offering of divine fellowship in Christ through the Holy Spirit. My thesis is that this creates the environment in which a seeker can intelligently decide for, or against, spiritual transformation and following Jesus—which is what it means to be a Christian. This new covenant relationship with God through union with Christ and the Holy Spirit empowers the new believer to move beyond forgiveness to a full life of transformation and spiritual maturity. Now the new Christian may live in and be transformed by God's "divine expectations" for the fullness of the Spirit in discipleship. This is the burden of Shelton's salvation theology as interpersonal covenant relationship based on God's faithful divine commitment and the covenant disciple's grace-empowered accountability.

Todd Hunter
President, Alpha, USA

Author's Preface

Through teaching Christian theology and history to undergraduate and graduate students in Christian universities and seminaries for many years, I've learned how our culture is constantly changing. The illustrations, humor, and even vocabulary I have used in the classroom over several decades have undergone significant change. The nuances of words and metaphors gradually came to connote concepts that were off target from my intentions. Theological concepts and vocabulary, too, have changed. A particular concern of mine was how the story of Christ's salvation work on the cross was being heard. For the last quarter century, I have been hearing more and more concerns about why God required the agonizing death of his innocent Son in order to forgive guilty humanity. The increasing sensitivity to human rights issues, the suffering of the marginalized in society, and the misuse of power have tended to shape perceptions of how historical and biblical issues are understood. My students were becoming more disturbed and less impressed by the traditional theologies of Christ's death as the necessary penalty God required from humanity in order to reconcile them to divine fellowship. These concerns are not new, but they are becoming increasingly problematic for clear communication of God's love and liberation of persons in spiritual captivity and alienation. Furthermore, the increasing distrust of the institutions of society by the growing postmodern culture diminishes the credibility of traditional institutions—such as the church, government, and legal establishment, in particular. The use of legal models to explain God's nature as justice has become less compelling for the telling of Jesus' story of redemption to this generation.

Searching for biblical ways to communicate Jesus' work and God's love led me to the covenant relationship that the Bible presents as God's way of working. The biblical concern for maintaining the vital covenant community relationship with God and one another seemed to address so many of the issues I was confronting in the classroom and in the youth ministry in which I worked. This, along with the spiritual searching that accompanied the suffering of my heart transplant experience, led to deeper research and a growing conviction that here was a neglected diamond mine of resources for telling the salvation story. It was based on loving relationships and not legal justice, although love always includes justice. The opposite, however, is seldom true. This generation is not impressed with justice concepts, for those who are charged with fulfilling them have not always done so effectively, at least in their eyes. Furthermore, those who have most needed justice so seldom received it.

Further experience in cross-cultural mission situations has confirmed my convictions that the covenant love concept is universally winsome. It does not presuppose a Western civilization view of law and order and retribution as a context for explaining God's saving activity. It is from this concern to rethink the meaning of God's saving work in Christ in a form that is biblically based, culturally neutral, and universally accessible that I present some of the insights to which I have been led. Many others have seen these same issues, but their insights have not always found their way into the public forum. Our goal is to increase the accessibility to these ideas, and to the Christ who motivated them, and to encourage the missional effectiveness of those who preach and teach Christ's saving message.

R. Larry Shelton
George Fox Evangelical Seminary, Portland, Oregon

Acknowledgments

While it would be impossible to catalog all the tributaries of influence that have forged my theological and personal development and therefore contributed to this work, I do want to acknowledge the formative impact of Robert Traina in shaping my approach to the biblical text and pointing out the centrality of interpersonal relationships in the atoning work of Christ. The encouragement of various other colleagues along the way has also been influential in critically influencing my thinking: Billy Abraham, Howard Snyder, Kenneth Kinghorn, Stanley Grenz, John Hartley, and numerous others. Particularly significant in demonstrating the missiological significance of the atonement is the work of John Driver, referenced in Chapter 8. The frequent dialogue and critical feedback of my present colleagues at George Fox Evangelical Seminary have been invaluable: Chuck Conniry, Kent Yinger, Daniel Brunner, Steve Delamarter, Laura Simmons, MaryKate Morse, and Jules Glanzer. Their support has kept me going in discouraging times.

I also want to thank the administration of George Fox University for supporting me in this project through sabbatical and writing grants. And I am particularly indebted to David Wilson, whose friendship, research assistance, and expert management of my manuscript have been crucial to this project. My gratitude must also be expressed to Robin Parry and Volney James of Paternoster/Authentic Publishing for their critical reading and preparation of this manuscript, to Susan Wood for her editing skills early on and to Andy Sloan for his careful and helpful editing. And finally, to my students over the years who have challenged me to critique, clarify, and expand my treatment of this issue. Their insights and support have been essential to this project.

R. Larry Shelton

1

Introduction: The Postmodern Challenge

The twenty-first century presents numerous challenges to the communication of the Christian message. The rise of the various perspectives of postmodernism has challenged the rational and empirical approaches to truth that characterize modernity. Serious questions are being raised about key issues of the faith, such as the doctrine of salvation in general and the concept of the atonement in particular. Why is Christ's death necessary? What does it mean? How does his death resolve the issues of salvation and bring reconciliation with God? While this study does not attempt to present a thoroughgoing critical review of postmodern culture, others are in the process of doing this.[1] But in order to communicate the gospel effectively, we must understand the culture to which we are speaking. The apostle Paul effectively contextualized the Christian revelation to a Hellenistic world centuries ago, proclaiming, "For though I am free from all *men,*[2] I have made myself a slave to all, so that I may win more. . . . I have become all things to all men, so that I may by all means save some" (1 Cor. 9:19, 22 NAU).

This apostolic principle of cross-cultural communication and contextualization has been employed effectively for hundreds of years in ministries to countless cultures. For example, each of the traditional theories of the atonement reflects characteristics of the cultures out of which they were developed, as we shall presently demonstrate.[3] However, attempts need to be made in every generation and culture to reinterpret the Christian message into thought forms and language that have the culturally equivalent meaning of the historic biblical revelation.[4]

This burden for relevance in the Christian strategy for evangelism has led many evangelical Christians to rethink how to communicate the gospel in view of the increasing ineffectiveness of traditional evangelistic approaches in the Western world. Brian McLaren, a participant in the Emerging Church dialogue,

for instance, calls for a "rebooting" of our theology of salvation to view it not simply as a way of assuring our going to heaven after we die, but as salvation within
this life that includes a radical vision of new life in Christ by grace—involving
personal life, family life, community life, social life, and global life. Numerous
other Christian leaders, such as Dallas Willard, Richard Foster, Bill Hull, Leonard
Sweet, Todd Hunter, Joel Green, and N. T. Wright are also speaking from this
same missional perspective.[5]

The postmodern tendency to reject exclusivist truth claims may be one of
the most difficult obstacles for communicating the Christian faith. How can we
communicate convincingly the classical Christian message of reconciliation and
justification by faith through Christ alone in a cultural context that automatically
rejects any form of exclusivism? What *is* effective is the interpersonal sharing of
the transformational experience of our own faith. Leonard Sweet writes: "The
difference is that Truth is not a principle or a proposition but a Person. Truth is
not rules and regulations but a relationship. God did not send us a statement but a
Savior. . . . Surrendering to Jesus is . . . merging one's personal story into the story
of the Son of God and the Savior of the world."[6]

This approach recognizes the convicting and empowering role of the Holy
Spirit in the evangelizing process. Effectively presented in a narrative/story, or
through the media of arts and aesthetics, a presentation of the biblical message
that emphasizes the loving and sacrificial nature of Christ's life will gain the attention and, hopefully, the faith commitment to Christ of many postmoderns. In
addition, addressing the Christian message to issues of human concern for postmoderns, such as for the poor, world hunger, world peace, and ecological stew-
ardship, also provides a bridge for communication.[7] Howard Snyder notes in this
regard: "The gospel is good news not only about Jesus as a person, however.
It also concerns God's purpose to bring reconciliation or shalom to all creation
through Jesus Christ."[8]

Furthermore, the power of story as a communication form must be integrated
into the task of witnessing to the postmodern generation. Logical, apologetic,
linear, doctrinally focused presentations of the gospel will reach fewer and fewer
people as this culture becomes more pervasive. Narrative evangelism enables us
to merge our story with God's story in an interpersonal interchange that includes
the hearer. As the Holy Spirit works within our story, with Christ as the center, a
collision of narratives, or "narrative convergence," takes place. As the postmodern sees the storyline of Christ living in our storyline, he or she will be more likely
to integrate this storyline into his or her own.[9] This is how the postmodern will be

enabled to experience the truth that leads to the transformation of the mind into the image of Christ.

From a Christian perspective, the divine intention of covenant fellowship was expressed in an inclusive covenant story—with all humanity created to live in covenant relationship with God and each other—and this declaration has been renewed in Christ's universal message (Matt. 28:19; John 3:16). This inclusive covenant exists by God's will prior to human agreement, although humanity must accept or reject its effectiveness. Furthermore, even when it is accepted it is often not fully realized because of the brokenness of human persons and communities. Thus, in some form the model of covenant shapes the internal structure of virtually every kind of meaningful human relationship, including the divine-human relationship with God. This relational foundation for moral behavior and accountability creatively addresses many of the postmodern's personal and ethical concerns.

The need for resources for communicating the biblical and theological concepts of the Christian faith to a twenty-first-century audience is urgent. Many key Christian concepts have been called into question, including the whole issue of salvation and what it means. And it is problematic that many of the models and motifs of Christendom have their basis in Latin Catholic and Western European intellectual history, while postmoderns have cast doubts upon that entire Western modernist intellectual and social tradition. Many of them have therefore looked to the East or to the occult for answers. The Christianity to which they have been exposed has not appealed to them for various reasons. This seems to be especially true of the traditional expressions of the doctrine of the atonement of Jesus Christ.

The postmodern culture is profoundly concerned, however, to address the existential alienation of separation from the foundations of meaning in their lives. They are concerned about how ultimate issues relate to them. In short, an atonement concept that promises to explain for them the issues of how one relates effectively to the God of the universe will require attention to their immediate existential concerns as well as faithfulness to the biblical witness. A relational theology that is profoundly biblical but relevant to their sociocultural situations shows promise for twenty-first-century ministry, as Sweet contends.[10]

The old wineskins of traditional theological categories are often inadequate to build adequate cultural bridges for communication to most postmodern people today. For example, the legal, forensic categories in which Protestant theology has developed its doctrines in the context of Western European Catholic culture are problematic for many twenty-first-century postmodern persons. Not only are they suspicious of the very concept of judicial and institutional authority, but of intellectual and rational classifications as well. The explanation that the death of Christ on the cross is an example of God's capital punishment against wrongdoers in order to meet legal requirements that are objectively necessary to maintain some inflexible universal law of justice is simply incomprehensible to many postmoderns. That is not to say that the Holy Spirit cannot effectively bring many of these persons to faith in spite of this cognitive dissonance, but if we are serious about following the biblical precedent of contextualizing the faith into forms understandable to the receiver culture, we need to look at our expressions of atonement afresh. As the central tenet of salvation, the atonement must make sense to a very relationally oriented culture. The biblical covenant forms the core of the doctrine of salvation in the Scriptures and is itself a contextualized interpersonal model of the divine-human relationship.

Christ's sacrificial act of submissive obedience to God is the supreme historical revelation of God's self-giving love. It is the vicarious expression of obedience for all humanity who will participate in Christ's life and death by faith. Christ's work enables a grieving God to believe in us again and an alienated humanity to again trust their Creator. The love that goes to such lengths to win back a "crooked and depraved generation" (Phil. 2:15) creates hope anew for a world that is lacking in integrity, trust, community, and hope. Such a positive message of hope is critically necessary for a generation disillusioned by global ecological crises and continual threats of nuclear destruction and made cynical by unending and pointless bloody wars that often display bestial genocidal behavior. In this context, we must ask if the traditional categories of penal substitutionary atonement are the only valid way of construing what Christ's work is about. The message of God's taking the initiative to seek out humanity to reconcile and love it back into a vital relationship with its Creator is the word that we must be able to translate to them in meaningful terms. The relational and narrative character of the "divine expectations" of the biblical covenant concept provides a framework for communicating meaningfully the atonement ministry of Jesus Christ in terms of God's expectations upon their lives.

And it is not only the unchurched twenty-first-century world that needs a renewed, interpersonal biblical approach to their faith. A close friend of mine told me of the struggle her daughter went through as a freshman at a leading evangelical Christian college recently. Raised in a Christian home by outstanding parents who had served in Christian leadership all over the world, this young woman grew up in a context of vital, global Christian faith. During her first year at the Christian college, she encountered in her religion classes a form of rigid, evangelical orthodoxy that emphasized a theological dogmatism and rationalism she had never before encountered. The exclusively forensic and penal views of salvation and the judgmental rejection of any alternative theological positions shocked and confused her until she was in a state of serious spiritual conflict. When she returned home for the summer, both her parents, who are themselves veteran evangelical Christian theologians, international ministry leaders, and professors with a vibrant faith at a prominent Christian university, spent the entire summer counseling and guiding her to overcome the destructive experience that had so disillusioned her faith. She chose to continue her education in a different context. This is only one of many experiences reported to pastors, counselors, and other religion and theology professors who interact widely with Christian young people. The need for a more loving and biblical model of Christian faith is necessary not only to win unchurched persons to Christ, but also to maintain the faith of Christians searching for an authentic and relevant message of hope.

The covenant concept provides an "ancient-future"[11] framework for understanding and communicating the atonement of Jesus Christ in a relational, transcultural, and community-oriented way that presents the gospel in the form of a narrative with compelling appeal to the twenty-first-century culture. As we effectively communicate the divine expectations and loving promises of the *shalom* of the covenant relationship with God in Christ through the empowerment and clarity of the Holy Spirit, the mission of Christ will be enhanced in the twenty-first century. This study seeks to provide resources for Christians to use in reconceiving the gospel in terms that are both biblically based and culturally relevant. Using the interpersonal, relational covenant concept of atonement as an integrative motif for developing narratives and stories that communicate the cross of Christ and his love to a twenty-first-century world will hopefully result in more persons responding to and fewer rejecting the gospel. It is tragic that often what they are really rejecting is not the love of Christ but the old wineskins of some of our theological language and traditions that do not communicate the intended biblical meaning of atonement in this culture. To that end of mission, this study is dedicated.

2

A New Heart: A Personal Covenant Narrative

In seeking to express the atonement of Christ in terms understandable to the twenty-first-century culture, we need to identify imagery that is culturally meaningful yet faithful to the concept of the reconciliation and interpersonal union expressed in the covenant renewal concept of atonement. We thus need new models for many of our theological ideas, particularly for salvation and the atoning work of Christ.

My own story of a heart transplant provides a fresh interpretation of the atonement that I believe works with the biblical covenant framework and can communicate the nature of salvation to a contemporary, even postmodern, audience. The image of organ transplantation is well-known in this cultural context, although the spiritual, psychological, and incarnational implications experienced by the transplant recipient are largely unexplored as a vehicle for communicating spiritual formation. Since I, as a heart transplant recipient, have reflected on the resources of this transplant imagery, the narrative presentation of my story is one example of using this metaphor to communicate some of the existential meaning of a covenant-relational understanding of the atonement.

A New Look at a New Heart

> Moreover, I will give you a new heart and put a new spirit within you; and I will remove the heart of stone from your flesh and give you a heart of flesh (Ezek. 36:26 NAU).

What was promised to Israel spiritually, I have been blessed with physically. I was given a new heart through transplant surgery in 1995. I was in critical need, having been given two years to live after a heart attack and bypass surgery. I

7

had lived three years since that diagnosis, so I was at least ahead of the statistics game.

Nevertheless, I had hoped that before I went into surgery researchers would come up with some other transplant techniques. Medical science is now very close to being able to transplant pig hearts into humans. In order to avoid suppressing the recipient's immune system to prevent it from attacking the new organ, doctors put the patient's chromosomes in a pig so that it grows up with the person's antibodies. Then when the time comes to harvest the organ and put it in the patient, the heart isn't rejected—it gets along just fine. The recipient's body thinks it's a cousin, so to speak. I had hoped to benefit from that new medical technology. There are some side effects, however; for instance, they say you tend to grow real big hips! I figured I could deal with that. But then I also like ham, and I would have a problem with eating my relatives!

In any case, when the transplant opportunity came, it was a real blessing. Driving from a retreat at Mt. Angel Monastery in central Oregon to Seattle after I got the message, I kept thinking: *This is what we've been waiting for, what we've been praying for.* I had the radio tuned to a Christian music station and was singing and praising the Lord all the way. And yet the whole idea of an organ transplant is profound—a very weighty matter. It is sobering to think that someone lost his/her life and now you are able to live because that person died. It gives you something to really reflect on. What about that person? What has he/she gone through? What is his/her family going through?

As I have reflected on my life-saving transplant experience, I have been struck by the similarities between my experience of literally having been given new life through someone else's death and the meaning of Christ's atonement for our salvation. He died that we might live; but it doesn't end there. It is because he also lives, and lives in us, that we can be resurrected to new life in the Holy Spirit.

While the various historical models of the atonement, such as the ransom, satisfaction, and penal theories, had relevance when they were developed, I believe they do not fully communicate to today's culture. The covenant model, I think, has much to offer. As a biblical model, it shows that salvation is a relational issue. Sin is a brokenness and alienation from God; and he has established, through his covenant with humanity, a way of reconciling the distance between himself and us. The transplant metaphor seems to me an excellent expression of that covenant model. I see it as an interpersonal kind of model in which we can understand salvation as the renewal of an interpersonal relationship between us and God. I also believe a theology of suffering is relevant to the idea of redemption. There's something about suffering that brings out grace, gratitude, and faith.

I think many in our society have tended to develop an attitude of entitlement: *I am entitled to happiness. I am entitled to so and so. I deserve a Mercedes because the commercial says I deserve it.* We really need to evaluate the concept of entitlement. In doing so, we need to understand indebtedness and lostness and dependence and accountability. These concepts enlighten us about salvation. Christ's purpose in giving his life was to reestablish an interpersonal union between humanity and God. That's what being created in the image of God leads to: the right relationship, the interpersonal union, the bond that exists between a person and the Father. When one is in right relationship to God, there is a capacity for open communication with God. When Adam and Eve sinned, they abandoned communication with God and tried to hide in the garden. God had to pursue them. That alienation revealed the consequences of disobedience. God never has to pursue someone if communication is open. But this openness requires an attitude of complete trust, an attitude of the subordination of your will to the Father's. In short, it requires obedience.

Sin, the asserting of our own will over God's will, strangles the relationship. It is like the medical condition known as *ischemia,* in which a narrowing of the blood vessels results in oxygen deprivation and asphyxiation of the cells of one's organs. A constant assertion of our own will—a refusal to submit, to subordinate our own selves and our own will to his self and his will—prevents any spiritual nourishment from reaching our souls. Then the life-giving "oxygen" of the Spirit of God is gradually pinched off and our souls die.

Humanity has choked off this relationship by our rejection of God's offer of intimacy and harmony with us. The reality of ischemia has become very familiar to me. That was the basis of my problem. The buildup of plaque in my arteries choked off my heart so that it was gradually starved of oxygen, and slowly and imperceptibly it deteriorated and ultimately failed. Spiritually, that's what happens when our relationship with God is strangled. Deprivation of spiritual oxygen from the direct relationship with God results in the deterioration of ourselves so that we become spiritually ischemic and further and further estranged from the source of life. And we ultimately die.

Sometimes our reaction to pain and suffering chokes off God's Spirit, and we begin to suffocate like the goldfish in the asthma commercial. We need to overcome this broken relationship to inhale God's oxygen. We need to restore the life-giving love of God. This is what atonement means: to be restored to a

Spirit-inspired relationship with God. What else does the paradigm of the heart transplant have to teach us about the atonement?

The Transplant Is a Gift

In Ephesians, Paul wrote: "God, being rich in mercy, because of His great love with which He loved us, even when we were dead in our transgressions, made us alive together with Christ . . . and raised us up with Him. . . . For by grace you have been saved through faith; and that not of yourselves, *it is* the gift of God; not as a result of works, so that no one may boast" (Eph. 2:4–9 NAU). God made us alive because of his great love for us. That is grace. God gave us the gift of new life: a new heart.

When a person's heart fails and the only treatment left is transplant, only the fact of death—someone else's death, and a voluntary gift of his or her organ—makes life possible for that person. When the medical staff talk in the background about the patient with terms such as "end-stage heart disease"—as I began to hear them speaking about me—one realizes that it is just a euphemistic way of saying, "His illness will kill him unless something is soon done." In 1992, when I had a heart attack and a quadruple bypass and nearly died, the doctors gave me approximately two years to live without some sort of other procedure. And nothing else could be done other than a transplant; there wasn't enough of the heart left to graft in any more arteries. Three years later I was still alive. That was a miracle! Another miracle was that I had survived the heart attack—up on beautiful Bear Lake in British Columbia, several hours away from medical help—to begin with.

It is very sobering to realize there is only one thing that can save you, and that is the death of someone else. You don't really know whether to pray for that or not, because in praying for a donor you know that someone's life will be lost. This is serious. And this is how serious our salvation is. However, when we admit that something is so terribly wrong that it can't be fixed, when we break denial, then healing can begin. But there must also be a *new creation*. And this new creation is also based on whether someone else has enough love and grace to want to give a gift beyond his or her life. A donor must do that. There must be someone willing to give beyond his or her life in order to save you. We were dead but God made us alive in Christ; God did that for us spiritually.

This whole idea of Christ dying for us may not really hit home until we face death. When you see someone die, you see the finality of death. Or if you've been brought to death's door and have met it head-on and said, "If this is my time, then I accept that," you have a sense of complete helplessness.

So when you receive that organ, you realize there's nothing you can do to earn it. You can't build up an account that says, "All right, when I get so many points I'm going to get the next organ." A very sophisticated system that uses computer data analysis to research all kinds of factors selects who will receive a heart. The person in need of the organ has no part in the search process. The only role I played was to say yes to the offer of new life. When the hospital called my beeper, I was at a retreat at Mt. Angel Monastery. I thought: *This is really ironic. Is God telling me something? Have I come to a monastery to be prepared for transport to the other side?* And the question of the transplant supervisor—once I was able to find a phone in a monastery—was, "This is a really great heart. Do you want it, or not?" It was as if God had offered me life and it was my choice whether I took it. I could not have earned it, or bought it, or deserved it, for the fourteen-year-old donor deserved it much more than I did. But here it was—a gift. Would I receive it?

A life-giving heart transplant is a gift you can't ask for. There is nothing you can do to earn it or buy it. You can give a spare organ, like a kidney, if you are a really loving person. A young woman in a youth group I led back in the seventies, during the Jesus Movement era, had some severe problems, and I was able to get her out of a terrible life situation, with the Lord's help, and get her straightened out and on her feet. She is doing wonderfully now; she is a strong Christian and has a beautiful family. When she found out about my need for a transplant, she wrote me a letter and said that if it were possible she would be willing to give her heart for me because her life had been saved through my ministry. I don't think I have ever been so touched. "Greater love has no one than this, than to give one's life for a friend."

A donated heart is a tremendous gift. Several years ago, Nicolas Green, a seven-year-old boy from America, went to Italy. He was very precocious and knew all about the antiquities there and wanted to see the country. Nicolas and his parents and younger sister were driving toward a ferry so they could go to Sicily when bandits pulled up beside them and sprayed their car with bullets. They were able to get away; but when the boy's parents looked in the back seat, Nicolas was quiet. They checked him more closely, and he didn't move. Then his parents realized he had taken a bullet in his head and was brain-dead. They got Nicolas to the hospital where the doctors tried unsuccessfully to resuscitate him. The family then donated all of his organs to the Italian medical authorities to be used for transplantation.

Now Italy has the lowest organ donor response in Europe. For some reason Italians just don't like to give away their organs! But this act of love totally overwhelmed that nation. This free, unrequired gift of grace—giving a part of one's life for the sake of someone else—this magnificently unselfish gift from this family, brought this country to its knees. It became a national issue. Streets were named after Nicolas. Schools were named after him. The family went back a year later and received great celebrations on their behalf. They have been emblazoned on the hearts of the Italians. A TV movie has been made of his story and was recently shown in America. As I watched it, I was overcome with gratitude as I was reminded of God's supreme love shown in his Son Jesus Christ, who voluntarily, willfully, accepted death—with all of its horrors, darkness, and uncertainty. He went through death for you and me. "Love so amazing, so divine, demands my soul, my life, my all."[1]

The donor who gave me his heart is supposed to be anonymous, but I have friends in Seattle who are mutual friends with his family. They knew of the tragedy of this family and of my transplant, and they put two and two together. The donor was a fourteen-year-old star athlete. At 165 pounds—all muscle—he could bench-press 250 pounds. Furthermore, he was an absolute star person: a top student, an all-American type boy. He was playing in a junior high football game, which had just begun. Right off the bat, he tackled a guy extremely hard and just flattened him. And then one of the other team's players blocked him really hard. So he received two pretty hard hits, though he seemed to be all right. But then he lined up for the fifth play of the game—and collapsed. The paramedics called for Life Flight, and they got him on the helicopter. They tried to resuscitate him and get him to the hospital. They tried all night to save him but were unable to do so.

At 7:30 the next morning, the young man was pronounced dead. At 10:30, I was called. I was asked to come to the University of Washington hospital as the alternate, or backup, organ recipient. The transplant team always brings in two candidates for the surgery. However, the primary recipient, who had come first, had a kidney infection and was disqualified. By about nine o'clock that night I was prepped and ready to go into surgery. As I was being wheeled into surgery, my wife, Evangeline, finally arrived from Portland, Oregon. I only had time to give her a thumbs up and whisper, "Resurrection." Either way, by death or new life, I was going to be a new person.

The donor's family had donated all of this young man's organs, so there were five transplants that weekend: heart, lungs, two kidneys, and a liver. Five people's lives were saved. His family wanted his death to mean something.

Death does mean something. Death means salvation, in a spiritual sense. The death of Jesus Christ was not merely something God did to show how strong he is, or how just he is to come down and punish with his wrath all of the wickedness that we had laid on Jesus Christ. The nature of God is not to exact punishment. The nature of God is to establish righteousness and renew his creation into his image. His concern is not to get even. His concern is to bring us back into proper relationship with him.

My concern really wasn't to get a new heart. My concern was that my body could function normally again. If they could have done it some other way that would not have required someone to die, that would have been fine with me. But in this case it took a death to bring the gift of new life. Yet the death of this young man was not some kind of divine punishment; the gift of his organ was a sacrificial offering that brought me resurrection to a new life. This was a gift of love.

The Transplant Requires Submission

Salvation is not a do-it-yourself project, and neither is a transplant. You're eligible for it because of the need, not because of your ability to do something to please somebody else. Because you don't have the ability to save yourself, salvation is done for you. You can't perform the needed surgery on yourself. You may have heard about the logger whose leg became pinned under a fallen tree. He amputated his own leg to get free and save his life. Or remember Aaron Ralston, the hiker whose hand became wedged under a huge rock and who amputated his own hand to save his life. Now those are superhuman exhibitions of courage. Most of us don't have the courage and discipline to do something like that.

But no one can perform his or her own heart transplant. For one thing, you couldn't get the old heart out. How long are you going to stay conscious after you run the scalpel down your chest? Then you get the saw and start down your sternum—no, I don't think so! Instead, you have to be willing to put your life in the surgeon's hands and say, "OK, I trust you with my life." There is no sense trying to jump off that bed and challenge death.

In many ways we need to learn the lesson of total dependence upon someone else. I was reminded of that when I came out of surgery completely dependent on machines for breath and circulation and everything else. An artificial heart pumps blood for you; tubes go down your throat to feed you, a machine breathes for you; a machine circulates your blood; a machine maintains your blood pressure; all kinds of needles and high-tech machines manipulate all of the chemicals in your blood. And all of that is done artificially and externally. Without this technology you would die, even though you have already had the surgery. And furthermore, you can't fight that respirator machine—I tried that. It is going to breathe when it wants to breathe, and it is a lot bigger than you are! "So you'll take this breath now, thank you," it says.

As a patient in surgery, you don't say, "Let me help; let me suck the blood out of this little pool and let me cut on that place over there," or, "You don't have the thing positioned quite right—let me help you." No. You learn what dependency is all about. Likewise we really can't follow Jesus without learning that same lesson: total dependence on God is required for doing the work necessary to transform us, to take out the old heart of stone and give us a new heart of flesh.

Not only do we have to trust our spiritual doctor to perform the operation and sustain our lives through the whole process; we also have to allow that old heart to leave. We have to be willing to let go of it to be changed. We get so familiar with the way things are that even if they don't work right we don't want to change them. We are afraid of change. We are afraid to be transformed. I was reluctant to undergo the transplant process. I said to myself: *I know this old heart doesn't work right; it doesn't do half the job. But it is familiar. The idea of a new heart is so scary, I can't bring myself to let that happen.* I had to trust the surgeon if I was going to live. So too we have to trust God.

When the surgeon restarts the new heart and lets the warm blood begin to flow back through your new organ, it begins to turn pink and then slowly starts to beat under its own power. It's a phenomenal sight when that new heart begins to beat on its own. The new heart is not controlled by the involuntary nervous system because the cardiac nerve was cut when the diseased organ was removed. The new heart is controlled by the chemicals in the body rather than by the brain. But that heart has such a strong impulse to beat that, when the chemicals begin to flow back in with the blood, it senses the new life and says, "I want to beat whether I'm told to or not." And it starts on its own. There is a lag without the direct command to the heart; the chemicals have to build up to a certain point. But after the demand is put on it for a couple of minutes, it begins to pick up the beat and sustains life anew.

This new life is a free gift. If we can entrust ourselves to human surgeons, why do we so often leave the destiny of our eternal souls up to our own amateurish efforts to please God and find our way to him unaided? We have to really want to be changed. Our own efforts do not keep us alive, but we must choose to stay alive. When the doctor was ready to do the transplant, he kept saying, "Do you really want this transplant?" What he meant was, "Are you willing to submit your life to me? This will mean a daily discipline for the rest of your life. In return, I will give you the wonderful gift of life—a new chance, a new life, a new opportunity to feel good and move out and be strong. Now do you want it, or not? If you do, you're going to listen to me. You're going to play by the rules."

Now every so often I get a call from Victoria, my posttransplant supervisor. Vic pretty much has control over me. She is kind of like the Holy Spirit in this analogy. I could choose to manage my medications by myself, but I probably wouldn't live very long. The drugs I take are extremely potent, and they are lifelong. Every day, every moment, I am dependent upon them to stay alive. Salvation—like a heart transplant—is not a "set it and forget it" type of thing. It requires a continual relationship of submission to the Master Surgeon, the Great Physician, who gave his own life to preserve and transform mine.

The Transplant Must Be Maintained

I have to take medicines, watch for exotic infections, and go through biopsies (taking pieces of my heart out to check them). I must keep a dynamic relationship with this whole process; it changes every day. Once we have the new heart of Christ, the Holy Spirit has conditions for living the new life in Christ. The prescription requires ongoing obedience to that new discipline—continual, fresh obedience. *God, what are your directions today?* Only every day maintenance and nurture will prevent the rejection of this heart.

Only the recipient can cause a rejection. I find this interesting. The doctor doesn't say, "Well, I think I'll have his organ experience rejection for a while." No, if I don't take my medicine, if I'm not careful in avoiding infections, and if I don't follow the conditions for maintaining my new heart, I will suffer the consequences. And it will be my own responsibility. The same human weaknesses and disease that brought death to me the first time will bring death to me again if I do not maintain the conditions for life. The ischemia, like sin and Satan, remains constantly at the door; and I need constant vigilance. But I'm blessed with a physician who continually monitors my condition.

It is the same in our spiritual lives: "But except you abide in me and my words abide in you, unless my life flows through you and yours through me daily," as Christ says, then my ischemia and rejection will occur. We can't stay close to

Christ without obedience to the conditions for maintaining the vitality of the new life. But the Holy Spirit, like the transplant cardiologist, monitors us constantly, spiritually tweaking our hearts and watching for signs of alien invasion. The life in Christ is thus maintained by the Spirit who actually lives in us and gives new life to our mortal bodies: "If the Spirit of him who raised Jesus from the dead is living in you, he who raised Christ from the dead will also give life to your mortal bodies through his Spirit, who lives in you" (Rom. 8:11).

The Transplant Inspires Gratitude

Twice in my life I have been indebted to someone for my very life. When I was twelve years old, I went swimming in a farm pond while at a youth camp in North Carolina. I was having a great time as the big guys pushed the float out into the middle of the lake. I was lying on the raft, not paying any attention. When I jumped off and started to swim, I realized we were farther out than I expected. But I thought I could make it. I became exhausted a number of feet from the bank, and I went down twice. As I was going down for the third time, I can remember looking up and seeing the top of the water above me. I was totally exhausted, and I then realized I was in real trouble. Then all of a sudden a big, strong hand grabbed my arm and jerked me back up out of the water and dragged me out of the lake. After I was able to breathe, I turned around, looked, and saw great big 240-pound Harold Holmes, a football fullback and one of my heroes. Harold Holmes has been my hero all my life because he saved my life. Because of him, I am alive.

The second person I am indebted to for my life is David who gave his heart to me. It is really ironic that all my life I've worked with young people—students— and tried to give all I could to them. And now at the end of my life when I need my life saved, one of them gives me back the life I've given. There's something about transplants, there's something about salvation, that calls you to respond to the sacrifice you've been given. It calls for faith, obedience, and then gratitude; there is no other appropriate response. Mere thanks is kind of thin. Your whole life has to be an expression of gratitude in response to the greatness of the gift that has been given you. As I contemplate David's life being lived in me, I am made aware of Christ's life transplanted in me and that the life I now live is lived in the strength he provides in me.

Our brokenness becomes the story of life. Nicolas Green's family giving his organs was an unexpected response to tragedy. That is not the kind of response to violence that people expect. They expect retaliation, not the giving of the body of the very victim himself. When Jesus was reviled, he did not revile in return. Seven people benefited from Nicolas' organs. A nurse was comforting one little boy as he was being wheeled into surgery to have his kidney replaced. She was trying to keep him from getting his mind on the operation and becoming nervous. She kept saying things like, "Don't be afraid. Think of all the things you will be able to do. You can run and be healthy." The little boy replied, "Don't talk to me. I'm not thinking of anything but Nicholas. He saved my life."

This is the meditation of worship. This is gratitude. It is the worshipful contemplation of the one who died for us. The face of Jesus Christ is our hope. In turn, the response to a life freely given is gratitude, faith, and obedience. So what a new heart really means is that we have a new sense of total dependency and submission. We have an abiding need for daily spiritual discipline. And we have an undiminishing gratitude to the one whose gift gives us new life. You are not your own. You have been given to God in Christ's sacrifice for you. Therefore, glorify God in your bodies. Amen.

3

Understanding Divine Expectations

A covenant relationship involves divine commitment and human obligation. But although the term *covenant* is a central and well-known concept within biblical theology, the broader unchurched twenty-first-century culture does not recognize it. "Divine expectations" may be a more useful label today. In a relationship between two persons, each has expectations about its meaning for the other. What kind of relationship is it? Is it formal or informal? Is it most likely to lead to friendship, business opportunities, or possibly romance? What kind of accountability to the other person does it imply? What are its boundaries? Without some idea of the answers to these questions, the relationship will create anxiety or uncertainty in those involved in it. In fact, people often clarify the boundaries and accountabilities for their relationship by either formally or informally establishing the purpose of the relationship. For example, a man and woman may agree that they are attracted to each other and would like to formalize the arrangement in some way, perhaps even by becoming engaged. When the relationship begins to become defined with a sense of expectations, boundaries, and accountabilities for the partners, a covenant is being formed.

The tension between divine commitment and human obligation is the core of the covenant motif.[1] It is the context in which the theme of salvation is developed, and its dynamic appeal lies in its interpersonal nature. God is presented as a personal Being who interacts with those persons created in the divine image. In Abraham's vision, God made specific promises to him: "On that day the LORD made a covenant with Abram and said, 'To your descendants I give this land, from the river of Egypt to the great river, the Euphrates'" (Gen. 15:18).

What is a covenant? It is a formal or informal agreement between two parties that stipulates the nature and purpose of the agreement, the expectations of the arrangement, and the accountability of the parties for the consequences of failure to fulfill the terms of the agreement. If the agreement is more impersonal and exclusively for the purpose of a business transaction, it is usually called a contract, and the terms of the agreement may be enforceable by civil law. A covenant is more of an interpersonal agreement based on the goodwill and trust that exists between those involved in it.

The covenant theme is the perspective from which all atonement metaphors may most effectively be evaluated, as we will demonstrate. The key issue and divine objective in the biblical teaching on salvation is the restoration of covenant fellowship, not simply the removal of guilt. The disposition of guilt and sin is part of the salvation process, but not the entire issue. Covenant fellowship with God is the goal for which humanity was created and which it has lost as a result of its fallenness. The key question for all atonement theories, then, is how this alienation from God can be overcome and the covenant relationship restored. The idea that the Creator of the universe intended to enter into relationships with the humans he created is best illustrated through the metaphor of the covenant. Michael Lodahl says:

> These ideas about relationship are no better demonstrated than in the Bible's stories of the covenants (Lat., **co** = together; **vene** = come) that God initiates. The idea that God is the God of covenants, of pacts or agreements, is much too often ignored in theology to its own detriment. To say that God is a covenantal God is to suggest a divine interest in our cooperation, a divine commitment to partnership, a divine power that is empowering and affirming of the other. A biblical theology of covenant relationships would suggest that God is not interested in performing solos. Instead, He invites our participation, our cooperation, in the tasks of creation and redemption. Of course, God's very act of creating the universe as other, and of creating us as others from himself, is what makes covenant relationship possible.[2]

Those metaphors for salvation concepts that arise from cultural and intellectual contexts outside the covenant matrix suffer from foreign and alienating elements that intrude impersonal models into the atonement mix. For example, the forensic metaphors that interpret the legal aspects of biblical teaching in terms of objective civil law categories tend to distort the interpersonal character of the legal elements of the covenant (hereafter denoted as "Law").[3] The biblical covenant idea may most effectively be used to serve as a hermeneutic that evaluates all the atonement metaphors, not vice versa. The covenant itself was the primary contextual framework God used to communicate and interpret divine love to an alienated humanity in terms they could understand.[4] This precedent already establishes the mission purpose of the atonement and its models. The various expressions of covenant love in the Bible—to Adam, Abraham, Moses, David, and others—are specific applications of the nature of God's "divine expectations" for humanity in general and Israel in particular.

Metaphors that introduce elements alien to covenant thinking—such as civil law, feudal hierarchies, governmental models, and retributive vengeance—suffer from allowing the cultural elements to diminish the faithfulness to the biblical ideas they represent. Furthermore, the more culturally conditioned the metaphors are, the less universal and timeless they become—being mere fads at the extreme, such as the "What would Jesus do?" (WWJD) theme, which has become popular in recent years. The historical background to this seemingly innocent expression of folk piety is the liberal moral influence point of view of Charles M. Sheldon in his very popular novel of a century ago.[5] The strongest metaphors are the ones that are universal, inductive to the text, and translatable into a variety of cultural settings. Steven McKenzie observes:

> It is through the series of covenants in the Hebrew Bible especially that we learn of God's desire to establish a relationship with humans and see the history of the divine commitment to humans that supplies one side of the covenantal relationships. At the same time, in the Hebrew Bible we come to understand better what God wants of humans—the human obligation that God imposes on covenantal partners. While Christians no longer follow the ritual practices prescribed in the Hebrew Bible (such as sacrifice), they do value the same virtues and internal qualities that the Hebrew Bible lauds. . . . Many of these are ideals associated with covenant.[6]

Faith-union with Christ, new life in the Spirit, and a transfer of lordship from sin and flesh to the Spirit of Christ, as presented in Romans 6 and 8, are all a part of the atonement process of a covenant restoration of relationship. To understand the atonement exclusively as a legal satisfaction of a penalty, as is often the case in popular understanding, is to miss the rich theology of the spirituality of interpersonal union with the Christ, not only through the cross but also through the resurrection. It also serves to minimize the profound role of the Holy Spirit in the reconciliation and regenerative process of the new life in Christ. The divine expectations of the Trinity for accomplishing salvation for humanity are met not simply with the satisfaction of a penalty, but through repentance and faith result-ing in a reconciled relationship of obedience and faith-union with Jesus Christ.[7]

It is also crucial that we understand the entire salvation process in the Trinitarian sense of divine unity and cooperative activity after the process of cre-ation itself. As part of the whole salvation process in the eternal mind of God, the atonement of Jesus Christ must be seen not as a contest or standoff between God the Father and Christ the Son, but as a unified action on the part of the Godhead in which each divine person fully participates in the restoration of humanity. Any view of atonement that tends to pit members of the Trinity against each other is not a faithful representation of either biblical or theological history.[8] Henry Spaulding II is undoubtedly correct in noting that Wesleyan-holiness theology after John Wesley, for example, has been notoriously deficient in reflecting on a Trinitarian ontology other than in "purely experiential-expressive ways." This is also true in various ways of the rest of evangelical theology. As Spaulding notes, the satisfaction and penal theories of the atonement, which are virtually ubiqui-tous in evangelical circles, have reflected a deficient Trinitarianism in assuming that the "real problem in the atonement is with God. . . . Inevitably this pits Jesus against the Father." He goes on to say that this is "sub-Trinitarian" and perhaps even "anti-Trinitarian."[9]

The emphasis on a "social Trinity" by Stanley Grenz, on the other hand, provides a perspective that is consistent with a biblical covenant relational under-standing of the Godhead and the divine/human relationship.[10] The biblical cov-enant relationship motif is helpful in explicating the relationships of the social Trinity and the cooperative partnering of the Godhead in the work of creation and salvation. In fact, the covenant concept may well be so effective in forming a pic-ture of God's relationship with humanity because it is first of all the dynamic, re-ciprocal, and faithful relational pattern observed within the Trinity itself. In John 10:30, Jesus says, "I and the Father are one" (NAU). In John 16:14, Jesus promises, speaking of the Holy Spirit, "He will glorify Me, for He will take of Mine and will disclose *it* to you" (NAU). And Paul writes, "The Spirit Himself testifies with our spirit that we are children of God" (Rom. 8:16 NAU). In other words, as the members of the Trinity represent and complement each other in the community of the Godhead, we are created in the image of the Godhead, to reflect also that social, covenantal, relational community as a part of that image.

There is also a need to consider other concerns about the penal interpretations that some have associated with the atonement idea itself. For example, feminist objections to the concept of atonement relate to the perceived abuse of power.[11]

Rita Brock expresses concern that the predominant models of the atonement teach that God's character comes across as a "paradigm of parental punishment . . . (at the expense of) 'the one perfect child' . . . The shadow of the punitive father must always lurk behind the atonement. He haunts images of forgiving grace."[12] This perception of violence in the penal model tends to make it vulnerable to distortions or even to rejection of the reality of the atonement itself, particularly for those with a history of domestic abuse. Others from the peace traditions, such as Denny Weaver, also perceive an anomaly between God's nature and the penal view, which Weaver addresses through a "narrative Christus Victor" model.[13] The covenant perspective avoids these concerns with the concept of participation and the *ḥesed* (union) of covenant love. The divine-human relationship cannot avoid the idea of God's power over creation, but it can introduce redemptive concepts of therapeutic healing of abusive wounding, reevaluate the appropriate use of power, and correct concepts of sexism which tend to connect God exclusively with attributes of maleness. Covenant thinking can provide a context in which this kind of critical reconceptualizing of atonement can be accomplished. This sets us free to find new metaphors for old truths—for example, viewing organ transplants as metaphors for sacrifice, understanding therapeutic Eastern Christian models for salvation experience, picturing salvation as the restoration of the image of God, and understanding submission and sacrifice as heroic self-giving rather than affirmation of dominance and abuse. Such concepts seem more true to the foundational biblical context than are the more forensically oriented, merit-transference themes found in the tradition of the satisfaction and penal substitutionary atonement models.

In what follows, we will examine three key aspects of the biblical concept of covenant that relate most closely to the atonement. We will later use aspects of the divine-human encounter as criteria for evaluating various atonement theologies against the biblical patterns.

God Expects to Have a Relationship with Persons

God reveals himself in the Old Testament as being transcendent over the world as its Creator.[14] Yahweh is holy, righteous, and loving and stands in direct relationship with the world. He relates to the world as the Giver of Life and interacts with people because they all live by divine power and need God's love, mercy, and grace. This relationship of interpersonal communion is categorically different from any other conceptions of God in the ancient world. This was not just a legal relationship. Yahweh characterized his relationship to Israel thus:

> The LORD, the LORD, the compassionate and gracious God, slow to
> anger, abounding in love and faithfulness, maintaining love to thou-
> sands, and forgiving wickedness, rebellion and sin. Yet he does not
> leave the guilty unpunished. . . . I am making a covenant with you.
> Before all your people I will do wonders never before done in any
> nation in all the world (Ex. 34:6–7, 10).

Described in profoundly personal and intimate terms, such as *hesed* (union)
and *'emeth* (faithfulness, steadfastness), this intimate bond of loving, faithful
union between God and humans provides a safeguard for even the most threat-
ening and distressing situations of life. On the basis of this love, God expresses
the relationship with Israel in the form of a covenant (Ex. 19:4ff). This covenant
with Israel is a token of divine love, of the communion between Yahweh and
the people. Though unspoken, this relationship of covenant-union had existed
between God and humans since creation, as expressed in the intimate communion
with Adam and Eve in the garden.[15] In fact, the divine/human relationship finds
expression in the creation of humanity as the image of God. The Genesis narrative
describes the relationship in this way:

> God created man in his own image, in the image of God he created
> him; male and female he created them.
>
> God blessed them and said to them, "Be fruitful and increase in
> number; fill the earth and subdue it." (Gen. 1:27–28)

And again:

> When God created man, he made him in the likeness of God. He cre-
> ated them male and female and blessed them. And when they were
> created, he called them "man." (Gen. 5:1–2)

In the ancient Near East, the purpose and function of the concept of "image"
consisted of representing someone. An image, or statue of a god, was considered
the real presence of that god. Addressing prayers to it was the equivalent of addressing the god it represented. In Egypt, the term "image" was first applied to
a man who was supposedly generated from the divine world and functioned as
the representative of the gods. But it is exclusively in the Old Testament that the
idea of humanity functioning as the representative of God appears. Thus, as the
"image of God" humanity serves as the ambassador or intermediary of God on
earth. Humanity expresses this intermediary role in dominion over the animals
and nature.[16]

This representative role requires, further, that humanity remain in relationship with and in dependence upon God, for whom it is the only representative. Old Testament theologian Edmond Jacob says in this regard: "To remain an image man must maintain his relationship with God, he must remember that he is only an ambassador and his dominion over creation will be effective only in proportion as that relationship becomes more real."[17]

The central element of being created in God's image is humanity's being in relationship with the Creator. The divine motivation for creation was love, which establishes the foundation for this relationship with Yahweh and mirrors the interaction of the Godhead and allows humans the privilege of "response-ability" in interpersonal dialogue with God. The loving, relational aspect of this divine image is extended to the human couple he has created. They are created "male" and "female" (Gen. 1:27): that is, with the capacity for relationship with each other, not only sexually, but also in loving partnership at every level of their existence, as the Godhead is interrelated as a social Trinity.[18] This ability to dialogue is at the heart of the image of God. "God creates us for conversation, for an ongoing dialogue with the rough-and-tumble of historical existence," says Lodahl.[19] It is this interactivity of interpersonal dialogue which enables humans also to respond to God's loving initiative of a covenantal relationship. We are created for conversation with God, and we are answerable for our relationship to him.[20] This accountability to covenant expectations is uniquely available to the human creature within all the created order. This relationship of coming into being by the inbreathing of the divine Spirit is what sets humans apart from the rest of the animal creation. This gives us the sense of self-identity as we receive that identity from mirroring the divine image. We learn who we are by the response of others toward us. When that Other is God, and when that appraisal is "very good," humanity is blessed with a secure self-image patterned after God's own character.[21]

This loving relationship with Yahweh and each other forms humanity into a community, which is a major expression of the covenant concept. Indeed, since man could not find community with the created animals, God creates woman as his equal. Looking at her in admiration, the man says, "This is now bone of my bones and flesh of my flesh" (Gen. 2:23). In this fellowship humans find their fullness of life. The creation was not complete until the family relationship was put in place. This expression of the family as an image of the divine communion is further worked out in the Old Testament in the esteem in which family relations are held. The family is the constitutive element in the life of the tribe and the larger community. The nation itself is an extension of the family community.

Based on the spiritual relationship as fellow-worshipers and images of Yahweh, the family, tribe, and nation enjoy community based on the common covenant relationship with the Creator. In its religious expression, Israel's family is formed into a congregation of those called by God's decree. It was made uniquely God's people by the covenant with Abraham, linked together not only by blood ties but by the spiritual ties of covenant fellowship as the creation of God.[22]

As the divine representative living in interpersonal relationship and dialogue with the Creator, humanity is also endowed with responsibility for the maintenance of the created order. God's commission to "fill the earth and subdue it" (Gen. 1:28) is a call for partnership in creation. Obedience is called for as the boundary requirement for this covenant relationship. Humanity is not to exploit the resources of creation, but to be God's representative partners in caring for natural resources. This care is related to humanity's role in naming the animals, participating in giving structure to chaos. In like manner we, too, have a role in and accountability for continuing to bring order to God's creation.[23] This partnership in creation and management of the earth is based on loving accountability to and dialogue with the Creator. At the point where humanity rebels against this assignment, the relationship of "image" in partnership with God is endangered because the trust and ecological accountability upon which it is based is eroded.

The implications of the loss or distortion of the image of God relationship resulting from disobedience are catastrophic for humanity. The forfeiture of humanity's role as divine representative, the distortion of relationship with the rest of creation, and the deprivation of self-identity resulting from the loss of God as a mirror for self-understanding all bring into existence a dysfunctionality in the divine-human relationship that must be healed. Guilt and shame accompany the demise of unspoiled reality and unlimited possibilities. This only compounds the alienation from God and self. A profound sense of loss accompanies the estrangement from God, the source of being. The attitudes and behaviors known as "sin" now characterize relationships.[24] This thwarts God's divine expectations for a relationship with humanity and firmly establishes the need for a means of restoration of a healthy, loving relationship with God.

Covenant Expresses Trinitarian Spirituality

The covenant community of the Godhead brought creation into existence out of the loving mutuality of the divine will. God as Creator, the Word which spoke creation into existence, and the Spirit brooding over chaos define a cooperative relationship throughout both the Old and New Testaments (Gen. 1:1–3; John 1:1–4;

1 John 1:1–3). Yahweh, the Spirit of God, and messianic references indicate the unity-in-diversity activity of a Trinitarian Godhead. The numerous references to these different ministries of God express the covenant concept in the form of community, which finds expression in the community of Israel and its spiritual life of covenant obedience, seen in both personal piety and community religious expression.

As the new covenant finds its definition in the ministry of Jesus, the Trinitarian nature of God is more clearly defined. This participation of unity in diversity is expressed in Christian theology as *perichoresis*, the intercommunion and participation of the Godhead among itself. In the baptism of Jesus, for example, the Father is heard to speak, the Son is spoken about, and the Spirit appears as a dove. Here we find the diverse members of the Godhead engaged in a unified sacramental activity simultaneously. Matthew reports the incident thus: "As soon as Jesus was baptized, he went up out of the water. At that moment heaven was opened, and he saw the Spirit of God descending like a dove and lighting on him. And a voice from heaven said, 'This is my Son, whom I love, with him I am well pleased'" (Matt. 3:16–17).

In this baptism the covenant finds the fulfillment of its promises for a restoration of the relationship between humanity and its Creator. Jesus, who is God, takes on his identity as "the one, true Israelite" and true humanity in continuity with John's prophetic expression of the servant who is obedient to the covenant.[25]

God desires and makes it possible for us to have a restored and vital relationship with him through the atonement of Christ and the creative ministry of the Holy Spirit. This is a Trinitarian understanding of the work of salvation that maintains the unity of the Godhead in the process of reconciling and transforming persons into the image of Christ and incorporating them into the community of faith. This growth in spirituality under the direction and power of the Holy Spirit must be based in an understanding of Scripture that affirms the full process of salvation. This spirituality includes not only the forgiveness of the guilt of sin, but the restoration of the loving oneness with God which is promised in the covenants with Israel and the teachings of Jesus, Paul, and other New Testament writers. This process of renewal of relationship with God is called "atonement."

God Expects Us to Be Faithful to Divine Expectations

The failure to fulfill covenant expectations tends to injure the relationship that exists and endangers or ends friendships by unfaithfulness to the covenant. A covenant has two sides. It does have conditions if it is maintained. The conse-

quences of unfaithfulness to one's marriage vows after entering into the covenant
of marriage are an example of this. Once that covenant is broken, its restoration
requires an often difficult and painful process of regaining the trust of the one
who was offended, which is not always successful. However, the covenant of
marriage is intended to be a positive relationship that enables the partners to understand what is expected of them in order to enable the relationship to grow and
mature. The covenant has force because its participants pledge their loyalty to it
and its expectations and take accountability for maintaining the relationship in
good faith. The love and integrity of those entering into the covenant agreement
form the basis of the credibility of the relationship. Faithfulness to one's promises
is the key to maintaining a healthy covenant relationship. In such a relationship, a
person may gain the security and ability to entrust her/his most vulnerable inner
self to the other. In such a relationship, a community may begin to develop—a
family may come into existence and be nourished by the healthy environment of
love and trust.

This is the kind of relationship the Creator of the universe offered to those
who owed their existence to the Divine Being. The purpose of God's covenant
was to identify and guarantee a specific relationship of communion between God
and Israel, and through Israel to all humanity. It is the description of what God's
"divine expectations" are for humanity. But how does this covenant work? Is it an
impersonal legal transaction? Is it an understanding between God and the nation
of Israel alone? Just what is it, anyway? These questions remain for the following
chapters.

God Fulfills the Divine Commitments

The spiritual thread that runs through both testaments concludes with Christ's
revelation as the last phase of God's faithfulness to his covenant commitments of
salvation to Israel, and through that nation to the entire world. God reveals his
faithfulness and love in keeping covenant promises in the firmly established relationship and bond of union between himself and Israel. This is the covenant-keeping love, known as "lovingkindness," expressed in *hesed* and *'emeth* (faithfulness,
steadfastness). Repeatedly in the Old Testament, these words are used to describe
the covenant faithfulness which characterizes God's relationship with the nation
(e.g. Gen. 32:10; Ex. 20:6; 34:6–7; Num. 14:18–19; 2 Sam. 7:15; Ps. 36:5; Isa.
7:9b; Hos. 2:19–20).[26]

These covenant promises come to fulfillment in Jesus Christ, who remained
faithful to his mission even while he was betrayed. During the Last Supper with

his disciples, he shares the Passover meal with them and reinterprets the meal as the renewal of the covenant and its final offering of forgiveness: "Then he took the cup, gave thanks and offered it to them, saying, 'Drink from it, all of you. This is my blood of the covenant, which is poured out for many for the forgiveness of sins'" (Matt. 26:27–28).

In the carrying out of this promise of covenant renewal, Jesus expresses the loving nature of his mission (John 17:23) and fulfills all the divine covenant promises of salvation in the atonement work of his incarnation, cross, and resurrection. Through his incarnation he identifies all that is God with all that is human. And in his own sacrificial gift he takes humanity through death to sin and resurrects them to new life to reestablish the image of God relationship. This he does through his transforming grace to a life of discipleship empowered by the Spirit of God.

Guiding Principles for Retelling God's Covenant Story

An appropriate study procedure for Christians to use to understand God's covenant story will involve openness to truth, creative approaches to the proclamation of the gospel, the contextualizing of biblical realities, and an inductive attitude which resists the intrusion of alien categories into biblical revelation.[27] A fresh examination of the usefulness of the biblical covenant model may well reveal a satisfactory context for describing God's work in terms that are culturally relevant today. John Calvin was fond of talking about what he called "divine accommodation." Because God loves us and wants to be in relationship to us, he accommodates to our level of understanding. Calvin put it this way: "God lisps to us." That is, God willingly alters the divine speech, speaking through ordinary means that we can understand.[28] The biblical concept of covenant describes an interpersonal relationship, and the biblical metaphors for salvation, such as husband-wife and father-son, are profoundly personal. In order to think clearly about the nature of God's divine expectations in the covenant, we should follow careful hermeneutical principles to guide our interpretation of the biblical and historical discussion of the issues of the atonement, both in the Old Testament and in Christ.[29]

The Need for Fresh Motifs

In seeking to interpret the gospel accurately to the rapidly changing culture of the twenty-first century, Christians need to understand how this culture (or cultures) thinks. It is important to seek dynamically equivalent words, metaphors, and motifs that communicate meaningfully the content of the gospel to these per-

spectives. The proposal of this book calls for the examination of the biblical covenant concept as a possible hermeneutical context through which the theology
of the atonement of Christ can be understood and communicated effectively, not
only in a twenty-first-century Western culture, but cross-culturally as well.

Several other initiatives from evangelical scholars call for a rethinking of
theological motifs in view of the cultural shifts of the twenty-first century, such
as the "community of faith" motif of Stan Grenz, the "creative love theism" motif
of Clark Pinnock and Robert Brow, and the "recovering the cross" motif of Joel
Green and Mark Baker. Each of them calls for a recentering of our theological
perspectives on more culturally relevant and more biblical, rather than dogmatic
and forensic, theological themes. All of these motifs are compatible with the "divine expectations," or covenant, view of atonement.

Community of Faith

Theologian Stanley Grenz calls for a "revisioning of evangelical theology."[30]
He calls for such a revisioning to include several things: a deep spirituality, a
balancing of the individual and corporate aspects of the faith, a sense of God's
people as a community of faith, and a theology that mediates the gospel in a way
faithful to Scripture and relevant to the culturally conditioned society in which
we live. To do this, we must clarify the "integrative motif" which forms the core
orienting concept around which our theology is organized. He sees the idea of the
"community of God" as being the most useful integrative motif.[31] Grenz states,
"In the biblical tradition, the goal of the human-divine encounter is to constitute a
community of people in covenant with God."[32]

Grenz notes that the Reformed wing of the evangelical tradition has tended to
define *evangelical* in terms of its connection to the Reformers and the theological
categories of orthodoxy, while the Pietistic expression has focused more on a personal experience of salvation, spirituality, and a social consciousness. The funda-
mentalism of the late nineteenth and twentieth centuries further defined orthodoxy
in terms of a set of exclusive theological categories declared to be "essential"
to set the movement apart from liberal modernity. The "new evangelicals," after
World War II sought to recover the focus on spirituality and shared behavioral
convictions that make the Bible come alive in personal and community life.[33]

The relevance of this concern for community life is underscored by the late
twentieth century cultural shifts from modernity to postmodernity. The individualism of Enlightenment modernity is reflected in the evangelical focus on individual
salvation, often minimizing the broader community implications. In addition to

the need to rethink evangelical theology in terms of more biblical, covenant concepts, the redemptive story must be reframed in community terms, since the culture of postmodernity relates negatively to perceived institutionalism in any form. The church must be seen as a believing community reflecting the presence of the kingdom of God.[34] The Holy Spirit forms the church as the community of love that reflects the unity of love shared in the Trinity. Evangelical theology, then, needs to revision its understanding of salvation and the church to reflect the loving character of God and the new covenant people in witness to divine grace.[35]

Creative Love Theism

Clark Pinnock and Robert Brow articulate an integrating model in which God is dynamic and loving and compassionately seeking a reconciled relationship with humanity. This approach understands God's love as extending to all persons. This is a parental, interpersonal, and therapeutic kind of love, which works through the cross in a revelation of compassion, not vengeance.[36] For example, in looking at God as judge and father, creative love theism does not conceive of God as a law court judge, as in the forensic model of theology, but as a judge of the biblical type who set about liberating oppressed people and putting things right. In the forensic courtroom-type judge, God can show parental love only after the penalty for lawbreaking has been fully paid. God's wrath over sin must be satisfied before his love can flow. In creative love theism, by contrast, sin is understood more as "estrangement from God and as an oppression that impacts us from birth and from which we need liberation." Rather than seeing Christ as bearing the legal penalty for sin and dying to absorb that penalty and then transferring his righteousness to our account, creative love theism understands sacrifice in the biblical sense not as a legal metaphor of payment of the penalty for sin, but as the obedient handing over of one's life to God in loving surrender. While forensic theism sees the cross as payment of a penalty, creative love theism views it as the historical expression of God's own suffering heart for humanity. This view understands that "at the cross the three persons of the Trinity experience the hurt of loving sinners and, by this act of sacrifice, open up a path to reconciliation."[37]

Creative love theism asks how the relationship with God, broken by sin, is healed and fellowship with God restored. The cross heals this broken relationship, and restores life and hope to humanity. Pinnock and Brow explain this process as representation: "Humanity has been raised from death to life in the person who acts as its representative. In Jesus, death is overcome and life is promised in the new Creation. The *representation* of the one on behalf of the many is a key for understanding the cross and resurrection. Humanity endures death and judgment in the person of Christ, its representative."[38]

Pinnock and Brow critique Western theology for its preference for an abstract legal theory of the atonement. This perspective reads the cross through the eyes of a forensic view of God that sees sin as a violation of justice and the cross as an infinite appeasement of God's wrath over the broken law. This projects God as "an implacable judge and avenger. This implication has burdened countless Christians and created who knows how many atheists," they say. Creative love theism would prefer to interpret the Christian message "in the family room, not in a courtroom setting." The real issue in atonement is a broken family relationship, not simply a breach of a legal contract. In a relational understanding of the cross, God is understood as healing broken relationships and drawing wayward children back into right family relations. As Pinnock and Brow state it, "Suffering love is the way of salvation for sinners. Jesus takes the pain of divine love on himself in solidarity with all of us. . . . Jesus did not die to change God's attitude toward us but to change our attitude toward God."[39]

This motif brings a much-needed corrective to an evangelical tendency to see atonement exclusively in legal and penal terms. The covenant understanding of atonement provides the biblical balance which maintains the emphasis on family relationships and views the legal language in the context of biblical covenant Law rather than in the abstract, principle-centered Western view of civil justice. Also, because of the diversity of models and frequently dysfunctional examples of family, covenant love seeks healing for the dysfunctionality of the family. God's purpose is to bring wholeness to human brokenness out of the restored covenant relationship.

Recovering the Cross

Joel Green and Mark Baker, as well as numerous others seeking to reach the present culture, encourage the use of new and timely metaphors to describe the atonement in relevant ways.[40] The biblical richness of the meaning of Christ's dying for us has been seriously diluted by the tendency of Christians to reduce the meaning of the cross to a single metaphor. They say: "Even though the pages of the New Testament and the landscape of historical theology are replete with many and diverse metaphors for rendering plain the meaning of the cross both in and outside Christian communities, the affirmation that 'Christ died for our sins' has, in the last two centuries, increasingly been articulated in the form of the doctrine of 'penal substitution' or 'satisfaction': Jesus satisfies the wrath of God by enduring the punishment we deserved on account of our sin. In fact, for many American Christians 'penal substitutionary atonement' interprets the significance of Jesus' death fully, completely, without remainder."[41]

Their concern is profoundly warranted. Indeed, even within churches whose history has not emphasized the atonement as a legal act of substitution of penalty, the penal view has become ubiquitous. The Western ethnocentrism reflected in this fusion of atonement models into a single legal theory that reflects Western categories of justice and ignores the concerns of other cultures which have different criteria for alienation, such as shame, is a serious hindrance to the communication of the gospel, not only in postmodern America, but in the Two-Thirds World as well.[42]

The Heart Transplant Metaphor

In seeking narrative ways of communicating the atonement story to the broader culture of the twenty-first century, other metaphors have also proven useful as well as consistent with the biblical covenant narrative. One which has come through my own personal experience is that of a heart transplant, in which the loss of one life makes possible the saving of another.

For Old Testament audiences, the word *blood* may have evoked images of animal sacrifices. Today, *blood* more than likely brings to mind scenes from television shows such as *ER*—or by one's own hospital experiences. My associations with blood and new life have been radically altered by the experience of receiving a heart transplant several years ago. While I was recovering, someone asked me if, since I had a new heart, I would have to be saved again! I laughed at first but soon realized that although the question was in jest it was not entirely superfluous.

As I reflected on the meaning of my rebirth by transplant, I began to see similarities between my experience and the meaning of the atonement of Christ as he sacrificed himself for you and me. It was a sacrifice for the family of the young organ donor to give his body even for the lifesaving mission of saving mine. The gratitude I felt at being given a second chance at life brought to my mind many issues that related to spiritual salvation. The innocent young man whose death brought me life did not deserve to die. His death was not some sort of moral penalty. It was not a ransom paid to set his family free from debt. Nevertheless, it was an expression of sacrificial love from his family to a person they did not even know. My sense of unworthiness at gaining my life at the expense of his was profound, yet I was eternally grateful.

This lesson gave me deeper insight into how Christ's death opened up the potential of new hope and new life for humanity. God the Father and Christ the Son made possible the creation of a new being through the work of the Holy Spirit in this sacrificial act of unselfish love and divine grace. The life of Christ was transplanted by faith and energized by the Holy Spirit in desperately needy humanity which was as good as dead because of its sin. As Paul says, "But if Christ is in you, your body is dead because of sin, yet your spirit is alive because of righteousness . . . he who raised Jesus from the dead will also give life to your mortal bodies through his Spirit, who lives in you" (Rom. 8:10–11). God released them from the sentence of death, but not just by having the divine anger against them satisfied. Christ transplanted a new life in them that actually made them new creatures. As in my case, these "new creations" may have the same bodies that will eventually die, but they are "new" in their focus and function. This transformed their entire spiritual perspectives and life purposes. Thus, theologically speaking, the source of Christ's transforming love that underlies his dying for us to make us new is the character of God that is expressed in the covenant relationship with the people of Israel and, ultimately, with all humanity. After all, God created humanity in the first place to have fellowship with the Godhead. The garden of Eden story depicts the participatory relationship with God in the entire creation account in Genesis 1–3. It is all about interpersonal obedience, social community, and spiritual intimacy. The motivation for creation was the creative and transforming love of God. God pictured and explained this love to humanity through the concept of a covenant between God and humanity. God's "divine expectations" expressed the desired community relationship to be expected between the covenant parties.[43]

Conclusion

The Christian message for a twenty-first-century audience is in need of restatement in terms understandable to the unchurched. A particularly important theological issue is that of the atonement. Since it has tended to be presented in evangelical Christianity in exclusively forensic terms in a penal substitutionary interpretation, the history of the doctrine needs to be revisited in terms of biblical theology. Indeed, an analysis of the concept of covenant shows it to be perhaps the central salvation theme in the Bible. The characteristics of the atonement set forth in the covenant context provide a set of hermeneutical guidelines by which the historical atonement theories may be analyzed to provide a more integrated and focused basis for a narrative presentation of the atonement. The story of covenant renewal has relevance to a postmodern audience and is yet true to the biblical theology upon which Christianity is based.

I certainly agree with Grenz that the community is a central concept of the Christian gospel, but I would like to step back behind community and look at the concept of covenant as a possible primary integrative motif and the basis for formation of community. As Steven McKenzie says, "covenant is the principal image used in the Bible to express the relationship between God and humans."[44] Ron Youngblood concurs, "Many students of the Old Testament believe that the concept of covenant is the most fundamental and overarching theme of the entire Bible."[45] In fact, a graduate theological student who has been recently studying the biblical covenant motif said to me, "For me, trying to look at theology anymore without the lens of the covenant is like trying to watch a 3-D movie without the glasses!"[46] The covenant between God and Abraham is what constituted the community in the first place. Also, the community of faith preserves its integrity by maintaining its proper relationship with the divine expectations of God's covenant with humanity as they are expressed in the Bible. In fact, although the term "covenant" is not used, the concept of a defined relationship based on promises and accountability characterizes the relationship between God and humanity in the garden of Eden narrative.

The maintenance of the covenant was the goal of all the Old Testament expressions of faith—sacrificial rituals, obedience to the law, and love for God. Certainly with regard to the atonement which reconciles humanity with God, the renewal and maintenance of the covenant relationship with God is the goal not only of creation but of Israel's hope of realizing God's promises to their community and to the nations of the world beyond. It is from this perspective that we propose the covenant model as the "integrative motif" for the theology of the atonement as a "cultural bridge" for communicating salvation in both Western and Two-Thirds World contexts of mission.[47] My own experience with the heart transplant metaphor has demonstrated that it can be used as a story narrative to communicate effectively the covenant relationship as the core of atonement in the relationally oriented postmodern cultural context.

4

The Old Testament and Divine Expectations

As I learned the power of new life through my own organ transplant experience, I began to see more clearly how God used the concept of covenant to enter into a life-giving relationship with humanity through the divine offer to Israel to participate in a covenant community with him. The biblical writers contextualized God's message into the cultural thought forms of the ancient world. One of these concepts was the covenant, which was a widely known legal formula for formalizing agreements and relationships in the Near East. In its biblical usage, however, the covenant formula took on a distinctively interpersonal flavor as it was used to describe relationships between God and Israel. While a significant body of literature deals with the historical and critical sources of the various covenants reflected in the Hebrew Bible, the major concern here is the theological concept of covenant that is formally expressed in the Old Testament covenants such as those with Abraham and Moses.[1] However, to begin to recover the biblical richness of this critically important issue we must step back behind the metaphors and look at the cultural context in which the biblical atonement concept is developed. This has to do with the profound relationship between Creator and creature. It is a relationship of love, which has the characteristics of a covenant, yet one that has been transgressed by unfaithfulness. How this covenant relationship of trust can be restored, while taking seriously the sin that destroyed it, is the question at hand. This process of restoration of covenant relationships is known as "atonement." Brevard Childs defines the term as "the restoring of a right relationship with God which has been disrupted through sin by means of a substitution of life."[2]

Old Testament Teaching on Covenant

Beginning with the creation narrative, we see God deeply involved with humans and the world. Birch, Brueggemann, Fretheim, and Petersen note: "The God of the opening chapters of Genesis is portrayed as a relational God. Most basically, God is present and active in the world, enters into a relationship of integrity with the world, and does so in a way that both world and God are affected by that interaction. . . . The rest of the Old Testament witnesses to this kind of God."[3] The reality of a covenant relationship predated the actual formulation of a specific covenant, such as the one God made with Abraham, and the general concept of covenant relationship pervades the Old Testament. The specific covenants made between God and certain persons for particular purposes operate within the overall context of the general covenant fellowship between Yahweh and creation. We see the reality of covenant relationship even where the word covenant does not appear, such as with Adam and Eve, or with Job. After all, God created humanity in the first place to have fellowship with the Godhead. The garden of Eden story depicts the participatory relationship with God in the entire creation account in Genesis 1–3. It is all about interpersonal obedience, social community, and spiritual intimacy. The motivation for creation was the creative and transforming love of God. God pictured and explained this love to humanity through the concept of a covenant between God and humanity. God's "divine expectations" expressed the desired community relationship to be expected between the covenant parties.[4]

In spite of their sin, by God's grace human beings are called upon to be cocreators with him, stewards of creation with responsibility and accountability for caregiving (Gen. 3:22–24; 9:1–7). Instead of presenting the Creator as all-powerful and the creatures as powerless, for the sake of relationship God shares creativity in the naming of the creatures and in granting humans freedom and independence. At the same time, in his wisdom God provides limits for human behavior, establishing boundaries in the prohibition of the tree of the knowledge of good and evil (Gen. 2:17). This is done out of a concern for their own well-being. Then, even after sin enters the picture and brings disharmony between humanity and God and among themselves, communication with God remains possible.[5]

It is on the foundation of this general covenant relationship and what it reveals about God that the Old Testament faith and Israel's birth as a people are built. And it is this foundational relationship that gives authenticity to the specific covenants, such as those with Abraham and David.[6] The Law, or Torah, is the moral pattern of behavioral expectations that God gives to guide Israel in maintaining the "divine expectations" of the covenant. This covenant relationship has been described as "divine commitment and human obligation."[7] Israel's success or failure depends upon its meeting its obligations to the covenant Law. Its test of faithfulness to the covenant is its exclusive worship of Yahweh, and the danger of breaking the covenant expectations is the reason for purging those who worship other gods (Deut. 7:1–5; 17:2–7). This danger must be weighed against Yahweh's patience, however. Only after centuries of repeated covenant-breaking did he allow destruction to come to Israel (2 Kings 17). Even then, the covenant provides grounds for hope. It is because of the covenant that all of Israel is not destroyed (2 Kings 13:23).[8]

In using the conception of covenant, which resembled the social and political law of the day, God introduced a well-known formula to depict his countercultural interpersonal relationship with Israel.[9] This relationship had been established early on in the divine relationships with the patriarchs and formalized with the exodus, as God had chosen Israel for his own purposes. The "covenant was a way of making a picture out of the relationship, so that the people would understand what it meant."[10] It thus functioned as a metaphor to depict the normal, peaceful relationship that God desired to exist between himself and Israel. As the norm for the proper relationship with God, the covenant guaranteed that Yahweh's ready assistance and faithfulness in delivering Israel from Egypt could continue as long as the behavior of the people was subjected to definite standards. These standards were not arbitrary, nor did they stifle Israel's freedom. On the contrary, the Law itself was a gift of God's grace.[11] Indeed, the covenant Law was a response of God's grace to establish clearly Israel's obligations to him for their salvation (Ex. 20:2).[12]

The Old Testament Meaning of Berith

Although the etymology of *berith*, "covenant," is somewhat unclear and its usage controversial, the frequency of its usage indicates its importance in Old Testament theology.[13] Davidson notes that the term *berith* occurs nearly 300 times in the Old Testament, in addition to many allusions to the concept of covenant.[14] Etymological analysis of *berith* yields meanings as different as "bind" and "cut or cleave."[15] Thus a literary usage analysis of *berith* is more fruitful for understanding its biblical meaning. As James Barr has shown, *berith* functions quite idiomatically, according to its context. Furthermore, *berith* is virtually lacking in synonyms, and is used in very limited contexts.[16] All in all, however, the concept of covenant reflects a relationship that is interpersonal rather than an objective, impersonal statement of law.[17]

The phrase "cutting a covenant" apparently refers to the preparation of the animal sacrifice with which the parties of the covenant formalize a set of existing arrangements and relationships.[18] It provides a particularly apt metaphor for the relationship between God and Israel. The Mosaic covenant in Exodus 19–24 and the covenant in Joshua 24 are examples. Particularly at Sinai, the covenant metaphor is used to describe a divinely initiated agreement that is ratified by Israel's response (Ex. 24:3–8) and conditioned upon Israel's obedience. Only if certain stipulations are followed is there a guarantee of continued fellowship between Israel and God. Israel will enjoy the benefits of the covenant promises only if it obeys the demands articulated by God at Sinai. Indeed, the conditionality of covenantal fellowship with God is explicitly stated in Leviticus 18:24–28, Deuteronomy 4:25–29, Jeremiah 4:1–4, and Ezekiel 33:23–29.[19]

The sacrifices involved in "cutting a covenant" were not a result of any applied penalty, but rather they functioned as an oath which validated the promises and guarantees that were the substance of the covenant. In the ancient world, the ceremonial sacrificing of an animal ratified or solemnized a covenant. Jeremiah 34:18–20 describes such a ceremony: "The men who have violated my covenant and have not fulfilled the terms of the covenant they made before me, I will treat them like the calf they cut in two and then walked between its pieces. The leaders of Judah and Jerusalem, the court officials, the priests and all the people of the land who walked between the pieces of the calf, I will hand over to their enemies who seek their lives."

The Sinai Covenant

At Sinai, the relationship between Yahweh and Israel that had begun with Abraham—and even before—was formally expressed. "The Sinai covenant (Exod. 24:1–8) does not establish the God-Israel relationship. As with other major covenants (Noah, Abraham, David), the Sinai covenant is made with those who have already been elected and delivered and have responded in faith and worship. Sinai is a more specific covenant within the Abrahamic covenant; the latter remains in place throughout the narrative (32:13)."[20]

While Israel's redemption occurred at the exodus from Egypt, the relationship did not receive its definitive interpretation until the covenant at Sinai. Yahweh's offer to make a covenant with Israel was an act of grace, for Abraham had not merited the promise that "in thee shall all families of the earth be blessed" (Gen. 12:3 KJV). Yet there were obligations. Joshua says, "Now fear the LORD and serve him with all faithfulness. . . . If you forsake the LORD and serve foreign gods, he will turn and bring disaster on you and make an end of you, after he has been good to you" (Josh. 24:14, 20). McCarthy notes that Israel's special relationship with

Yahweh is maintained only as it continues to obey the divine commands. It was in this relationship that Yahwah continues to guide and teach the covenant nation.[21]

In the biblical narrative of the Sinai covenant, God promised to continue his faithfulness and aid as long as Israel met specific standards. Although it was Yahweh's covenant and conditions, the covenant took on the aspect of mutuality only when the people responded by accepting the terms and promising to be obedient.[22] God thus forbade behavior that damaged the covenant relationship between himself and his elect nation. Every breach of this Law was a personal offense against the God whose concern and love had been so explicitly expressed.[23] As long as Israel remained obedient to the Decalogue and observed the standards of the sacrificial system, God would continue to assist and deliver her. The covenant was both initiated and maintained by obedience to its stipulations, and the ritual of the sacrificial system mediated the expression of this obedience and covenant communion with Yahweh.[24]

In this context of sacral communion, the rite of blood-covenanting symbolized the bringing together of God and Israel in a mutual union. This did not reflect, however, the pagan concept of magical power residing in the sacrificial victim. Instead, the covenant sacrifice resulted in a personal and moral commitment to God and a union with Yahweh that gave Israel life and strength.[25] While pagan rituals had to be continually repeated in order to maintain the cycle of nature or appease the gods, in the Israelite covenant the sacrifice was not repeated in order to maintain a magical nature cycle, but to commemorate the establishment of the relationship and to express faithfulness to it.[26] Thus the relationship between God and Israel took the shape of an interpersonal covenant that became the basis of Israel's history.

Further, since all sin is essentially relational, the means of overcoming the curse of sin must be personal and relational. The sacrifice, for example, is an endeavor to remove the barrier between God and the person created by sin. It is important to remember that it was God himself who initiated and established the sacrificial system for the purpose of Israel's making atonement for sin. However, the sacrificial ritual is limited to inadvertent sins. Intentional sins are not covered and some may not be atoned for at all (1 Sam. 3:13–14; Isa. 47:11 NAU). For those sins covered by sacrifice, the person who has violated the covenant obligations must avoid God's wrath by a proper use of the sacrifice. In the Old Testament, the essence of atonement, or *kipper,* is what occurs in this process of avoiding wrath.

Israel's Covenant Shared with the Church

Before we proceed to examine in detail some key Old Testament passages and then the primary characteristics of Israel's covenant, we need to make explicit its relevance for understanding the biblical doctrine of the atonement today. In order to appreciate the relevance of the covenant motif for communicating the gospel to contemporary culture, it is important to see that Christianity shares the same covenant as Judaism. The purpose of the Law, the epitome of Judaism, is also the purpose of Christianity. The prime directive under the Mosaic covenant is the same as that under Jesus: love God with all your being by obeying his commands in an attitude of covenant love.

Paul shows in Ephesians that the Gentiles, who had been "strangers to the covenants of promise," are now "brought near by the blood of Christ" (Eph. 2:12, 13 NAU). In Romans 11, he writes of God's plan for Israel, which is described as a tree that has branches broken off and others grafted in. The tree seems to represent God's covenant with Israel, since, in verse 27, Paul quotes from Isaiah 59:21, "This is my covenant with them." This means that the relationship Christians now have with God is not a brand-new covenant, but an old one into which they have been grafted. For Paul, Christianity's "new" covenant is connected to the covenants in Israel's history. The previous covenants are not abolished with the new covenant in Christ, but have come to their fullest purpose and significance. Paul says that "the gifts and the calling of God are irrevocable" (Rom. 11:29 NAU), and "all Israel will be saved" (Rom. 11:26 NAU). The "new" covenant in Christ is related to those of the community of Israel; they share the same family tree.[27]

We can see in the canonical writings a tension between God's covenant faithfulness and the requirement that the people obey and remain faithful to the covenant relationship. Thus the church's interpretations of the canonical writings ultimately see the resolution of this tension only in Jesus Christ as he embodies both God's perfect grace and humanity's perfect agreement in the obedience of faith.

The Covenant Relationship and Atonement

The covenant community life of Israel derives from the overarching covenant relationship between God and the community, a relationship the church now shares. We must examine the characteristics of this covenant community life in more detail in order to understand this major integrating motif underlying the biblical concept of atonement.

Obedience and Faith

God initiated the covenant, established the conditions, and guaranteed the validity of the covenant relationship through his holiness, love, justice, and grace. However, the people of Israel also had a part to play in maintaining the relationship. They were called upon to respond with obedience in an attitude of faith and love. Not only were they reminded of their duties and obligations in occasional covenant renewal ceremonies, but each new generation needed to pledge again its loyalty to God in covenant obedience.[28] An example is when Moses "took the Book of the Covenant and read it to the people. They responded, 'We will do everything the LORD has said; we will obey'" (Ex. 24:7).

The maintenance of the covenant, then, necessitated a moral response. Yahweh promised to give the land of Canaan to Israel if it obeyed his commandments. He said: "See, I am setting before you today a blessing and a curse—the blessing if you obey the commands of the LORD your God that I am giving you today; the curse if you disobey the commands of the LORD your God and turn from the way that I command you today by following other gods, which you have not known" (Deut. 11:26–28).

This faith, obedience, and love had direct and explicit implications, which, upon Israel's disobedience, the prophets poignantly declare. Micah states the covenant requirement in rhetorical questions: "He has told you, O mortal, what is good; and what does the LORD require of you but to do justice, and to love kindness (*hesed*), and to walk humbly with your God?" (Micah 6:8 NRSV). The editors of the NRSV add the following note, "In this single sentence the prophet sums up the legal, ethical, and covenantal requirements of religion, and sounds major notes of Amos (5:24), Hosea (2:19–20; 6:6), and Isaiah (7:9; 30:15)."[29]

With election—God's choice of Israel to be his covenant people—comes responsibility. The covenant community was to be exemplary in its attitudes toward God and each other. Indeed, the key to Israel's relationship with God lay in its obedience. Its very status as the chosen people of God and its very survival in the Promised Land were at stake. Yahweh had brought them out of Egypt, preserved them in the wilderness wanderings, and continued to remain faithful to his promise to Abraham. But the burden of acquiring and retaining the land fell on them and depended on their obedience (Deut. 5:33; 11:26–32) and their children's obedience (Deut. 6:2, 6–9, 20–25). Disobedience—failure to uphold the divine expectations—would result in loss of the land and the scattering of the people (Deut. 8:19–20; 11:16–17), an utter catastrophe to the community. But the essence of the faith of Israel was not that they were coerced to act according to the laws of morality because Yahweh was moral. It was that Yahweh had been and still was their savior, and he had saved them to do his will.[30]

The ceremony on Mounts Ebal and Gerizim described in Deuteronomy 27–28 recounts the alternative attitudes toward God and his covenant expectations and their consequences: blessings for obedience and curses for disobedience.[31] Injustice and disobedience disrupt the state of *shalom*, which is the goal of the sacred Law. While Yahweh set the conditions and guaranteed them on the basis of divine lovingkindness, grace, and holiness, the people of God also had responsibilities in maintaining the covenant relationship.

While it is clear the covenant structure was not egalitarian, or equal, debate continues on whether the covenant was bilateral or unilateral, conditional or unconditional. Although we can see elements of both, since each party to the covenant had responsibilities for its maintenance, the Old Testament covenant structure appears to have been conditional, not unconditional. While the covenant was divinely ordained (Ex. 6:7), it was also conditioned upon the human obligation to accept its demands and fulfill them (Ex. 19:5–8; 24:7–8).[32] The tragic consequences that followed the fallacy of believing that the covenant was unconditional are seen in the messages of the prophets during the time of the fall of the northern and southern kingdoms.

The expectation of obedience in the covenant relationship was not understood as a drudgery, however. Sanders points out that obedience not only maintains participation in the covenant, but also demonstrates that one loves God. Not only is it the proper behavior, fulfilling the commandments is Israel's response to the God who chose to redeem them. Israel's obedience expresses its motives and attitude of gratitude toward God.[33] Through obeying, with an attitude of faith, the behavioral laws as well as the ceremonial rituals of sacrifice, Israel conforms to God's covenant expectations; and their sacrifices remove any reason for alienation from God, so that any wrath they have incurred is expiated—that is, removed as a barrier to covenant fellowship.

Covenant Kingdom and Community

The covenant relationship represents a religion of the heart and the family that affected a person's entire being. In the security of the covenant laws and promises, Israel flourished as a people in community with God. Brueggemann says, "This 'being with' is not merely ethical, cognitive, or intellectual, as a thin, Protestant theology of the word might have it, but it is holistic and involves the full engagement of the whole person in the gathered community."[34] The people of Israel are Yahweh's "special property" because he has a covenantal relationship with them. God says in Amos 3:2a, "You only have I chosen of all the families of the earth." His care and provision for them in the covenant community led them toward the covenant goal of *shalom*. In this relationship of community fellowship with God, Israel experienced his care and provision. On the other hand, with relationship comes responsibility. Because of their sinfulness in exploiting their familiarity with God's ways, their presumptuousness becomes their downfall, as God goes on to say in Amos 3:2b: "Therefore, I will punish you for all your sins."

God desired Israel to live in a community relationship with himself and each other. This community drew no clear line to exclude strangers but absorbed outsiders into its ranks. Furthermore, readiness to submit to the will of the God of the covenant was the requirement for admission, not natural kinship.[35] The key to entrance into the covenant was faith in Yahweh and subordination to his Law which was signified and sealed by circumcision (Gen. 17:11–12). The spiritual lineage of Abraham participated in the covenant by faith, not merely by being his physical descendants. Others who were not Israelites were to be included in the blessings of Abraham, for Yahweh had said that all the nations would be blessed through him (Gen. 12:3). In fact, the covenant community reflects a different sort of social life and practice. While repudiating the conventional modes of exploitative and hierarchical social organizations, Israel adopted core community values of equity, justice, and compassion.[36]

Yahweh can be known and desires to be known by his people in the covenant. So, in Jeremiah, Yahweh connects Israel's knowledge of him with those characteristics described by the covenantal requirements. The prophet admonishes: "Thus says the LORD: Do not let the wise boast in their wisdom, do not let the mighty boast in their might, do not let the wealthy boast in their wealth; but let those who boast boast in this, that they understand and know me, that I am the LORD; I act with steadfast love, justice, and righteousness in the earth, for in these things I delight, says the LORD" (Jer. 9:23–24 NRSV).

Thus the covenant restricts any sense of self-seeking, self-indulgence, or self-righteousness while elevating love, justice, and righteousness. The well-being of others takes precedence and even eliminates what Brueggemann refers to as a "self-arranged pattern of well-being."[37] The boasts of wisdom, might, and wealth demonstrate circumcision "only in the foreskin"(Jer. 9:25 NRSV), but not in the heart. True circumcision and knowledge of Yahweh and his covenant are known only in obedience. As Brueggemann writes, "There is no knowledge of God that can focus on the things of heaven to the disregard of the affairs of earth."[38]

Covenant diminishes the advantage to the wise, mighty, and wealthy as it elevates knowledge of Yahweh. This knowledge that comes only by covenant obedience implies a preference toward the poor and needy. Yahweh cannot be known through power or exploitation, nor will Yahweh accept the offerings of those who mistreat the poor (cf. Amos 5). The covenant may particularly appeal to the underdog and the downtrodden. The weak are often empowered by their weakness, and being on the bottom opens one to humility and receptivity to any signs of hope from God.

Covenant Law

As a key expression of love for Israel, Yahweh bestowed on the nation his Word, which guaranteed the presence of divine guidance throughout its history.[39] The Torah was the expression of the revealed will of Yahweh and the means of ordering the nation he had chosen in a manner befitting his own people, a manner suitable for their highest well-being. The negative prohibitions of the Law forbade behaviors that would invalidate or disturb Yahweh's covenant relationship with his elect nation. Hartley notes that God's holiness required that the people must also seek sanctification in order to approach the divine. God's giving of his will through the Law provided the ceremonial rituals as a means by which a sinful people could maintain the covenant relationship. It was through the sacrificial ritual that Israel's sins could be expiated and God's presence could be restored through the people's obedient actions of repentance, praise, and worship.[40] The Law was thus not an oppressive element of tyrannical divine authority, but a direct proof of love, since it gave Israel tangible evidence of its elect status and superiority over all pagan attempts to proclaim God's will (Deut. 4:6; 30:6–15).[41] God gives the Law because of his gracious concern for Israel's welfare: "Walk in all the way that the LORD your God has commanded you, so that you may live and prosper and prolong your days in the land that you will possess" (Deut. 5:33).

In the Law, Yahweh expressed the appropriate reciprocal behaviors for Israel to express its love for him. The distinctive personal character of the Torah sets it apart from the legal codes of the surrounding cultures. With Yahweh, unlike with pagan gods, people knew where they stood, and this created an atmosphere of trust and security in which Israel found strength to grapple with life in a hostile environment. This prevented Israel from falling into the impersonal and magical external rituals of the Canaanite religions, for example, and suffering from the arbitrariness and caprice of the pagan gods.

The way Moses brought God near to the people with the Law made it clear that its demands were those of a personal will seeking to conform Israel to the mind of God.[42] The concept that the covenant was based on Yahweh's grace alone provided an inherent defense against the danger of a legalistic distortion of the relationship into a mere agreement between two partners of equal status. The awe with which Israel viewed the sovereignty of this personal God as he acted in history stopped all thought of a sheer mercenary agreement or of a relationship of parity with him. Any attempt to substitute personal merit for the unmerited favor of Yahweh was effectively stifled by the very thought of the sovereign Lord of the universe condescending, in his lovingkindness, to enter into a covenant relationship with human persons. Indeed, worship expressed in the covenant ritual was Israel's appropriate response to their deliverance.[43]

Not only is the Law based on grace and given to assist Israel in maintaining its personal relationship with God, but the basic meaning of *Torah,* which is usually translated "Law," is not really *law. Torah* means "instruction" or "teaching." Deuteronomy, often called "the Book of the Covenant," contains what is known as the "law code" (Deut. 12–26). But the term *law* is misleading. It is not only a collection of laws, but contains much more. And though it contains civil legislation on public affairs, even this legislation is religious in nature. It deals with religious celebrations and personnel, ritual cleanness, sacrifices, and issues like warfare (or "rules of engagement"). Furthermore, the law code contains preaching; the religious rationale for certain laws, such as treatment of the poor; practices to avoid, such as wrongful sexual behavior; guidelines for personal hygiene; and management of finances.

The religious nature of the covenant Law, then, distinguishes it from other Near Eastern codes, such as the Code of Hammurabi.[44] The entire description of the culture of the nation of Israel in the biblical narrative does not have a civil or legal tone. Its laws have a religious and interpersonal nature. They guide behavior, they are instructive, and they have an instructive (parenetic) rather than a legal (forensic) perspective.

Rightly conceived, then, Israel and its covenant laws create a true community in relationship with God that is distinct from any culture before or since. To conceive of issues that affect this relationship, such as sin or salvation, in terms other than interpersonal ones distorts and impoverishes the richness of the covenant conception of righteousness. This is not to say that atonement does not deal with the issues of civil law and lawbreaking, but that interpersonal covenant reconciliation is clearly the prevailing conceptualization.

The covenant provided the pattern to organize the community around the Law, and in this sense it constituted the society which Yahweh had elected. It likewise provided for the institutions of the sacred shrine, cult, and covenant Law that expressed Israel's religion.[45] Thus in Israel, all law, whether related to everyday nonreligious issues or sacral observances, has its foundation in the covenantal relationship with God as expressed in the Torah/Law. E. P. Sanders points out that those who choose to deny God's right to command them choose to remove themselves from the covenant. A narrow legalism does not translate into a purely civil, forensic understanding of law, even in later rabbinic Judaism.[46] Sanders challenges the perception that intertestamental Judaism had become a purely legalistic salvation by works system in describing the spirituality of this period as "covenantal nomism."[47] As Dennis Bratscher points out, the Old Testament concept of *torah* has not been adequately interpreted in Christian theology: "The Old Testament concept of torah cannot adequately be understood forensically. Rather, torah is primarily a relational concept, providing the community of faith an anchor point in God's grace from which it can live out, in changing historical circumstances, its identity as the people of God."[48]

The Old and New Testaments are often contrasted as law and gospel, old covenant and new covenant. But law in the Old Testament can be positive, as well. In summary, the foundational concept of Torah is God's revelation of himself to Israel. As such, the Torah determines the structure of the Old Testament as it discloses the exclusive personal relationship between God and Israel that institutes a new state of *shalom*. The Law is not a series of secular commandments, nor an independent set of principles, but a description of Israel's well-being under God that is given in relationship to himself. It is thus this relationship of well-being, *shalom*, that describes Israel's basis for salvation—not the works-oriented keeping of the Law, as it is often caricatured.

This partnership with Yahweh gives Israel its identity, and God's self-disclosure places Israel before God at the center of his revelation. They become a people bound to God and to whom God is bound in a covenant relationship.[49] But the gifts of this salvation history are not just the establishment of a people and the giving of the land. The inward keeping of the Law as a positive ordering of life in relation to God, particularly during the exilic era, comes to be understood as the knowledge of God because the Law is written on the heart. Jeremiah 31:31–34 and Ezekiel 36:25–27 speak of a new covenant in which people, unlike in the previous covenant expressions, are drawn into the divine self-disclosure, and the sin that causes separation is overcome. The Torah will be understood as the knowledge of God placed in the heart by Yahweh himself. Hearts will be created anew and quickened with a new spirit (*ruach*), so that people obey the Torah completely.[50]

Overcoming Sin

Since this Law was the direct command of Yahweh spoken out of his love for Israel, any breach of it was an outrage against God. The covenant Law was based in the covenant context of relationship and maintained by obedience to its divine expectations.[51] Pagan law, such as the Code of Hammurabi, was invested with all the authority of the national god; but in Israel the Law was the very word of Yahweh. The divine Lawgiver laid down the Law personally, and any breach was a personal offense. In the new legal system established by the covenant, with its markedly personal quality, all of life relates to obedience to the will of God.

This raises Semitic law to a completely new level. A deepened sense of oral sensitivity and an appreciation of the higher value of human life informs the Book of the Covenant. It abolishes the death penalty for offenses against property, in contrast to the Babylonian Code of Hammurabi. The covenant code also rejects class distinctions in the administration of justice. Transgression of the Law carried no connotation of the formalistic, forensic objectivity and legal punishment by gross brutality as seen in Babylonian law. In Israel, the transgression was not the flaunting of an impersonal, juristic norm, but rather a conflict between two wills, the divine and the human.[52] Sin constituted a failure to fulfill one's vows to obey God. Wright describes sin thus: "Sin is the violation of covenant and rebellion against God's personal lordship. It is more than an aberration or a failure which added knowledge can correct. It is a violation of relationship, a betrayal of trust."[53]

The basic character of sin, then, is action contrary to the norm of the Law of Yahweh, a violation of the personal relationship with him. Three basic Hebrew words for sin illustrate this concept: (1) *hatah'*: "to miss the mark"; (2) *'avon*: "to veer or go aside from the right way," or "irregular or crooked action"—with the implicit idea that the agent is aware of the culpability of his action; and (3) *pesha'*: "rebellion or revolt."[54] Sin to the Israelite was unhealthy, for it rendered one incapable of living with others or with Yahweh.[55] When a person insisted upon acting in a manner contrary to God's order, he or she negated the covenant purposes of fellowship with Yahweh. This was a moral transgression, not a legal one. It required a moral antidote, not a legal one. The seriousness of individual sin was compounded by the belief that the ties of blood and common interest imbedded the individual so deeply in the community that an offense by one person not only affected his or her relationship with God, but also that of the entire community.[56]

Sin, however, not only violates a relational law, but the destruction of the personal bond with God estranges the sinner's very being from its purpose for existence, which is to live for God and from God's perspective. This fundamental distortion of purpose and being corrupts the very center of the person. In an existential sense, the sinner has forfeited his or her life. This situation so fundamentally affects the sinner's existence that the guilt of the sin cannot just be taken away. Otfried Hofius points out that the only way the sinner can win back this forfeited life is to surrender his or her life to God through death itself.[57] In fact, as will be shown later, this is exactly what Paul calls for in Romans 6 in the Christian's union with Christ.

Thus, the whole of Old Testament atonement, represented by blood sacrifice, includes all the components discussed in this chapter: obedience to the Law, faith commitment to Yahweh, participation in the covenant community, a response of gratitude for God's gracious election, rejection of whatever sin mars the covenant relationship. These elements appear in the various feasts and sacrifices described in significant detail in the Torah. The following chapter will look in greater detail at the role of these feasts and sacrifices in God's expectations for Israel.

5

The Divine Expectations in the Old Testament Feasts and Sacrifices

As new life flowed into my body through the pulsing power of my new heart, I more and more felt like celebrating the anniversaries of my transplant event. One month, then one year, then two years passed, then ten. My health returned, and in the joy of remembrance as each fifth day of October approached, I was again impressed with a desire to mark the anniversary with an expression of gratitude to the organ donor and to God. I understood more fully how profound Israel's feasts were in giving thanks and praise to Yahweh, as well as commemorating his deliverance of the nation. Yahweh's personal commitment and deliverance motivates Israel's gratitude and obedience in its response of worship.[1] The animal sacrifices, as blood-covenanting rituals, also symbolized the coming together of Yahweh and Israel in a mutual covenant union. Israel was not using some magical power residing in the sacrificial victim to manipulate the deity, which was the pagan concept in the surrounding Canaanite religions. On the contrary, Israel's sacrifices reflected a personal and moral commitment to God and a personal union with Yahweh that gave Israel its moral vitality. "Worship that is visual, active, dramatic, and all-comprehending was a thing of joy for Israel, not a burden," says Brueggemann.[2] Such worship involved both feasts and sacrifices.

Feasts

The annual feasts, such as Passover and Tabernacles, demonstrated Israel's participation in the covenant. They were initiated as ways to maintain communion with Yahweh and to sanctify life by dramatically reminding Israel of God's saving activity from generation to generation. Symbolizing participation in community with God, the feasts expressed the fellowship aspect of the covenant life.[3]

As one of the most significant forms of ceremonial response, through celebrating these feasts the faithful in Israel demonstrated their commitment to Yahweh and to maintaining the covenant communion. The Passover, for example, was a memorial meal of Yahweh's delivering Israel from Egypt (Ex. 12:14–28). These ceremonies expressed the historical character of Israel's religion, as a kind of anniversary of the historical events in which Yahweh's power had been manifested.[4]

Perhaps the clearest way to explain Israel's memorial feasts is to contrast them with pagan nature religions. In these religions the gods were identified with the natural forces, and they represented no moral or ethical values. These religions resorted to myths as a means of explaining the natural cycles. Since the earthly society was believed to be dependent on the movements of nature, the worshipers believed that the faithful performance of ritual acts effected the renewal of the cosmic powers and enabled their activity. The worshipers used mimetic or sympathetic magic rituals to establish a sympathetic relationship and to coerce the cosmic powers to act favorably. The cult or ritual became the means of maintaining the status quo and keeping the cycle of nature in motion. New vitality could be given to the natural forces, they believed, by mimicking natural processes such as the giving of life. There was no concept of the gods acting in historical events, no sense of a divine purpose in history.[5] Nevertheless, these religions exerted a powerful temptation toward syncretism in Israel. The prophets' intervention sought to combat these tendencies and maintain Israel's monotheistic focus. The prophets never tired of lamenting Israel's failures on this issue. Elijah's contest with the Baal prophets provides a powerful example of this conflict (1 Kings 18).[6]

In contrast, Yahweh was not a localized, natural force. As Creator of nature, he was powerful over the entire universe. God was active in nature, but not identified with it. Since Yahweh was not continuous with nature, mythical ritual acts that were based upon continuity between the natural and supernatural worlds were irrelevant for Yahweh worship.

Israel's cultic rituals for the present, in contrast to the pagans', included the commemoration of Yahweh's past acts (Deut. 6, 26; Josh. 24). Israel conceived of history not cyclically, as in the pagan scheme, but as a linear development of God's purposes. The cultic recitals told of Yahweh's past acts, but seldom were attempts to coerce him to do again what he had done before. The pagan mythical cult attempted to reproduce the cosmic cycle; Israel saw history as the unfolding sovereign plan of God. The recital of God's actions in Israel's rituals was not to support the status quo, as in the pagan recapitulation ceremonies, but to challenge all of the status quo that was not in harmony with God's will.

As the feasts reenacted the past events of redemptive history, the past was made contemporaneous in Israel's experience.[7] By remembering what Yahweh had done, Israel projected itself into the past and reexperienced it in the present. This was not an attempt to recapitulate past events, but to focus on reexperiencing the once-for-all-acts of God. By symbolically reenacting these past events, such as in the Feast of Tabernacles, Israel gained a fresh, contemporaneous experience of the meaning of Yahweh's past acts for their present redemptive history. By doing this, Israel reaffirmed and reexperienced the profound meaning of the covenant relationship in the context of the community of faith.

Sacrifices

The covenant Law established the ritual practice of animal sacrifice as a means of restoring Israel's relationship with God. The alienation that resulted from sin was inconsistent with the fellowship of the covenant, and a process was needed by which the worshiper could become reconciled to God. Indeed, maintaining fellowship with a holy God, which was the very purpose of the covenant, was possible only if the people had an effective means of atonement.[8] A proper act of sacrifice had to be more than a mere outward ritual. Before the sacrifice could achieve anything, the Law required the confession of sin from a penitent heart. In the offering of the sacrificial animal, the offerer was understood to be dying along with it—not physically, but spiritually. In the case of the sin offering, the offerer identified with the victim by laying a hand upon the animal's head so that its death symbolized the offerer's death to sin, or to whatever stood between himself and God. In the other offerings, the animal's death symbolized the offerer's surrender of self to God in thankfulness and humility. The sacrifice mediated fellowship with God.[9] In fact, the communal nature of the sacrifice, particularly in the Day of Atonement sin offering, served to restore normal relationships between God and the people.

The Laying On of Hands

In his "Excursus: Laying On of Hand(s)," Hartley discusses a significant body of scholarly literature on this issue. One interpretation states that this ritual of hands *(semikah)* transfers the sins of the offerer to the animal. This view is less than satisfactory, Hartley argues, since only the Day of Atonement ceremony (Lev. 16) depicts the laying on of both hands and the transference of the nation's sins onto the goat, thus defiling it and necessitating its removal into the wilderness. This instance of sin transference has been read into the other offerings of Leviticus 1–7, which do not all have reference to removal of sin and which specify the laying on of one hand, not two.[10] The other major interpretation of the laying on of hand(s) claims that in the ritual the offerers make an identification between themselves and their sacrifice.[11] The ideas of "exclusive substitution" and "inclusive substitution" thus find expression in the two main interpretations of the meaning of the laying of the offerer's hands on the sacrificial animal's head: (1) the transference theory and (2) the identification theory.

The Transference Theory. This interpretation sees the laying on of hands as transferring sins to the animal in something of a concrete way. This understanding of the laying of hands on the animal makes the animal a substitute-bearer of one's sins. This prevalent approach takes the scapegoat passage in Leviticus 16:20–22 as its primary text, although the other sacrifices also mention the laying on of the hand (Lev. 1–7). In the scapegoat ritual, Aaron the priest facilitates the literal transfer of the sins of the nation upon the goat as a substitute for the people. But there are problems with this explanation: (1) The animal that is slaughtered as a sacrifice on the Day of Atonement is not the one upon whose head the two hands of the priest are laid. (2) The transferral of sins on the Day of Atonement is a separate procedure from the laying on of a hand (singular) in the sacrifices in the rest of Leviticus. Confession of sins while laying on the hand is not a part of the ritual of any of the other sacrifices, including the individual sin offering ritual in Leviticus 4–7. (3) Atonement is not made by the killing of the animal, but by the fulfilling of the entire cultic ritual, whether performed by the individual or by the priest in the tabernacle or temple (Lev. 5–7; 16:6–19).[12] Furthermore, while the scapegoat passage in Leviticus 16:20–22 does indicate transference of sins, we must consider the context of all other references to laying on of hands.

The ritual is also widely used in the Old Testament to appoint a successor (Num. 27:18, 23; Deut. 34:9) and to indicate consecration (of Levites, Num. 8:10). These examples, however, argue for identification and against transference. Even in Leviticus 16, laying on of hands is not used for both the sacrificial animals; the goat slain as a sin offering in Leviticus 16:15 does not have hands laid on it as does the goat in verse 21 (at least it is not in the text), even though it is used in the sacrifice of atonement. Instead, both hands of the priest are laid on the scapegoat, and the confession is spoken so that the sins are explicitly transferred to the animal. Thus the atonement of the first goat and transference of the second goat are seen as two parts of the same atonement ritual. The laying of hands on the scapegoat testifies to the goat's purpose of demonstrating the removal of sin and the deliverance from sin's power and dominance as a consequence of the work of atonement.[13] Atonement is thus accomplished on the Day of Atonement through the dual ritual of the two goats—one through sacrifice, the other through deliverance. The first goat has already been slain and offered as a sin offering before the hands of the priest are laid on the scapegoat and the sins transferred to it.

Further evidence against the transference theory suggests the annual laying of hands on the scapegoat and the laying of one hand on other animals in the routine atonement sacrifices in Leviticus 4–7 are different rituals. The purpose of the *semikah* differs as well. If the laying of the hand on the animals to be used for routine sin offerings (e.g., Lev. 4:24, 29, 33) involved the transfer of sins to the animal and then the taking of the sin-laden animal into the Holy Place for slaughter, this would have brought contamination into the place of atonement which had already been cleansed by the previous priestly purification sacrifice (Lev. 4:1–11). In this same vein, Hartley notes that the scapegoat has been disqualified from being brought into the Holy Place as a sacrifice by virtue of its uncleanness from the sins of the people being transferred to it.[14] In addition, nothing in the Leviticus text indicates that the goat sent into the wilderness is considered a sacrificial sin offering.[15] Instead, the priest performs a priestly role in confessing the nation's sins over the goat and putting them on the goat's head. It is then taken out into the desert and released, thus separating sin and its bondage and oppression from the people.[16]

In summary, if the transference theory were correct, then atonement would have been accomplished on the Day of Atonement when the first animal was killed as the punishment of death for the people's sins. Yet the entire Levitical code includes elaborate rituals of purification and preparation that accompany the animal atonement offering, as well as requiring the proper attitude of the offerer.[17] The event of the death of the first animal does not in itself effect the atonement. Otherwise, the prerequisites of repentance and obedience and the role of the scapegoat would have been superfluous.

The Identification Theory. The distinction between the laying on of one or two hands in the rituals raises significant issues. The laying on of both hands signifies the transference of something from one thing or person to another, such as passing on some special power or, as in this case, the transfer of sin to the scapegoat. Other explanations argue that the laying of a single hand on the offering identifies the animal as the offerer's own. These views see this as the offerer's identification with the animal so that he participates in the death of the animal as the sacrifice and thus surrenders his life to God.[18] Therefore, the more likely explanation of the laying on of one hand *(semikah)* understands the act as an identification of the life *(nephesh)* of the sinner with the animal's *nephesh,* which then is taken into the sanctuary where it comes into contact with that which is holy. Rowley notes that this identification with the animal symbolizes that in its death the offerer also dies spiritually, for the death of the victim denotes the offerer's death to sin, or to anything that stands between the person and the surrender of oneself to God in thankfulness and humility.[19]

Furthermore, the atonement is accomplished not only by the animal's death, but by the commitment of its life—representing the sacred life of the offerer. This seems to be the most consistent interpretation of Leviticus 17:11: "For the life [*nephesh*] of a creature is in the blood, and I have given it to you to make atonement for yourselves [*nephesh,* plural] on the altar; it is the blood that makes atonement for one's life [*nephesh*]."[20] Thus, by identifying with the animal the collective lives of the nation are symbolically offered up and incorporated into the holy so that they now have community with God.

The ceremony of sprinkling the blood on the altar and on the people conse-crates them both and renews the covenant binding-together of God and Israel. Sins are not simply wiped away or capital punishment inflicted to pay for them. Instead, in an identification symbolized by the laying on of hands, the *nephesh* is dedicated to the sanctuary and consecrated to the holy. Gese says, "In the inclu-sive substitution by means of atoning sacrifice, this ritual brings Israel into contact with God."[21]

In offering the sacrifice and in identifying with it, the sinner changed his[22] attitude toward God. As the offerer turned back to God and repented, he him-self became the gift-sacrifice to God through identification with the sacrificial animal.[23] In response to human repentance and self-offering, God accepted the animal sacrifice as a token of his reception of the offerer who had identified with it and forgave the sinner of the offenses. In this forgiveness God did not merely look upon the sinner *as if* he had offered himself, but he looked upon him as a true self-offering, since the offerer's very life had been given in the life of the animal. This is the critical distinction between the transference and the identifica-tion understandings of the laying on of hands. McKenzie writes, "We can with assurance decide the question of the laying on of hands by saying that it expresses an identification in the sense of a delegated succession, a serving in the place of, and not a transferal of mere 'sinful material.'"[24]

Because of the commitment of the offerer's life to what is holy, God did not simply consider the offering *as if* it were the offerer; it *really was* the offerer. The reality of ritual identification is not simply a fictional "let's pretend" action, but a genuinely realistic portrayal of the relational reality that was represented by the identification between the subject (offerer) and the object (offering). Thus the norm of a righteous covenant relationship is realized by the obedient and faithful actions of the identification with and offering of the animal. This relationship *is* the fulfillment of covenant obligation. It is not a substitute for the expectations of covenant relationship.

The Function of Israel's Sacrifices in Contrast to Pagan Sacrifices

In establishing a covenant relationship with Israel, God put in place a system of sacrificial offerings, each designed to express some aspect of the covenant relationship in a ceremonial ritual, or cult. While these kinds of rituals were commonplace in Near Eastern culture, God seems to have used these common rituals, contextually reinterpreted, in ways distinctively meaningful to Israel.[25] The ancient world practiced sacrificial rituals widely, as they were used to tangibly express agreements, contracts, and covenants of all kinds.

How were the Jewish sacrifices different from the pagan ones? In Israel's life, the Law was given to define the way to use the sacrifice to maintain the covenant relationship and to give expression in Israel's worship to its relationship with God. This was countercultural, in a sense, in that Israel's covenant and its sacrificial expressions were understood in terms of the nation's relationship with Yahweh. It was not just a legal contract, but an interpersonal expression of love and compassion that enabled Israel to understand its moral boundaries in relationship to a personal God who actually interacted in the community's life. It also gave tangible expression to the divine expectations of covenant living. The role of obedience and the relation of blood to obedience were also elements distinctive to Israel's covenant community. Birch and his coauthors point out:

> Thus in the offering the worshipers submit *themselves* to God. The sacrifice is thus a *tangible sign of faith*, a concrete way in which one offers the self to God; no theory of how the worshiper is related to the animal is involved. Thus it should come as no surprise that, elsewhere in the Old Testament, sacrifices are not considered necessary for forgiveness (as with the Lord's Supper). Repentance and trust in God are sufficient. . . . Hence, by definition, expiation does not involve a penalty. The focus is on the rite as a saving event. Moreover, the language of substitution is not explicitly used in these texts; the animal is not a substitute for the bringer of the offering.[26]

It is imperative to understand that in Israel the sacrifice was not primarily a means of placating God, but it served to restore and reorder the social relationships between the community and God and to restore "confused categories." Davies notes that the sin offering was also used in this sense in the restoration of lepers to full status as members of the covenant community after their healing.[27] Even though the sin offering was made to obtain forgiveness of sins, one must remember that the real sacrifice of self-surrender and repentance had to be made by the sinner alone. There was nothing in this ritual resembling the pagan externalism of *opus operatum* (i.e., the ritual itself automatically effecting the change).[28] An attitude of repentance and obedience was critical.

In this vein, Vriezen also writes: "The cult is the means of grace that again and again restores . . . the covenant relation. [However], . . . the sin and guilt-offerings can only atone for sins committed *bi-shegagah* (through ignorance). This condition shows . . . [that] the danger of becoming automatic—a danger that threatens every cultic sacrament of penance—is avoided."[29] The offering of a sacrifice is simply the overt expression, or seal, of the worshiper's repentance and renewed commitment to the covenant relationship. Brueggemann also emphasizes that the restoration of relationship is the point of the sacrificial ritual, as seen in Leviticus 16: "The astonishing claim of these texts, and of the vehicle to which they witness, is that *Yahweh has granted to Israel a reliable, authorized device whereby Israel can be restored to full relationship to Yahweh.*"[30]

Not only must atonement involve something that changes the sinner's relationship with God (propitiation), but something must also change the sinner's attitude toward sin (expiation). Thus the personal repentance of the sinner resulted in the personal forgiveness of God and the restoration of the relationship of covenant love between God and the penitent. This forgiveness did not result in a positional righteousness in which God looked at humanity through the sacrifice, but in an actual righting of interpersonal covenantal relationships between humanity and God. The symbol was the animal; the reality was the changed relationship between humanity and God. The offering really made things right with God because presenting the offering in an attitude of obedience and repentance was what God had commanded in the first place. The sin offering resulted in forgiveness because that is how God told Israel to express its repentance. Covenant renewal and salvation is about restoring health, or *shalom,* to the relationship between God and Israel.[31]

The Kinds of Sacrifices

The sacrificial system that God calls for is presented in Leviticus 1–7. These chapters prescribe the regulations for the respective sacrifices and explain the purposes of the offerings. At the center of Leviticus (chapter 16), which is also located at the center of the Pentateuch, is introduced the legislation on the Day of Atonement. Its strategic location signals its importance as the culmination of the mandatory system that affects the entire community of Israel. It is important to understand the theological significance of these sacrifices in context because the New Testament assumes them as presuppositions for several theological points relating to the atonement of Jesus Christ.

The entire system of organized service to a deity is known as the "cult." In Israel's case, the cult included the Tent of Meeting, furniture, artifacts, the priests, rituals, sacrifices, feasts, and sacred seasons in the calendar. The rituals performed at the sanctuary were the formal part of worship that was intended to develop spiritual communion between God and Israel.[32] The first three kinds of sacrifices could be presented as the offerer desired to express praise, gratitude, and fellowship with God. These were the burnt offering, grain offering, and fellowship offering. The last three were for the expiation of sin: the sin offering, guilt offering, and the sacrifice on the Day of Atonement.

The Burnt Offering or Whole Offering (Lev. 1:3–17). The burnt, or whole, offering was the main sacrifice offered by individuals and the entire community. It was offered daily in the morning and evening, and at additional times on high days such as the Sabbath, Day of Atonement, and festivals. This was a more expensive offering than the others, since nothing of the offering was returned to the offerer. This offering involved expiation in rendering the offerer acceptable to God and therefore free to offer the fellowship offering and celebrate in praise to Yahweh. Also, the aroma rising from the offering may have been understood as stimulating Yahweh's memory, thus reminding him to be favorably disposed toward the worshipers.[33]

The Grain Offering (Lev. 2:1–16). While it could be made on its own for thanksgiving, the grain offering was usually made along with an animal sacrifice, thus making a meal of the bread and meat. At the Feast of Weeks, one presented a new grain offering consisting of two loaves baked out of fine flour with the addition of yeast to express the joy of harvest time.[34]

The Fellowship Offering or Offering of Well-being (Lev. 3:1–17). A fellowship offering, or offering of well-being, was usually made by an individual as an expression of reverence for Yahweh. On special occasions, these sacrifices were made quite freely. There seems to have been a couple of reasons for this: (1) the joyful nature of the sacrifice fit in well with the nature of the festivities; and (2) it provided meat for the feasting. There were three kinds of offerings of well-being: a praise offering (to praise Yahweh), a votive offering (to fulfill a vow made to Yahweh), and a freewill offering (to express a thankful heart overflowing with joy). Since the bulk of this sacrifice was returned to the offerer to be used as a festive meal, it served as a reminder of the covenant in tangibly expressing the relationship between the people and Yahweh.[35]

The Sin Offering or Purification Offering (Lev. 4:1–5:13). Individuals or the congregation made this sacrifice because of a specific sin, or a particular need for purification. The purification offering was to make expiation for sins committed accidentally or because of human weakness, and it required the sinner to reflect a contrite and repentant spirit in offering the sacrifice in order to expect Yahweh to grant forgiveness. Furthermore, it was only for the inadvertent sin, not a flagrant or intentional one. Sins of inadvertence are committed accidentally, out of negligence or because of a weak will, in contrast to those done "with a high hand," or intentionally (Lev. 4:27–31; 5:1–13; Num. 15:22–31). Some inadvertent sins were hidden in some way so they were unknown, such as carelessly taking an oath or touching something ceremonially unclean, even if one was unaware of it. Also, they might involve contact with something that makes the person unclean for an extended period, such as contact with a corpse (Lev. 5:1–7; Num. 19:11–16). Sin offerings might involve rituals of consecration or some other form of purification. One specific type involved purification offerings in preparation for major festivals marking the seasons and their transitions.[36]

The Guilt Offering or Reparation Offering (Lev. 5:14–6:7). The reparation offering was for the expiation of a sin that required restitution, such as mishandling another's property or violating anything sacred.[37] These kinds of sins were apparently connected to this offering for expiation because the person doing such things elevated the level of the offense to that of a breach of faith against Yahweh by falsely swearing an oath of innocence in Yahweh's name before a court to clear himself of wrongdoing. Since this is using Yahweh's name in vain, it moves the sin into the category of a flagrant offense beyond the means of an expiation, rather than allowing it to remain at the level of inadvertence. The purpose of the guilt offering then, in such a case, was that the repentance and restitution included in the offering were critical to genuine repentance and reduced the intentional sin to the level of an inadvertent one for which expiation could then be made through the sacrifices.[38] Other sources simplify the distinction between the sin and guilt offerings to the issue of restitution. The NIV Study Bible note on Lev. 5:15 notes, "The major difference between the guilt and sin offerings was that the guilt offering was brought in cases where restitution for the sin was possible and therefore required (v. 16). Thus in cases of theft and cheating (6:2–5) the stolen property had to be returned along with 20 percent indemnity. By contrast, the sin offering was prescribed in cases of sin where no restitution was possible."[39] While this is true, the type of sin that necessitated restitution involved in some way a breach of faith against Yahweh. This might involve theft by deception, swearing a false oath and thus profaning the divine name. This made the offense more flagrant and beyond the means of expiation in the offering for inadvertent sins.[40]

The Day of Atonement (Yom Kippur). The culmination of all the atonement sacrifices was the Day of Atonement, held once a year and representing the entire nation of Israel. The atonement accomplished here included the purification rituals and all the sins of the people not previously expiated through the other sacrifices, including the willful sins not covered elsewhere. "This is to be a lasting ordinance for you: Atonement is to be made once a year for all the sins of the Israelites" (Lev. 16:34).

The manipulation of the blood of the sacrifice by the priest provides important insight into the purpose of the sacrifice for sin. In all the offerings where blood is used, Aaron first sprinkles the blood of the sacrifice on the base of the altar and smears it on the horns of the altar before the sacrifice is burned. The description of the Day of Atonement ritual in Leviticus 16 provides the reason this is done. The preparations for the ceremony emphasize the need for ritual cleanness. Aaron puts on linen undergarments but must first bathe because the garments are sacred (16:4). He then offers a sacrifice of a bull for himself and his family to make atonement for them (16:11). Then he takes some of this sacrificial animal's blood and sprinkles it on the atonement cover, the "mercy seat" (16:14). The priest then takes two goats and presents them to the Lord. He slaughters the first goat as a sacrificial animal for the people and sprinkles its blood on the atonement cover (16:15) in order to make atonement for the Most Holy Place and for the Tent of Meeting, because these stand in the midst of the uncleanness of the rebellious Israelites (16:16). These actions first make atonement for the priest himself and his family, the Most Holy Place, the Tent of Meeting, and the altar before the atonement process for Israel is allowed to begin (16:17). Then he takes more blood of the goat and puts it on the horns of the altar and sprinkles it on the altar in order to cleanse and consecrate it from the "uncleanness of the Israelites" (16:18–19).

It is important to notice that the Leviticus account of Aaron's performance of the atonement ritual here has not mentioned his laying his hand on the sacrifices, nor that the people have laid their hand on the animals they have brought.

Apparently, the ritual here is routine and would have involved the same laying on of one hand by the person bringing the sacrifice (the priest and/or the people), thus signifying their identification with it. Also, notice that the blood does not play the role of appeasing God, nor is it represented as some form of penalty. It simply serves to symbolize the purification of sin from those places that are consecrated for God's use, as well as indicating the pouring out of the life of the animal (and the people) to bring their life into the presence of Yahweh whose presence filled the Holy Place (Lev. 17:11). Also, in the succeeding description of the ceremony, the sins of the people are placed on the head of the second goat, the scapegoat, and it is sent out into the wilderness, thus removing their sins from them and making atonement (Lev. 16:10). It seems that if the sacrificial goat used also for atonement were to be considered an appeasement to propitiate God's wrath so that he would forgive their sins, Aaron would have transferred the sins to this animal to bear the penalty of the people, rather than to the scapegoat, which is not killed. But no two-handed transference of sins to this first sacrificial goat is stated in the text.[41]

Nothing in any of the sacrificial texts indicates that the purpose of the sin offering is to punish Israel by exacting a penalty offering before forgiveness can be given. Instead, Israel's action was obedience to covenant expectations. Thus the sacrificial legislation does not provide biblical evidence for the penal substitutionary explanation of the role of the blood sacrifice.

In addition to the complex rituals of purification of the Tent of Meeting and the sin offering for the priest and his family, the atonement ritual for the entire congregation was twofold: two goats are selected for the atonement (Lev. 16:7–11). One is chosen by lot to be slain as a sin offering before the Lord, thus effecting atonement and forgiveness for the people. The other, known as the scapegoat, was not slain, but instead the high priest laid both his hands on its head and confessed over it all the wickedness and sins of the Israelites and put them on the goat's head, thus ritually identifying it as the bearer of the sins of the nation. It was then not slain, but taken out into the desert to a solitary place and released (Lev. 16:20–22). Its purpose was also to make atonement for Israel (16:10), but not by shedding its blood. It symbolized the forgiveness and separation of sin from the people, thus making atonement between God and Israel. The man who handled the goat was then required to bathe and wash his clothes before he could reenter the camp (16:26). Hartley notes: "The purpose of this ritual was to remove the sins from the area where the people lived, to return them to their source, and to leave them there in order that they would have no more ill effect within the community. The rite *completely broke the power of these sins over the people of God.*"[42]

In no way does the text indicate that either the sin offering or the scapegoat represented a penalty that absorbed God's wrath against Israel and thus made it possible for him to forgive them. Instead, the Day of Atonement was a solemn day of fasting and penitential prayer as the people sought God's forgiveness, a day that ended with the blessed assurance of atonement.

The Purpose of Sacrifices

One of the rescue workers at the World Trade Center following the tragedy of September 11, 2001, was asked by a reporter, "Wasn't this quite a sacrifice for you to take all these risks and endanger yourself to try to rescue these victims?" This question reveals the common contemporary understanding of the word *sacrifice* as an obligation or act of drudgery. The worker replied, "Oh, no. It wasn't a sacrifice. It was a gift!" While his attitude is certainly commendable, this understanding of "sacrifice" does not match the biblical meaning. A sacrifice is not a drudgery or penalty imposed because of God's displeasure. It is a life-saving, life-giving opportunity and privilege to restore a living relationship with the God of creation.

Sacrifice Is *Not* an Appeasement of God. There is a persistent tendency among Christians to understand sacrifices as some kind of substitutionary blood penalty, even with regard to the first three types of sacrifice that are made for purposes of celebration, community, and thanks. This reflects a basic misunderstanding of the nature of sacrifices in the religious life of Israel. While pagan religious sacrifices display a concern to propitiate, appease, or bribe to counteract a god's vengeance, Israel reinterpreted sacrificial practice in a countercultural way; the sacrifices were used in the context of covenant maintenance and renewal as a "divinely appointed way of dealing with sin."[43]

According to Hartley, the primary purpose of all the Old Testament sacrifices was to preserve the covenant relationship between God and the worshipers. They function as gifts to God, a means of expiation, and a means of communion with God. They are tokens of obedience, not *ex opere operato*[44] bribes that automatically propitiate or appease him. On account of such an attitude of obedience, God accepted Abraham as righteous. Even though he did not have the formal legislation of the sacrificial system, his behavior reflected the attitude of covenant obedience, which is God's understanding of "righteousness." Sacrifices were used by Israel, Hartley notes, in several ways.[45] How they operated and accomplished their purposes is a matter of extensive discussion.

The prevailing popular understanding of atonement is that God's wrath is propitiated, or appeased, so that he can then be implored to forgive sinful humanity. But both the textual and grammatical evidence refutes this assumption. In the Bible, God is never the object of the terms *atonement, propitiation,* or *reconciliation.* Humanity is the object of these terms, all of which have to do with changing of attitudes. God is not called upon to become merciful, to be conciliated, to be reconciled or appeased or propitiated. (Note, for example, 2 Cor. 5:19 NAU, "God was in Christ, reconciling the world to Himself."). God is the Reconciler, not vice versa. Bernhard Anderson notes that God showed, by the giving of the covenant and the Law, and by providing the entire sacrificial system, that "appeasement" of himself is inconsistent with the entire biblical theology of atonement. God is thus the subject of "makes atonement for" (2 Chron. 30:18 his translation), and the one who takes the initiative to cancel the results of sin (as in Isaiah 6:7, "Your sin is forgiven"). Ultimately, we see by God's sending of Christ that he is already merciful and gracious.[46] Love is his nature. His covenant promises of love never change. God is not at war with humanity. God does not need to be reconciled.

As soon as Adam had sinned, he fled in terror and hid, thus projecting onto God his own sense of alienation. The change in Adam's heart made him believe God had changed. It is humanity who needs reconciliation. P. P. Waldenström says, "Reconciliation is a work which proceeds from God and is directed towards man, and aims not to appease God, but to cleanse man from sin, and to restore him to a right relation to God. . . . God is love from everlasting to everlasting."[47] Jacob Jocz concurs, observing that God saves by his condescending presence, ultimately in Jesus Christ: "The thrice-holy God, before whom no sinner can survive, stoops to the point of man's greatest need and unreservedly offers Himself at the risk of rejection. This is God's sacrifice. . . He places on the altar for the sake of sinners. The Cross can be described as an act of "propitiation" if we care to use cultic terms, but it is propitiation in the reverse order: it is God who propitiates. He is the acting agent: He sacrifices, He dies, He initiates an act of At-one-ment in which all mankind becomes involved."[48]

Sacrifice Is a Gift to God. It is clear that the primary Old Testament sense of sacrifice is the presentation of a gift to Yahweh. The generic term for sacrifices is "gift, oblation" *(kipporet).* This gift recognized Yahweh's sovereign lordship. In the same way that a person would not approach a king without a gift, so the worshiper would not presume to approach the Lord of creation without a gift or present in tribute of his lordship. The different sacrifices represented different kinds of gifts. The whole offering was a gift of homage and devotion. The offering of well-being was a present of praise or gratitude. The purification offering was a present of contrition and supplication.[49] To interpret these symbolic practices as payment of penalties God had assessed is to distort the entire spirit of the sacrificial ritual. Gifts are not coerced. The Law specified the appropriate protocol to follow in approaching God, and the sacrificial practice gives expression to the covenant fellowship between God and the people.

The use of the term *blood* to refer to the entire process of atonement is widespread in the Old Testament. As explained below, it functions as a synecdoche, a figure of speech in which a part of a larger concept represents the entire concept. In a sacrificial or atonement context, *blood* represents the giving of life as the offerer of the sacrifice of atonement presents the offering in obedience to the commands of covenant Law. The sacrificial legislation in Leviticus 17 explicitly shows that the blood represents the life of the animal: "For the life of a creature is the blood, and I have given it to you to make atonement for yourselves on the altar; it is the blood that makes atonement for one's life. . . . You must not eat the blood of any creature, because the life of every creature is its blood; anyone who eats it must be cut off" (Lev. 17:11, 14).

The sacrificial use of this blood functions to renew the covenant relationship with God.[50] But as we have seen, even offering the sacrifice with its blood will not accomplish atonement and reconciliation if the offerer is not repentant and obedient in spirit. Furthermore, atoning sacrifice for sin may even be made without a bloody offering if the offerer is unable to give an animal. Leviticus 5:11–13 reads: "If, however, he cannot afford two doves or two young pigeons, he is to bring as an offering for his sin a tenth of an ephah of fine flour for a sin offering. . . . In this way the priest will make atonement for him for any of these sins he has committed, and he will be forgiven."

Since the sacrifice is a gift and not a payment of penalty, the relative value of the gift is not relevant to what it accomplishes in restoring the covenant relationship between God and the penitent sinner. What is offered to God is a gift that represents life, usually in the form of a blood sacrifice. But it is important to understand that the blood itself stands for the entire concept of giving one's life through identification with the sacrificial animal, rather than for payment of a penalty or bribe for propitiation of God, as was the case in the pagan rituals in the surrounding cultures.[51] Determining which terms and phrases to translate and interpret literally instead of figuratively can make a world of difference in one's religious practices and spiritual life. For example, scholars from John Calvin to contemporary experts have noted that in Hebrews 9:23 the phrase "without the shedding of blood there is no forgiveness" is a synecdoche, and that the forgiveness of sins involves much more than the ritual killing of an animal. Calvin writes: "By mentioning blood alone he did not mean to exclude other parts of redemption, but rather to include the whole of it in a single word, and he mentioned the blood, in which we are washed. Thus the whole of our expiation is denoted by taking a part (blood) for the whole (redemption)."[52]

A synecdoche uses a word associated with an idea to stand for the entire concept. Forgiveness involves, in the Old Testament at least, not only the sacrificial ritual, but the attitude of repentance as well, which includes the making of restitution and continued faithful obedience to the expectations of the covenant with God. Thus the blood of the sacrifice is only a part of the covenant forgiveness process, and we should not interpret "blood" literally as the essence of atonement. Instead, we understand it as a synecdoche in which "blood" means the entire atonement process.In fact, as E. P. Sanders notes, an obedient attitude to the covenant, rather than blood itself, may be the most essential part of atonement.[53] The prophet Samuel confronts King Saul with the statement, "Behold, to obey is better than sacrifice, *and* to heed than the fat of rams" (1 Sam. 15:22 NAU). The prophets strongly rebuked Israel when it began to emphasize the external doing of the sacrificial ritual instead of nurturing an inner faith and an obedient spirit.[54]

Israel treated blood differently than other religions. Blood was the substance of life. It was not magical, but sacred. By the shedding of the blood of the sacrificial animal, the life of the person was ritually offered up and surrendered to what is holy, so that his life (*nephesh*) was dedicated and incorporated into the holy through the blood ritual. What is more, we see in Leviticus 1–7 that God provides the gift that the offerer brings in obedience and submission.[55] The focus lay not in the act of killing the animal, as if that dramatically represented the beast's becoming a substitute absorbing the penalty of death that rightly belonged to the sinner. Rather than a penalty, sacrifice is a tangible expression of offering oneself to God. Birch and colleagues emphasize that these obedient relationship expectations predated even the Sinai agreement: "This makes it clear that to obey the voice of God entails more than obeying the laws given at Sinai. Obedience is a way of exhibiting trust in the God who speaks the word in *any* time or place (for a similar NT perspective, see 1 John 2:3–6)."[56]

The tendency to define *sacrifice* as a penalty is a rather recent linguistic usage. Yet the events in the 9/11 terrorist attacks have restored some of the term's correct historical meaning of "gift." In the medal ceremony for heroes of the tragedy, Secretary of the Army Thomas White said, "There is no greater virtue than to risk one's life to save another."[57] The firefighter mentioned earlier did not regard the risks he took as a sacrifice, saying instead, "It was a gift." The popular usage of the word *sacrifice* to mean "penalty" or "mandatory service" may not match the biblical understanding, but the firefighter's attitude captured exactly the meaning of sacrifice in the Old Testament covenant ceremonies.

Furthermore, there are numerous Old Testament examples where Yahweh forgives without payment of sacrifice, such as in the repentance of David, Nineveh, and other situations. In the intertestamental period when the temple was not available and sacrifices could not be offered, the rabbis were very concerned about how atonement could be achieved without obedience to the commandments to offer sacrifices. Since none of the sacrifices of the Old Testament had been seen as efficacious without repentance, the rabbis came to see that as long as a person's intention was to remain within the covenant, atonement is biblically fulfilled by genuine repentance. Suffering was also sometimes seen as a means of atonement, based on the legislation in Leviticus 26:40–46: "But if they will confess their sins and the sins of their fathers—their treachery against me and their hostility toward me, which made me hostile toward them so that I sent them into the land of their enemies . . . I will not reject them or abhor them so as to destroy them completely, breaking my covenant with them. I am the LORD their God. But for their sake I will remember the covenant with their ancestors whom I brought out of Egypt in the sight of the nations to be their God."

It is because of their suffering that the Israelites can be redeemed if they repent. The rabbis interpreted this passage (Lev. 26:40–46) as teaching that if a slave is abused and the master maims him in some way, the slave's suffering constitutes atonement that obtains his redemption as a consequence. Suffering, reasoned the rabbis, leads to repentance and cleansing and is a costly sacrifice to pay for atonement.[58] Thus the main idea of covenant renewal was not to demand a particular payment to God, but to repent of the behavior that brought estrangement to the covenant relationship and to humbly and in faith seek God's forgiveness.

Sacrifice as a Means of Expiation

Another purpose of sacrifice was to enable a person who had violated the covenant obligations, committing a sin covered by sacrifice, to avoid God's wrath. This avoiding of wrath is the essence of atonement, or *kipper.* Much controversy surrounds the meaning of *kipper,* however. It can mean "make expiation," "wipe away," "forgive," "appease," or "propitiate," as well as carry a number of other nuances. Its Akkadian roots render it as "wipe off" or "smear," with reference to buildings, people, and other objects purified by magical rites. The Old Testament usage can convey a similar idea of ritual purification of worship-related objects. The more common idea, however, is that an act that "expiates" removes pollution and counteracts sin. The idea is that God had purged or removed the sin so that the person finds forgiveness (Ps. 65:3; 78:38; Ezek. 16:63). In other words, "expiation" describes the removal of sin and its effects on the person or nation.[59]

The debate over the proper translation of *kipper* relates primarily to whether atonement means "expiation," "propitiation," or both. *Propitiation* suggests that God, who is angered by sin, requires that something be done to appease or neutralize that anger before forgiveness can be offered the sinner. Whether the offended character of God must be appeased, as in the pagan cultus, or simply that his desire to restore normalized relationships must be addressed, is also an issue in defining *propitiation*. The question here is whether the sacrifices are intended to appease God (propitiate) or to remove sin (expiate). The answer depends on the context. Hartley notes that *expiation* focuses on the removal of the sin that has obstructed the expression of God's love, and this is usually done through sacrifice.[60] While he has possibly overstated his case, C. H. Dodd has argued that *kipper* is most accurately rendered "expiate," since God is not an irascible deity whose anger must be appeased by sacrifices and bribes so that his reluctance to forgive may be overcome. Dodd notes that the biblical writer portrays God as the one who initiates forgiveness rather than as a capricious and vindictive deity who must be bribed back into a good mood by sacrificial gifts. Thus "expiation" better represents the nature of the sacrifice that removes or annuls the sin so that God can forgive with integrity since the cause of his anger has been removed.[61]

The strength of this argument is that it denies a hindrance to reconciliation resulting from God's reluctance to forgive. Its weakness lies in its unwillingness to admit that there is divine wrath and judgment (Rom. 2:5–6) and hence a propitiatory element, although not pagan appeasement, in the biblical usage of *kipper*. For example, propitiation is certainly the intended meaning in Numbers 25:1–13. Here God's anger was being executed against those who had worshiped Baal Peor. However, his wrath ceased when Phinehas the priest slew a blatantly guilty couple.[62] The penalty of death upon the sinner does not have to be exacted, however, when the person obeys God and thus functions in a righteous relationship to God (Matt. 6:12–15; Mark 2:10, 11:25; Luke 6:37; Col. 3:13; Heb. 8:12; Rom. 4:1–17).

Others, such as Leon Morris, object to the expiatory interpretation of atonement (removal of the cause of God's anger) because they believe it gives inadequate consideration to the moral nature of God, whose anger at sin is based on his holiness and integrity. Morris does not see God's wrath as impersonal retribution, for God has provided a just means for averting his wrath. However, he stresses the propitiatory means of satisfying God, although not in the pagan sense of giving a gift to appease anger. These propitiatory ways of purging sin include destroying the wicked city (Deut. 13:12–18), putting away heathen wives (Ezra 10:14), and repentance (Jonah 3:6–9).[63]

Birch, Brueggemann, and others emphasize that the object of the verb *kipper* is sin, never God. The action of expiation effects the forgiveness of sin, not the appeasement of God. By definition, the expiation of sin does not involve a penalty. The focus is on the saving aspects of the ritual.[64] Bernhard Anderson agrees that translating *kipper* as "propitiation" reflects the theological view that God, "who is angry and alienated by human sin, requires something to appease divine anger before showing favor to the sinner." This is inconsistent with God's demonstrations of forgiveness to Israel. In contrast, the "expiation" translation reflects that the obstacle to right relationship with God is in the sin of the sinner, and God initiates a way to restore that relationship through grace.[65] God is the one who pardons (2 Chron. 30:18–20), forgives (Ps. 78:38; Isa. 6:7), and makes atonement (Deut. 21:8; Ezek. 16:63). It is God who takes the initiative to cancel the consequences of sin, and this is also Anderson's interpretation of Isaiah 53:10, in which he sees the Servant's sacrifice as a sin offering which restores the covenant relationship with God.[66]

The important issue, then, is how God's judgment against sin can be averted and a loving covenant relationship restored. Ultimately, atonement is achieved, in both the Old Testament and New Testament, by some means of expiation that results in propitiation. Sacrifice, repentance, or some other means, such as prayer, expiates sin and removes the cause of judgment because the covenant has already been renewed by the penitence and obedience of the worshiper. This removal of sin and the corresponding repentance and obedience of the person as expressed in the sacrifice results in the removal of God's wrath. God is no longer wrathful because his intention was to maintain the covenant fellowship in the first place. Whatever makes possible the restoration of that fellowship with God, whether it be sacrifice, prayer, or the destruction of the guilty party, reconciles humanity and God.

A further problem with interpreting *kipper* as "propitiation" is that it is very difficult to show from the biblical texts that God is first reconciled to sinful humanity and therefore humanity can then be reconciled to God (Lev. 6:30; 16:20; Matt. 5:24; Rom. 5:10; 2 Cor. 5:20). In fact, the *opposite* is true. Sinful humanity is alienated from God and must be reconciled. Indeed, God initiated the procedure for atonement and reconciliation. The action of God is always to restore the covenant relationship. Sinful humanity must be turned back toward God. "Expiation," the removal of the sin that alienates from the covenant relationship, is what the sacrificial system is intended to accomplish, so long as the sinner accompanies the sacrifice with an attitude of repentance, humility, and obedience toward God.

In fact, repentance in itself may serve to expiate sin, even without the use of sacrifice. Milgrom shows that repentance can have an expiatory function. While sacrificial atonement is useful only for involuntary wrongdoing, a deliberate sinner may mitigate his offense by confessing it and repenting. This is apparently the case with King David following his sins of adultery and murder (2 Sam. 11), when Nathan the prophet pronounces David's absolution—without the use of an animal sacrifice—after David acknowledges his sin (2 Sam. 12:13; Ps. 51). Through remorse and confession, the penitent reduces his intentional sin to an inadvertent one and thus makes it eligible for sacrificial expiation.[67] This may well have been what Moses was trying to accomplish for the people by praying for their forgiveness for sins not covered by the sacrificial system (Ex. 32:30). Also, after the Ninevites repented in response to Jonah's prophetic indictment, God withdrew his threatened judgment: "When God saw what they did and how they turned from their evil ways, he had compassion and did not bring upon them the destruction he had threatened" (Jonah 3:10). The sacrificial acts were not effective unless they were accompanied by true repentance.[68] Thus, in the Mosaic covenant the obedient performance of the sacrificial ritual is the means of restoring right relationship *(tsedaqah)* with God after it has been compromised by disobedience.

Even though the sacrifice was made to obtain forgiveness of sins, one must remember that the real sacrifice of self-surrender and repentance had to be made by the sinner. In offering the sacrifice and identifying with it by the laying on of hands, the sinner changed in his attitude toward God. He turned back to God and repented. In response to the offerer's repentance and self-offering, God accepted the animal sacrifice as a token of his reception of the offerer who had identified himself with it and forgave the sinner of his offenses. In this forgiveness God did not merely look upon the sinner as if he had offered himself, but he looked upon him as a true self-offering. This forgiveness did not result in a positional righteousness in which God looked at the person through the sacrifice, but it resulted in an actual righting of interpersonal relationships between the person and God. The symbol was the animal; the reality was the changed relationship. Since sin had broken the relationship, the covenant fellowship could not be restored so long as sin remained in the sinner's life.[69]

The penal substitutionary interpretations of the sacrifices are based on the forensic equality of value between a sacrifice and the life of the person offering it ("the punishment must fit the crime"). However, a sacrifice is not a *quid pro quo* ("this therefore that"—i.e., an exchange) because there is a great difference in the worth of a sacrifice and the one who offers it. And the covenant is not just another legal contract that must inexorably drive home its legal sanction. It is personal. God is free to exercise justice and mercy. Nevertheless, nothing is effective in restoring the relationship with Yahweh until the breach caused by unconfessed and unforgiven guilt is closed. When the sinner humbly acknowledges sin and recognizes that, since sin broke the relationship with God, it cannot remain while this relationship is restored, then Yahweh can forgive. But forgiveness is conditioned upon confession and repentance.[70] We see this illustrated in Psalms 32 and 51:

> When I kept silent *about my sin*, my body wasted away
>   Through my groaning all day long.
> For day and night Your hand was heavy upon me. . . .
> I acknowledged my sin to You,
> And my iniquity I did not hide;
> I said, "I will confess my transgressions to the LORD";
> And You forgave the guilt of my sin. (Ps. 32:3–5 NAU)

> You do not delight in sacrifice, or I would bring it; you do not take pleasure in burnt offerings. The sacrifices of God are a broken spirit; a broken and contrite heart, O God, you will not despise. (Ps. 51:16–17)

Through the sacrificial ritual prescribed by God's grace, then, the penitent expressed repentance and submission to the will of God and the broken covenant fellowship was restored. Obedience to the Law thus expressed love for God, who had established the covenant community. But it was the personal repentance of the sinner and the personal forgiveness of Yahweh that restored the broken relationship. The basic element in the restoration of this relationship was love of Yahweh expressed practically in a personal surrender to the Law (Deut. 6:4–9). Just as transgression threatened to disrupt the present order, love upheld it—because love was the essence of fellowship with God, and that fellowship was the purpose of the covenant order.[71]

In order to maintain covenant relationship with God and with other members of the community, the persons who committed a sin needed a specific means to overcome the consequences of their acts. The commission of sin results in a complex matrix of consequences. Furthermore, sins were considered to have differing levels of seriousness. Numbers 15:22–36 distinguished sins that were intentional and deliberate (literally, "with a high hand") from accidental and inadvertent sins. Deliberate actions such as bloodshed, adultery, idolatry, blasphemy, etc., carried a "cutoff" penalty, which placed their remedy outside the sacrificial system. Their penalty was death (Num. 15:30–36).[72] They could not be expiated within the power of the sacrificial system. Sins that were expiable, or forgivable, within the system could be atoned for through the sin offering. However, if sins classified as "inadvertent" involved violations of the sacred or were against property, the guilt offering was necessary in addition to the sin offering.

With the guilt offering, the sinner had to restore the property or make compensation for it, in addition to paying a penalty of 20 percent of the value of the item. This restitution aided in restoring the relationships within the community on the human level. Remorse and contrition on the part of the sinner were necessary for the sacrifice to be effectual. Furthermore, the expiation gained from the obedient offering of the sacrifices atoned for the sin and healed the relationship between the sinner and God. Only on the Day of Atonement could willful and intentional sins, or those that were against Yahweh, be expiated. The greater sins not expiated by the specific sacrifices were generally expiated for the entire congregation on the annual Day of Atonement.[73]

Hofius uses Gese's idea of "exclusive substitution" and "inclusive substitution" as a means of communicating the idea of the sinner participating in death.[74] In the forensic conception of "exclusive substitution," the sinner transfers the objective guilt, which will bring death to him, over to an animal. That animal takes the sinner's place and dies for the sinner as a substitute in some sort of "moral fiction," pretending as if the sin has been removed, like excess baggage, so that the sinner may go on living. The sinner thus escapes his merited death and remains alive. Gese rejects this "exclusive substitution" and offers the more appropriate view of "inclusive substitution." He shows that guilt cannot just be removed and transferred from the sinner as a tumor can be removed; this is far too mechanical an understanding of sin.

Sin is a part of the sinner's very existence, and the sinner must bring the corrupted, sinful self to surrender his to God. This process may be accomplished in the Old Testament ritual by an "inclusive substitution" enabled by a ritual gesture of the laying on of one hand. This does not just load the sins onto the animal so that the sacrificial slaughter removes the sins from the sinner. Rather, the laying on of one hand is an *identification gesture,* and the killing of the sacrificial animal is a surrender of life that includes the life of the sinner. The sinner—who has been identified ritually with the animal killed—participates by means of this identification in the death of the sacrificial animal. Hofius suggests, "The *blood ritual* expresses this aspect of the surrender of life to God."[75] The death of the animal victim symbolized the offerer's death to his sin. It is the "medium" of the offerer's fellowship with God.[76] As the blood is ritually applied to the altar, the life of the sinner/animal is surrendered to God himself.

In the blood ritual the priest took the blood of the sacrificial animal, with which the sinner had been identified through the laying on of hands, and sprinkled it on the horns of the altar of burnt offering and on the curtain in front of the Holy of Holies. On the Day of Atonement the high priest sprinkled the blood inside the Holy of Holies on the *kapporet,* the "means of atonement" or "mercy scat," on top of the ark, which symbolizes God's presence and glory and is where the sacrifice becomes effectual. This is not just a negative sin-removal, but a coming to God through the sentence of death. Atonement and reconciliation are accomplished as the sinner in the inclusive substitution is thus given to God through death. The sprinkling of blood brings the sacrificial life in the blood into contact with God's dwelling place, so that it connects with the life of God (Lev. 17:11). The newness of *being* that comes through the giving of life to God thus brings about in the person a new creation.[77]

Although we still do not understand the exact way the offerings functioned to expiate offenses against God, it is clear that they were not simply equivalent payments exchanged for atonement. The sin offering sacrifices were not equal to the offenses for which they were offered, and hence could not be considered payments or bribes. Furthermore, the sin and guilt offerings, which were the only types of sacrifices that could be construed as penal in nature, were efficacious only for inadvertent sins, not the removal of sins that violated the Ten Commandments. Even the Day of Atonement legislation does not portray the sin offering as being killed to absorb the sin of the nation. Instead, the sin offering reaffirms the covenant, but the sin itself is laid on the head of the scapegoat that is then banished into the desert (Lev. 16:20–22), thus removing Israel's sins and releasing them from their guilt. In summary, the expiatory purpose of the sacrificial rituals expressed God's saving action to restore the individual and community to wholeness in relationship to God and each other and to achieve the *shalom* that was the ideal state of society.[78]

Sacrifice as a Means of Communion between Yahweh and the Community

The meal provided by the sacrifice depicted the sense of fellowship between the worshipers and Yahweh, whom they knew to be invisibly present as an honored guest. In contrast to the cults of the surrounding nations in which the gods were sustained by the people's sacrifices, Yahweh was never believed to be dependent upon the sacrificial food for nourishment. Although the sacrifices were called "the food of God" (Lev. 21:6, 8, 17, 21), the sharing of fellowship was the purpose, not the literal feeding of God. The sharing of the meal of meat, grain, salt, oil, and wine from the offering of well-being, in particular, strengthened the spiritual bond between God and the family. Moreover, because the sacrifices were given in the context of the ritual as stipulated by the covenant Law, they were sacred and the meal was itself a sacrament.[79] This intimate fellowship that Israel had with Yahweh contributed to the spiritual formation of the community and established it with confidence as literally the family of God.

The sacrificial rituals thus functioned to restore the vitality of the covenant communion. The renewing of covenant relationship was effected through the atoning nature of the rituals. H. Wheeler Robinson expresses this concept clearly:

> The sacrificial act is in miniature the actual renewal of a relation. In the fundamental conception of a sacrifice as a gift, seen in the whole burnt-offering, acceptance of it restores some previous relation which has been broken, or reinforces one which exists. The peace offering works to similar ends by different means. Here the meat eaten by the worshippers and the blood poured out for the deity on the altar, coming as they do from the same consecrated animal, realistically unite the worshippers and their God. The sin-offering with its special manipulation of the blood . . . cancels what the anthropologist would call a broken taboo. . . . The guilt-offering centers in the necessity to make reparation for offences of a wider range, such as theft, in addition to restoration. Yahweh's will as well as man's right has been infringed; the offering, if accepted, restores the broken relation to Him.[80]

So the biblical sacrifice is a gift given to God by a sinner (1) who by that gift expresses obedience to the Creator God of the covenant; and (2) who desires intimate, interpersonal spiritual fellowship; and (3) who seeks the forgiveness that restores the covenant fellowship with God for which humanity was created. Through the atonement ritual of sacrifice in an attitude of repentance and faith, God's loving and saving action restores the individual and the community to a healthy covenant relationship with himself and with each other.[81]

Key Covenant Atonement Passages

Even when seeing that we share the same covenant that God initiated with Israel, the church has often failed to observe this covenant concept as a hermeneutical framework in which to understand the atonement. While other themes such as community, kingdom of God, and election have all been used as integrative concepts, the covenant concept seems to be the overarching and most pervasive biblical theme. Furthermore, when interpreting biblical passages dealing with atonement, the failure to place them against the background of covenant can lead to a disjointed focus on details of the rituals and actions of atonement that are often unrelated to their biblical context.[82] While the most extensive treatment of covenants is in Deuteronomy, which discusses various rituals and affirmations that accompanied the ratification of covenants in Israel, particularly in 26:16–30:20, there are two other key Old Testament passages that Christian theology needs specifically to interpret within the context of covenant: Jeremiah 31:31–34 and Isaiah 52:13–53:12.

Jeremiah 31:31–34

Upon the heels of his words of judgment on Israel for their unfaithfulness, Jeremiah holds up a message of hope: "'The days are coming,' declares the Lord, 'when I will plant the house of Israel and the house of Judah with the offspring of men and of animals. Just as I watched over them to uproot and tear down, and to overthrow, destroy and bring disaster, so I will watch over them to build and to plant,' declares the Lord" (Jer. 31:27–28). Then he delivers these prophetic promises in the language of covenant:

> "The time is coming," declares the Lord, "when I will make a new covenant with the house of Israel and with the house of Judah. It will not be like the covenant I made with their forefathers when I took them by the hand to lead them out of Egypt, because they broke my covenant, though I was a husband to them," declares the

Lord. "This is the covenant I will make with the house of Israel after that time," declares the Lord. "I will put my law in their minds and write it on their hearts. I will be their God, and they will be my people. No longer will a man teach his neighbor, or a man his brother, saying, 'Know the Lord,' because they will all know me, from the least of them to the greatest," declares the Lord. "For I will forgive their wickedness and will remember their sins no more." (Jer. 31:31–34)

The inability of persons to live in fellowship with God and to incarnate his commands into their actions demonstrates the need for the transformation of their hearts by the activity of the Spirit to bring about a deeper communion with God. It is by the "circumcision of the heart" that God's word "is very near you, in your mouth and in your heart, that you may observe it" (Deut. 30:6, 14 NAU). Eichrodt points out that although this passage in Jeremiah does not use the word *spirit,* it takes up the same issue, as does Isaiah 32:15, and context, as Ezekiel 36:26–27: namely, the new possibility that God himself creates in the faithful the ability to realize the will of God in human life.[83] This new covenant hope is the assurance of salvation that is based in the covenant faithfulness (ḥesed) of Yahweh's unmerited mercy. God promises those who are under the sentence of death his justification that removes their guilt and opens up a new life by his mercy. This promise of justification opens the way to the eschatological hope that is the theme of the prophetic promises.[84]

Now, more than ever, this future hope is based on the inwardness of God's moral convictions. The ethical requirements of the covenant Law remain unchanged. However, the faithful are no longer motivated by duty or obligation, but by obedience to their inward knowledge of God—a knowledge which transforms the Law from an external standard that legislates moral action into an internal spiritual attitude of God's Law written upon their hearts.

Since the dialogue between God and Adam and Eve in the creation narrative, the covenant concept has always called for this inward trust and fellowship with God. In this age of promised salvation, the Spirit of God brings to life the deepest meanings of the covenant relationship. The Law is now fulfilled through "inward communion with the lawgiver." This is the ultimate purpose of election: to separate from the nations of the world a people exclusively devoted to God. Through the restoration of this intimate covenant relationship, Israel comes to understand that love for God is, as Eichrodt phrases it, "the inwardly necessary response to the overwhelming gift of election."[85]

Isaiah 52:13–53:12

Christians almost universally interpret the Suffering Servant figure to connect in some way with the atonement work of Jesus Christ. Although we cannot adequately address the many difficulties surrounding the interpretation of this passage in this section, we do need to address the tendency to interpret it exclusively as a biblical example of the penal substitutionary theory of atonement. Here we can only briefly look at this common tendency and at alternative ways to view the passage in light of a covenant understanding of atonement as the integrative motif for the biblical view of Christ's work of salvation.

The affliction of the Suffering Servant in Isaiah does not demand interpretation as a punishment or discipline in line with penal theories of atonement. Statements such as, "He was pierced for our transgressions, he was crushed for our iniquities" (Isa. 53:5) certainly sound penal. However, the experience of vicarious suffering allows non-penal associations as well, such as the therapeutic understanding that has been the more pervasive view in the Eastern Orthodox Church and in the theology of salvation of John Wesley and others.[86] Daniel Clendenin notes the focus on suffering in the Orthodox tradition as the ultimate act of God's self-revelation, rather than as an expression of penalty or discipline. It is in times of great suffering that Israel discovers God, not so much in his revelations of power. This is "knowing God through the way of the cross," the *theologia crucis,* to use a Lutheran phrase for this concept.[87] To follow the Suffering Servant thus means to pattern one's life after Christ's life of self-giving and suffering. This is the way to wholeness, or *theosis,* which is the Orthodox characterization of this likeness of and union with God.[88]

Jesus interpreted his own priestly sufferings and death in terms of this passage from Isaiah. One of the reasons he did so, notes Vincent Taylor, lies in the idea of representative suffering reflected in the sacrificial system.[89] Verses 5 and 12, which refer to the Servant being "pierced for our transgressions" and "numbered with the transgressors," express the ideas of identification and representation. Through this suffering on their behalf, the Servant establishes a covenant between God and humanity and intercedes for them.[90] This idea of representation is central to the theme of the Servant's work. The Western tendency to view suffering as synonymous with punishment distorts the priestly understanding of identification and participation in the human experience. Here the Servant identifies with human suffering and alienation and represents it through his priestly intercession. Taylor says this is why Jesus interpreted his own sufferings and death in terms of the Suffering Servant passage. The meaning of his mission was based on the representative suffering motif in the Levitical sacrifices, and his sacrificial suffering functioned to establish a new covenant between God and an alienated humanity.[91] And as we have seen, sacrifices in Israel's ritual are not penal, but expressions of obedient repentance and faith.

Sue Groom, Morna Hooker, and others note the linguistic issues involved in identifying the Servant's role in this passage. They show that the Servant's relationship with the people is one of identification rather than substitution. In the same way that Moses links "bearing the guilt of others" to the priestly activity of atonement (Lev. 10:17), so the Servant's bearing of iniquities is a guilt offering of himself as a representative of the people to reconcile them with God. However, the guilt offering itself requires the people to recognize their own sin and make their own offering.[92] So, in the Servant's identification with them, the people are offering themselves in reconciliation. Thus the Servant's identification and suffering for the people involves not an exclusive kind of substitution, but rather, in Hofius' and Gese's words, an "inclusive substitution," or as Hooker describes it, an "inclusive place-taking."[93]

Bruce Reichenbach observes that Isaiah emphasizes in this passage the motif of healing through the suffering of another. He sees this Servant Song as describing the human situation of a life of pain, weakness, transgressions, and iniquities. The song also emphasizes the connection between sickness and sin. The Servant is bruised and punished for our sins, and also bears our diseases and sickness. This connection appears in the Old Testament in the Levitical legislation regarding the need for atonement for certain sicknesses or bodily discharges (Lev. 12–15). While neither the Old Testament nor Jesus taught that all sickness was caused by sin (Job; John 9), certain illnesses apparently required the work of atonement; and a function of God was to heal the sick (Ex. 15:26; Matt. 8:16–17). This linkage, then, between sickness and sin may properly form a backdrop for the motif of this Servant Song.[94]

Finally, while Christ portrays himself in terms of this Suffering Servant passage, in what way is the identification of the Servant identical to or different from that of Jesus' incarnational identification and participation with humanity in the New Testament? Bernd Janowski notes that while this Servant narrative does establish a precedent for Jesus' representative work, it differs in not being incarnational. While sinners do die and rise with Christ, they do not do so with the Servant in Isaiah 53. Because of Christ's divinity and preexistence, he enters into our place in a way that does not displace us but incorporates us. While he does not die in place of humanity, Christ dies while in humanity's place (participation). Christ does not simply come alongside us to remove sin and guilt, but has become identified with humanity through surrendering his life in order to lead us into fellowship with God through "inclusive place-taking." This is not simply taking another's place to "wipe away" his or her guilt, but the Servant helps people understand their responsibility and begin to change.[95] Incarnational identification in the completeness of humanity's suffering and death leads humanity to restored identification with God.[96] The Servant thus provides the preparatory model that informs the redemptive meaning of Christ's work.

Divine Expectations in the Old Testament: Conclusion

The covenant story is the framework in which all metaphors of salvation function. The story of the covenant relationship is God's love story of faithfulness to his promises and his presentation of divine expectations for us human creatures. Thus the concept of covenant reflects an interpersonal relationship rather than an objective, impersonal statement of law. It provides a particularly apt metaphor for the relationship between God and Israel. The covenant was both initiated and maintained by obedience to its stipulations, and the expression of this obedience and covenant communion with Yahweh was mediated through the ritual of the sacrificial system. These sacrifices did not indicate a penalty being applied, but rather they were an oath that validated the promises and guarantees of the substance of the covenant. The sacrifice mediated fellowship with God. It is not most adequately understood in forensic terms, since the forensic tendency is to reduce the covenant relationship to legal-contractual terms. Yahweh's intention and desire for his people is a loving familial relationship.

It is imperative to understand that the sacrifice was not a means of placating God. It was an act of renewal of the covenant relationship in obedience to God's command in the covenant Law to do so. In response to human repentance and self-offering, God accepted the animal sacrifice as a token of his reception of the offerer who had identified with it and forgave the sinner of the offenses. Thus the biblical sacrifice is a gift given to God by the sinner who by that gift expresses obedience to the Creator God of the covenant and who desires intimate, interpersonal spiritual fellowship with God through renewed inclusion in the covenant community. The significance of this understanding of sacrifice as a gift becomes evident in the New Testament presentation of the cross as it presents Christ's incarnational life reaching out in love to humanity and his sacrificial death as a love gift to both humanity and the Father.

Although not equivalent to the sacrifice of Christ, but similar in motivation, are a number of contemporary situations. In the Star Trek movie, *The Wrath of Khan,*[97] Spock sacrifices himself to save his colleagues when the Enterprise's nuclear power system melts down. Spock goes into the reactor room and deactivates the power while suffering a lethal dose of radiation. This is a willful sacrifice for the sake of others, not a penalty. It is understood as a loving act. Captain Kirk eulogizes him as a "sacrifice" and a hero. He says, "Spock understood that the needs of many outweigh the few, or one."

A sacrifice is motivated by love. It was love that motivated a teacher in North Carolina recently to give a kidney to a student, a woman in Portland to give a kidney to her mother, a pastor in Portland to give a kidney to his wife. It was love that motivated a family to donate the heart of their fourteen-year-old son to this author, thus literally giving me the gift of life. These are examples of bloody sacrifices that are gifts, not penalties. No wrath is being paid for, but love is being expressed. The biblical sacrifices are not the payment of a penalty, but the offer of a precious gift that represents faith and obedience to the covenant expectations and are a response to the love and mercy of the God of creation. Christ's sacrificial death expresses the profound lengths to which a loving God was willing to go to provide eternal life to the humanity he had created.

6

Divine Expectations in the New Testament

Since the prognosis of my heart failure was "terminal," my only hope was a heart transplant. Not only was that a very serious and frightening option, but it also required that someone else's life must be lost in order for my life to be saved. As I realized that this is, in some respects, what Christ has done for humanity in his death on the cross, I began to see other parallels between my organ donor's death and Christ's work. Since the donation of an organ is not based on a penalty pronounced upon the victim but on a gift of humanitarian love, and since renewed life would result from that gift, I could see some similarities to the death of Christ. Life does not result from the enacting of the death penalty. Life comes only as a result of a sacrificial gift. Like the gift of my donor's family, Christ's gift was voluntary; and it was also based on love. Both were given in order to bring life, not to ensure someone's death. Both were sacrifices that enabled others to live. But they were different in that my donor did not choose to die in the first place. That is where Christ's death is so astounding—he *chose* to take on himself all the brokenness and pain of human sin and death so that we might take on ourselves all the newness of life of a renewed relationship with God (Phil. 2:5–11; Rom. 6:8–10). Furthermore, since Christ has identified himself with humanity in the incarnation, we become participants with him in his death and his resurrection (Rom. 6). This opened up for me a deeper understanding of how our incarnational participation in this union with Christ leads us back into a reconciled relationship with the Creator.

This biblical idea of atonement, particularly when associated with blood sacrifices, is often simply inconceivable to contemporary persons without a biblical background. Hartmut Gese notes the numerous attempts to avoid the mention of blood in recent Bible translations and to explain the theology of the cross in ways that avoid mentioning what some would call the "outmoded" idea of atonement.

Particularly in the modern worldview that rejects the concept of the transcendent, says Gese, the result is that people attempt to ignore or control ideas with which they do not identify. He goes on to point out that the modern concept of atonement presented by those who believe in it simply does not adequately represent the biblical concept to the contemporary world. He writes, "Our concept of atonement is basically limited to the legal realm of transactions between persons, and its content [limited] to restitution through some symbolic action."[1]

Attempts to communicate atonement to the postmodern culture present a different problem than critical theologians are accustomed to facing. In contrast to moderns, the postmodern mind is relatively ready to accept the transcendent and to conceive of interactions between the human and the transcendent. The problem lies in how the transcendent is understood. Popular spirituality, in this culture, is often conceived in terms of an impersonal or magical life force. The idea of ultimate accountability to a divine person often creates the perception of a "dark side" kind of metaphysical Darth Vader-style blackmail. Furthermore, the postmodern suspicion of institutions and objective authority makes it very difficult for many to accept traditional atonement constructs such as inflexible legal codes, cosmic justice, and capital punishment imposed through forensic penalty. This concern is articulated effectively from the perspective of radical transformation by Steve Chalke in his controversial book, *The Lost Message of Jesus.*[2]

The widespread indifference to the gospel reflected in the growing secularity of Western Europe and North America is simply not being effectively challenged by traditional forms of presenting the gospel. The vital Christianity that formed the identity of Western civilization has become increasingly marginalized, and now Christianity's center of gravity is found in the Southern Hemisphere among the developing nations.[3] There are certainly many reasons for this, but the significance of Christ for this generation needs to be presented in a narrative that is contextualized in a way that is biblical as well as meaningful to the secular audience. The postmodern rejection of tradition, the increasing influence of Eastern religions, and the mindset of pluralism in religious issues raise serious issues for the perceived relevance of the Christian message.

While these perspectives raise challenges to effective communication of the atonement of Jesus Christ in the twenty-first-century world, the covenant itself was a contextualization in which God used cultural artifacts and categories to communicate divine love. How can we now understand the central meaning of the atonement in the New Testament for this contemporary world? The biblical covenant concept properly understood and presented with contemporary relevance will, I believe, contribute significantly to this communication of the gospel. Jocz says, "From beginning to end biblical theology is founded upon the premise of the covenant."[4]

In the New Testament, the significance of the atonement is grounded in the Old Testament story of God's loving pursuit of a sinful people and his gracious provision of the Law to provide moral direction for them in the context of his covenant love. The fulfillment of that saga of God's seeking and wooing of Israel is found in the New Testament message of Jesus Christ's incarnation, ministry, and loving, mediatorial sacrifice to accomplish finally the eternal restoration of covenant union with God.

New Testament Covenant Atonement in Light of the Old Testament

Steven McKenzie notes that through the history of the covenant relationships in the Old Testament God reveals the divine commitment to humanity that forms one side of the covenantal relationships, while the attitudes of obedience and observance of the moral and ceremonial practices required of Israel exemplify the human obligation expected of God's covenant partners. Though Christians do not follow the rituals called for in Israel's worship, God still requires the obedience, faithfulness, and penitent spirit characteristic of the faithful covenant partners.[5]

In the New Testament, the atonement of Christ serves a mediatorial role in initiating and maintaining God's new covenant with all humanity. While Christ's death is presented as a sacrifice and may seem analogous to the Old Testament sacrifices, it is not entirely so at every point. The Old Testament covenant does provide the foundation for understanding the New Testament message of Christ's incarnation and atoning death, but there are significant differences between the two versions of covenant understanding. For example, not only Christ's death, but also his life, is a revelation of God's love that works to mediate and reconcile an alienated humanity back to himself (John 3:16–17; Rom. 5:8; 8:32). Just as the Mosaic covenant established a new Israel, so Christ's sacrifice of death and his resurrection delivers humanity from sin and establishes a new covenant with God and a new people of God. However, Christ offers this new sacrifice once for all, so it needs no repetition for its effectiveness. Furthermore, he offers this new community universally to all humanity who will by faith be included in his new covenant.[6]

While the usefulness of the Old Testament sacrifices was limited to atoning for the involuntary sins of transgressors, Christ's sacrifice is for all people, regardless of their previous affiliation with God. It should also be noted that since the Old Testament sacrifices incorporated not only the sin offering but worship and praise offerings as well, analogously the sacrifice of Christ is certainly not limited to penal or judicial function. Indeed, the sin offering makes up only a small part of the entire sacrificial system, and sharing in Christ's new covenant also involves offering continued praise and thanksgiving to God for the divine blessings of covenant fellowship in the community of faith.

The Old Testament background to the New Testament's understanding of atonement will be examined with regard to the cross, the incarnation, and the Trinity. Then this chapter will look at what the New Testament says about this renewed covenant in the Gospels, Acts, Hebrews, and Paul's writings. Lastly we will see how the New Testament describes the covenant community and review key passages on the Eucharist, baptism, and the Law.

Atonement and the Cross

The New Testament presents Jesus Christ in light of the Old Testament atonement sacrifices. The death of Christ on the cross is the central focus of the Gospels and the Epistles. In Romans 5:10, Paul writes, "For if, when we were God's enemies, we were reconciled to him through the death of his Son, how much more, having been reconciled, shall we be saved through his life!" Paul's own experience of persecuting Christians and seeking to destroy the gospel of Christ placed him in the position of being an enemy to God. But God was never the enemy of humanity. Paul shows in this passage that God had orchestrated redemption while humanity was his enemy: "God demonstrates his own love for us in this: While we were sinners, Christ died for us" (Rom. 5:8). However we interpret the theology of atonement, the core concept is that we are brought back into covenant relationship with God in some way by means of Christ's death on the cross. However, the cross is never separated from its foundation in the incarnation and its outcomes through the resurrection.

How this dynamic exchange of Christ's death for humanity's life takes place has been a matter of theological reflection for millennia. But the universal human experience is that even while humanity was the enemy of God and under sentence of death because of sinful alienation from the life of God, God worked to bring salvation and reconciliation to them. In some way, the enemies of God have now ceased to be enemies and are at peace with their former nemesis through the mediation of Jesus Christ (Rom. 5:1). To accomplish this loving salvation of humanity, Christ had to die, as the writer of Hebrews says: "For this reason Christ is the mediator of a new covenant, that those who are called may receive the promised eternal inheritance—now that he has died as a ransom to set them free from the sins committed under the first covenant" (Heb. 9:15).

The problem for reconciliation is not God, because God created humanity and now has initiated the process of salvation (2 Cor. 5:19). The problem is with humanity. Because of sin, humanity is dying in relation to God (Rom. 8:6–11). Christ had to identify with humanity, even in death, in order to save humanity from sin and death. It was God's love expressed in the covenant promises of salvation, not just some objective sense of divine justice, that required the death of Christ. His death established the renewed covenant and restored the relationship between humanity and God.[7] The barrier to salvation is humanity's alienation, not God's justice. Sin and death had alienated humanity from God and had to be overcome. Therefore Christ, as the representative of both God and humanity, needed to die and be resurrected in order to overcome sin and death. Sin and death entered the world through humanity—Adam (1 Cor. 15:22: "In Adam all die"). Therefore sin, as the cause of death and alienation from God, had to be defeated by humanity—the second Adam, Jesus Christ (Rom. 5:12–19 and 1 Cor. 15:21–22.)—through participation in the full experience of humanity, including death. Dunning notes, "The most profound dimension of his identification with the human race is in his death."[8] He identifies so completely with the human sinner that he experiences the infinite loneliness of humanity's alienation from God in his cry on the cross. This taking of humanity into himself becomes the basis for his representing humanity before God in his encounter with evil on the cross.[9]

Christ's identification with and representation of humanity picks up the Old Testament idea of the sacrificial animal functioning as the sinner's representative before God. As we have shown in chapter 5, the offering of an animal sacrifice was an act of suffering, not punishment. Therefore, by his incarnational identification (Phil. 2:5–11), Christ participates in the suffering of humanity's death because of sin and serves to validate, mediate, and renew the covenant relationship with God, as in the Old Testament sacrificial ritual (Lev. 1–7). And, as in that ritual, the offerer must participate in this sacrificial action of Christ on the basis of faith-obedience and a repentant heart.

The primary terms Paul uses to describe what the atonement accomplishes are "justification," "reconciliation," and "union with Christ." Each of these concepts speaks of the saving activity of God based in the atoning work of Christ. Paul's conception of the divine attitude toward humanity is that God is behind the atonement seeking to bring alienated humanity back into covenant fellowship with himself. Christ's mediatorial work is the demonstration of God's willingness to acquit guilty sinners and restore them to a relationship with himself.[10] Indeed, the biblical understanding of salvation assumes an I-Thou relationship. God does not offer "salvation" as a thing; he offers himself. When God acts in Christ, he offers himself—not an experience or a legal standing.

This relationship of love is not just a legal declaration of acquittal from the fatal consequences of sin, but the *actual restoration* of the sinner to the life-giving relationship of covenant love. The covenant relationship with God lost with Adam's fall is recovered with Christ's incarnational atonement. It is only in the covenant context that God shows himself as being *for* us (*Deus pro nobis*). The covenant is the pledge and token of the fact that God has been for us from the beginning. And now, in his act of saving love through the cross of Christ, he again reveals his faithfulness as the covenant-keeping God.[11] Although we were not aware of it, God has been for us from the beginning; the covenant is the pledge of this reality.

Without the historical background of God's relationship to his people in the covenant relationship, concepts such as reconciliation, redemption, salvation, and justification are only theoretical theological concepts lacking concrete historical examples to give them meaning. The New Testament message of salvation functions as the revelation and validation of God's faithfulness (*ḥesed*) as the covenant-keeping God.[12] This is why Barth understands the covenant as the "presupposition of reconciliation."[13] God's righteousness, then, reveals its saving nature through the death of Christ. The cross is clearly the ultimate manifestation of God's love for sinners and the ground on which justification and reconciliation are made possible (Rom. 5:8–9). Justification is based not on the works of a person or even on one's faith, but on what God has done on our behalf through the death and resurrection of Christ. His work thus ties redemption to the cross, and justification and reconciliation rest on his death. Faith, however, is necessary for understanding and appropriating this sacrificial action. It is by faith that the believer surrenders his/her whole being in trust to Christ and identifies with Christ's rejection of sin and his acting in obedience to God. Faith means entering into a right interpersonal relationship with the covenant God through an obedient personal appropriation of the work of Christ in the continuing empowerment of the Holy Spirit.[14]

Atonement and the Incarnation

The significance of "the Lamb that was slain from the creation of the world" (Rev. 13:8) is that the atonement of Christ is not just the single act of the cross, but it is the "righteousness of God" (Rom. 3:21–22 NAU)—the eternal, saving activity of God himself demonstrated in the entire incarnation experience of Jesus Christ. The death of Christ is the "eternal, suffering love of God for man."[15] This suffering love may not indicate the absorption of God's own penalty as much as it indicates the extent to which he will go to restore a covenant that he did not break and to deliver helpless humanity from a bondage it brought upon itself. This is what grace is all about! God's loving identification with humanity in the incarnation of Jesus Christ initiates the New Testament descriptions of Christ's sacrifice. These descriptions imply that the incarnation was itself a sacrifice to God that fully and eternally achieved what the Old Testament ritual did only in figure and with repetition (Heb. 10:1–10). As God gave the sacrificial system as a way of making atonement possible for humanity in the Old Testament, so in the New Testament he gave Christ as the one who accomplishes reconciliation through his atoning work. As the obedient sacrifice, Christ also functions as a representative of all sinners. In his baptism by John the Baptist, he identified with Israel and the whole of humanity in giving himself to God.[16]

The incarnation is essential for the atonement. Christ cannot represent that with which he has not first identified. The second-century church father, Irenaeus, described this "divine exchange": "He has become like we are that we might become like he is."[17] The Gospel of John points out, "The Word became flesh and made his dwelling among us" (John 1:14). The New Testament understanding is not what Gese calls "exclusive substitution," which views Christ's incarnation as allowing the transference of humanity's death sentence for sin upon Jesus in a way that exempts humans from participation in the work of their own atonement. Rather, New Testament atonement is "inclusive substitution": believers identify themselves with all of Christ's life, death, and resurrection. Paul involves Christ fully in every experience that is human, even death, and humans in every experience that is Christ's, even resurrection (Rom. 6:3–11).

The point Irenaeus makes, then, is that Christ does not merely objectively represent humanity in his dying, but participates with humanity in the experience of death, so that humanity may participate with him in the experience of living. God initiates union with persons in Christ so that persons might participate in union with God through faith and be thus reconciled and restored to divine communion (Rom. 6:5–10). This incarnational identification and participation with

Christ also results in the restoration of the image of God, in which humanity was created but which was marred by sin and death. Only by participation in the full experience of being human could Christ participate as mediator in the salvation process of restoration and transformation of that sinful humanity into the image of God that it was originally created to be.[18]

Atonement and the Trinity

The concept of the Trinity can be seen, albeit in shadowy form, in the Old Testament covenant discussions. Jeremiah envisioned a new covenant and the divine expectations attached to it that would guide the people in renewing their obedience to God. This message of hope in the middle of a time of despair focuses on the offspring of Israel as God promises to make a new covenant with the houses of both Israel and Judah (Jer. 31:27–31). It is also called an "everlasting covenant" (Jer. 32:40). Through it God promises that the devastating history of the captivity will not be final. In Jeremiah 33:15, the promise of the Messiah—the "Branch" in Jeremiah's metaphor—is given as a promise of security. The Branch will restore justice and righteousness to the land. The nature of the Torah will be changed with this new covenant so that obedience and love for God will be written on the people's hearts (Jer. 31:33).

Where the old covenant was external and required external rituals and festivals, in the new covenant, the Torah (Jesus Christ) is placed within the heart. While the covenant relationship had always been a personal one with Yahweh, Israel's disobedience and sin had impaired that relationship significantly. The new covenant promised to communicate the intimate personal knowledge of God directly in an inward, interpersonal relationship. This relationship was to be immediate, and not mediated through priests and prophets and rituals. God says, "I will put my law in their minds and write it on their hearts" (Jer. 31:33). This is a similar promise to the one made to Joel, "I will pour out my Spirit on all people. . . . Even on my servants, both men and women, I will pour out my Spirit in those days" (Joel 2:28–29). Thus the people of God will be brought into intimate relationship with God, without human mediation, through the ministry of the Holy Spirit. So the Father promises a renewed and renewing covenant; the Branch is promised to bring justice; and the Spirit will enable access to God in radically new ways.[19]

Ezekiel also refers to the new covenant between God and his people that will be fulfilled by the offspring of David and will establish a new kind of relationship with God. This new covenant promises forgiveness of sins (Ezek. 16:63), and the Law will be placed in the heart along with a new spirit. Rather than the new covenant being a new code of laws that are out of reach of fallen humanity, the Spirit will enable obedience: "I will put my Spirit in you and move you to follow my decrees and be careful to keep my laws" (Ezek. 36:27).[20] Thus God the Father, the Messiah, and the Spirit can be seen in Ezekiel's presentation of the covenant hope.

Isaiah also speaks of the new covenant as an "everlasting covenant" (Isa. 61:8). Other aspects of this covenant are described in Isaiah 49. Here the servant of God is called a covenant, if the servant in verse 8 can be construed as an individual: "This is what the LORD says: 'In the time of my favor I will answer you, and in the day of salvation I will help you; I will keep you and will make you to be a covenant for the people, to restore the land and to reassign its desolate inheritances." Apparently the servant here is to function as a covenant. If this is the case, the form of covenant referred to is the promise-oath described in Genesis 15:17–19. The promise-oath secured the terms inherent in the covenant and promised a positive future for the offspring with the promise of a homeland. God's grace will bring forgiveness and renewal under the new covenant, who is personified in the "servant of God." Thus God's faithfulness to his promise looked to a new day when Jesus said, at the beginning of his passion as the sacrifice to ratify the new covenant, "This cup is the new covenant in my blood" (1 Cor. 11:25).[21] As the "servant of God," Jesus brought in the new covenant and validated it by the blood of his sacrifice of love on the cross, so that with the administration of the Holy Spirit the new covenant could be established in the heart of every person who identifies in faith with the Christ who had identified with them in his incarnation.[22] This was the vision of Jeremiah, Ezekiel, and Isaiah.

While the old covenant was unable to fully establish the covenant community universally among all nations because of the failure of the sinful human heart, the new covenant promised to bring life through the ministry of the Holy Spirit. Cranfield points out that the Law is misused without the Spirit, for it remains only an external letter rendered ineffective by human sinfulness. Only after the cross and resurrection and the gift of the Spirit did the Law come into its own as the Law that gives life (Rom. 7:10).[23] Paul describes the old covenant as fading in its glory because it did not last, since Israel's understanding of its glory was veiled and they misplaced their hope on their servitude to the letter of the Law devoid of the empowering of the Spirit (2 Cor. 3:6–18). Only when the Spirit takes away the veil can they see Christ. Only in the new covenant do they have the freedom to be transformed into his likeness. The old covenant administered obedience by conformity to the letter; the new covenant administers obedience through the inward obedience of the heart made possible by the ministry of the Spirit of Christ within the heart.[24] In that way the veil is lifted, and "we . . . are being transformed into his likeness with ever-increasing glory, which comes from the Lord, who is the Spirit" (2 Cor. 3: 18).

Thus we see the Trinity at work in the covenant. The Father initiates the covenant, Christ empowers and seals it, and the Holy Spirit administers it. The Spirit gives life, while the letter gives death. The New Testament retains the Law, but redefined as Christ indwelling through the Holy Spirit. The prophet described this redefinition: "I will put my Spirit in you and move you to follow my decrees and be careful to keep my laws" (Ezek. 36:27). Obedience is now made possible, not by a new code of laws, but by the personal ministry of the Holy Spirit.

Furthermore, God's nature is love, and Christ's indwelling is love incarnated in humanity through faith-union with him. The Holy Spirit is Christ living within and maintaining the constantly renewed covenant of relationship with God. "In Christ" is Paul's motto, and he means that through the ministry of the Spirit the covenant with God now lives in the heart with personal vitality through the ministry of the Trinity.

New Testament Expressions of Covenant

In the New Testament, the word used to translate the Hebrew word *berith* (covenant) is *diathekē*. The word literally means "last will," or "testament." Most of the New Testament passages using this term are either quotations or allusions to the Old Testament covenant idea. Thus the Hebrew Bible usage of "covenant" determines its New Testament usage. The term occurs thirty-three times in the New Testament: six times in the Gospels and Acts, nine times in the letters of Paul, seventeen times in Hebrews, and once in Revelation.[25] The term "covenant," in the New Testament expresses primarily the idea of forgiveness in connection with the work of Christ. Because of Christ, a relationship between God and humanity has become possible in a way previously impossible. What the Law could not do in overcoming sin, God has done in the incarnation of Christ (Rom. 8:3–4). The writer of Hebrews speaks of a "better covenant" (Heb. 7:22; 8:6 NAU). Paul compares the Law of the old covenant with a schoolmaster whose purpose was to lead Israel to Christ, while the new covenant is eternal, universally offered, and received by faith (Gal. 3). Morris writes, "Each time the New Testament refers to the new covenant as having been prophesied it links an explicit reference to forgiveness of sin with the new covenant."[26] There is, of course, a continuity of structure between the "old" and "new" covenant. The new covenant in Christ is "new" because it lasts, not because it is different in function. A promise is a promise, no matter how many times it is renewed.

The Gospels and Acts

The new covenant continues the heritage of covenant relationship expounded in the Old Testament. While Jesus internalizes and expands the covenant idea and also gives it a new and universal grounding in his sacrificial death, McKenzie notes he does not come to annul the previous covenants, but to bring them to their fullest expression.[27]

Apart from Luke's version of the Lord's Supper, Luke–Acts speaks of the covenant concept three times, and all three are references to Abraham. In Luke 1:72–73, the prophecy of Zechariah, the father of John the Baptist, connects God's "holy covenant" with the "oath he swore to our father Abraham." In Peter's speech in Acts 3:25, the apostle mentions "the covenant God made with your fathers" and then quotes from the promise to Abraham in Genesis. Finally, Stephen stated in his speech, in Acts 7:8, that God gave to Abraham "the covenant of circumcision," which is a direct reference to the account of the Abrahamic covenant in Genesis 17. All three examples recite the history of God's covenant relationship with Israel beginning with the covenant with Abraham. McKenzie sees this as suggesting that all later forms of covenant are extensions or refinements of the original one with Abraham, in the fashion of concentric circles each expanding the previous one.[28]

Another significant appearance of the covenant idea in the Synoptic Gospels comes with the statements of Jesus at the Last Supper. The word *covenant* is used by Jesus in all three Synoptic accounts: Matthew 26:28, Mark 14:24, and Luke 22:20. In addition, Paul quotes the same saying in 1 Corinthians 11:25. The Luke and Paul versions of the saying include the words, "This cup is the new covenant in my blood." In most manuscripts, Matthew and Mark omit the word *new* in their accounts: "This is my blood of the covenant, which is poured out for many"— with Matthew continuing, "for the forgiveness of sins."[29]

What is most significant, however, is that the phrase "blood of the covenant" is a direct quotation from Exodus 24:8 and shows clearly that Jesus is drawing an analogy between himself and the sacrificial covenant-making ceremony described in Exodus 24. It is noteworthy that Jesus' own self-description relates to covenant ratification rather than exclusively to the sin offering and procedures for the removal of guilt in the Law. In referring to the "blood of the covenant" from a sacrificial ceremony in which the Israelites promised to keep the divine expectations of the covenant, Jesus identifies his own blood and sacrifice as the means through which the "new" covenant between God and humanity is ratified.[30] These quotations also contain allusions to the Passover lamb of Exodus 12:3–13, the Suffering Servant of Isaiah 53, and the "new" covenant of Jeremiah 31. The early church saw all these fulfilled in the renewed covenant in Christ.

Matthew's genealogies also show that Jesus stands in the line of Jewish tradition with its series of covenants between God and his people. In the Sermon on the Mount (Matt. 5–7), as well, Jesus reflects the Old Testament tradition. For example, he does not replace the Law of Moses, but epitomizes the message of love that the covenants had always conveyed, and he focuses and epitomizes that love in himself by his own teaching and example. Matthew presents him as a lawgiver similar to Moses as he goes up on a mountain to present to the people a sort of "new law," in which the Beatitudes are remarkably similar to the Ten Commandments. He explicitly denies that he has come to abolish the Law or the Prophets (Matt. 5:17), but to fulfill them by bringing out their complete, intended meanings.[31]

The three Synoptic Gospels all present the "Greatest Commandment" concept, although they use different settings for the story. In response to the lawyer or scribe who asked him, "Teacher, which is the greatest commandment?" (Matt. 22:34–40; Mark 12:28–31), or "What must I do to inherit eternal life?" (Luke 10:25–28), Jesus gives the same answer, "You shall love the Lord your God with all your heart, and with all your soul, and with all your mind, and with all your strength" and "You shall love your neighbor as yourself" (NAU). The significance for the covenant theme in the New Testament is that Jesus' answer sums up the whole of Old Testament covenant Law and the Prophets—almost the whole of the Hebrew Bible—with a quotation of the *Shema,* the basic confession of Jewish religion (Deut. 6:4–5), and then the admonition to love one's neighbor. This is the essence of the covenant, for love for God is a covenant obligation, a divine expectation; and to obey his commandments, especially in the treatment of others, is the core concept of the Law. Thus the primary theme under the Old Testament covenant is the same as with Jesus: to love God with all your heart by obeying his commandments.[32]

Theological treatments of atonement often omit the insights of the Gospels in favor of Pauline constructs. While the Gospels do show awareness of the lostness of sinners, the overwhelming message is not the announcement of the wrath of God but the good news of the kingdom. The judgment of God on sinners is a part of the eschatological work of the Son of Man (Luke 17:20–37). The concept of God's wrath is also brought out by John the Baptist when he says, "Whoever believes in the Son has eternal life, but whoever rejects the Son will not see life, for God's wrath remains on him" (John 3:36). Also, the "Seven Woes" passage in Matthew 23:13–39 catalogs the variety of reasons that the unrighteous will receive judgment for their many hypocritical actions and thus will receive the consequences of their wickedness as payback for their shedding of righteous blood (23:35).

However, the Gospels make no link between a penal death of Christ and the avoidance of God's wrath. Rather, the emphasis lies on the life Christ gives (e.g., the "new birth" of John 3) that enables a person, by grace, not to be under God's wrath. Christ suffers at "the hands of sinful men" (Luke 24:7), and "repentance and forgiveness of sins will be preached in his name to all nations" (Luke 24:47). But his death is connected in the Gospels to forgiveness and love ("Greater love has no one than this, that he lay down his life for his friends," John 15:13) rather than God's wrath. Indeed, in the Gospels God honors and loves Jesus, and there is no talk of Christ working to appease God's wrath, although Jesus repeatedly warns that God's wrath is real for the unrepentant (Matt. 3:7; Luke 3:7; John 3:36).

Hebrews

The author of Hebrews uses the covenant theme to frame the entire message of the epistle, repeatedly arguing his main point that the old covenant was an incomplete version of the heavenly prototype.[33] This account develops its explanation of Christ's work primarily through analogies drawn from the sacrificial and worship context of the Old Testament covenant relationship. In the frequent references to *diathekē,* the writer presents Christ as the guarantor of a better covenant, and Christ assures the availability of this covenant. Chapters 8–10 discuss the superiority of this covenant at length, arguing that the priestly system of sacrifice in the community of Israel was only a shadow of the better, heavenly system that Christ has now revealed. In this new system, Jesus is the high priest with a "more excellent ministry" because he is the "mediator of a new covenant" (8:6 NAU).

The first covenant is obsolete because Israel broke it, and a new one is required. This new covenant is radically different from the old. Its focus is spiritual and its scope encompasses the forgiveness of all sins, not just inadvertent ones.[34] This seems to be a sharp difference between Hebrews and the other New Testament sources, which tend to see the new covenant as more of a renewing or refurbishing of the old covenants (Rom. 9–11). However, the writer of Hebrews shows in chapters 9–10 that what is obsolete about the first covenant is its ritual activities and sacrifices, because these are not able to purify the conscience of the worshiper in the way the once-for-all sacrifice of Christ can (9:9, 14). The obsolescence of the old covenant "does not mean that God's moral law is abolished, but that the old covenant was an imperfect version of the heavenly prototype. . . . It is only the ceremonial laws of the Hebrew Bible that have been superseded."[35] Thus Moses and Jesus agree that the moral laws and God's will for humanity remain the same, because they form the basis for the teachings of both.[36]

The Hebrews writer is therefore emphasizing the internal as opposed to the external nature of the new versus the old covenants. Hebrews is showing their differing levels of effectiveness, not their absolute lack of continuity. The new covenant becomes effective with the death of Christ because a will or testament requires the death of the testator to go into effect (9:15–17).[37] And Hebrews' references to the death that inaugurates the covenant allude to both the words of the Last Supper and to Exodus 24:8: "This is the blood of the covenant that God has ordained for you" (Heb. 9:20 NRSV). Hebrews 9:23–10:18 goes on to elaborate the further superiority of Jesus as high priest whose sacrifice is effective for all sins and for all time.[38]

Perhaps Hebrews' most helpful contribution to the understanding of atonement is the presentation of Jesus as our high priest. A major part of the epistle is devoted to showing Christ acting on behalf of God's people to offer a permanent and fully effective sacrifice for sins. Christ is presented as replacing the Levitical order and as the surety of a better covenant (7:11–22). He is perfect forever, in contrast to the merely human priests, and offers himself as the perfect sacrifice once and for all (7:27). He thus provides for us a better hope because he continues forever (7:19, 24). And as the high priest he has to present a perfect sacrifice, which he does by presenting himself as the sacrifice that ultimately cleanses perfectly from sin and reestablishes the covenant with God.[39]

Christ establishes this covenant through the shedding of his own blood. The writer of Hebrews, in 9:16–18, reviews several reasons the blood is shed: "In the case of a will, it is necessary to prove the death of the one who made it, because a will is in force only when somebody has died; it never takes effect while the one who made it is living. This is why even the first covenant was not put into effect without blood."

In addition to life being in the blood, blood also functions as a symbolic cleansing agent. Blood was sprinkled over the people, the scroll, the altar, and everything used in the ceremonies (9:19–21) because it signifies a ceremonial cleansing of all contamination from sin of those items dedicated to the covenant rituals. This is why there is no forgiveness without the shedding of blood (9:22).[40] Everything used in worship must be purified and rededicated to covenant service. And if it was necessary to carry through all this ritual for the earthly implements used in worship, how much more is it necessary to cleanse the "heavenly things" that are used to enter the ultimate Most Holy Place, heaven itself (9:23–25)? Through the sacrificial shedding of his own blood, Christ provides the means of atonement and the ground upon which the case for mediation, acquittal, justification, reconciliation, and union with Christ is freely given to the believer.

Christ himself was thus dedicated, as the priestly representative of all humanity. Because humanity is in Christ by our identification with him in faith, says Cullman, his own blood cleanses him as the representative Man and sanctifies all he represents. As Christ goes into the presence of God, we are thus cleansed and taken into the presence of the Most Holy One. We are consecrated to his service as those who in Christ have participated in the covenant renewal and consecration through obedience to Christ. The blood of Christ's sacrifice signifies obedience to and participation in the divine expectations of the covenant with God. Christ's work in entering heaven "now to appear for us in God's presence" (9:24) is described in 9:14: "How much more, then, will the blood of Christ, who through the eternal Spirit offered himself unblemished to God, cleanse our consciences from acts that lead to death, so that we may serve the living God!" Christ's priestly work, made effectual by the Holy Spirit, turns the spiritual cleansing of the sacrament inward—the sacrament is now *us,* the community of faith in him—and this empowers *us* to serve God. For this reason, Christ has mediated a new covenant, so that *we* who are in him by faith may enjoy the eternal inheritance promised to God's covenant people (9:15).[41]

Hebrews also answers the question of human obligation in the covenant structure, beginning with the call to persevere: "Since we have confidence to enter the Most Holy Place by the blood of Jesus . . . and since we have a great priest over the house of God, let us draw near to God with a sincere heart in full assurance of faith. . . . Let us hold unswervingly to the hope we profess. . . . Let us consider how we may spur one another on. . . . Let us not give up meeting together . . . but let us encourage one another—and all the more as you see the Day approaching" (10:19–25).

While the divine side of the covenant includes writing the Law on people's hearts and minds and forgiving their sins, the human side entails faith and obedience in response to God's covenant blessings. The kind of obedience God desires is the kind Christ showed when he obeyed to the point of death. Motyer says, "He nullifies the power of death by *sharing in it*."[42] Christ's total identification with humanity in his incarnation and his participation in suffering and death leads the Hebrews writer to designate him the "pioneer of their salvation" (Heb. 2:10).[43] Thus Hebrews clearly understands what Christ did in his life and death to be the perfect example of obedience, in order that by identifying with his example of perfect obedience the people might be saved. The writer of Hebrews expresses this emphasis on Christ as our prototypical example by calling him the "pioneer" *(archegos)* "of our salvation" and "of faith" (Heb. 2:10; 12:2).[44] In the exhortation section of chapters 12 and 13, Christ's priestly work and example blaze the trail to mark out a template establishing the boundaries of covenant behavior, enabling that behavior by his own example and empowerment (12:2–3). Christians are called upon to follow the covenant behavior that is expected of the new covenant and "fix their eyes on Jesus" (12:2) and participate with him in his deliverance because he has participated with them in their suffering.[45]

Hebrews concludes with the marvelous benediction and affirmation of empowerment through Jesus' covenant ratification: "May the God of peace, who through the blood of the eternal covenant brought back from the dead our Lord Jesus, that great Shepherd of the sheep, equip you with everything good for doing his will, and may he work in us what is pleasing to him, through Jesus Christ, to whom be glory for ever and ever. Amen" (13:20–21).

Paul's Letters

In 2 Corinthians 3:6, Paul writes that God has made him and his coworkers the ministers of a "new covenant," which is not of the letter but of the Spirit. This may be a reminder of Jeremiah 31:31–33, which describes a new covenant with Israel and Judah that is written on their hearts and its laws will be written in their minds. Paul is not saying here that the old covenant is obsolete, but that in Christ it is made spiritual, "written on the heart." Though not materially different from the old, this new covenant refurbishes and clarifies and internalizes the old, so that one can get its real message. In the same way, Paul interprets the ministry of Christ as permanently removing the veil that covered the Torah when it was not being read, so that the meaning already inherent in the Mosaic covenant could be understood in its true spirit (2 Cor. 3:12–18).[46] Thus, as Paul shows in Romans 11, this new covenant validated in Jesus Christ stands in line with the other covenants of Israel. McKenzie says: "It is part of the same tree, not an entirely new stock. This line of previous covenants is not abolished or nullified with the coming of Christianity. The new covenant is not a relationship that renders the older covenants obsolete. Rather, in Christ they reach their climax in terms of their real intent and significance."[47]

In Romans 11:27, Paul seems to connect the new relationship with God through Christ and the Christian mission with Isaiah 59:21: "This is my covenant with them." Thus Christ's people are grafted into the original covenant relationship between God and his people, as the root and branches imagery suggests (Rom. 11:17–24), thereby bringing the salvation intent of the covenant to its final definition and universal application.[48]

Ephesians 2:11–22 continues this same universal theme. In Christ, the Gentiles, who formerly were aliens outside of Israel, have now been made citizens. By the same token, they are no longer "foreigners to the covenants of promise" (2:12), but participants in those covenants. The new covenant in Christ is not a separate dispensation in which God starts over with "Plan B," but is the culmination of a preparatory relationship that began with Israel and now comes to its full meaning in Christ. So the new covenant operates in the same interpersonal relationship mode as its predecessors.

Through Christ's identification with humanity, God renews his relationship with humanity. The entire ministry of Jesus—his incarnation, sacrifice, and obedience—serves as a tangible sign of the election of Israel *and* the Gentiles as God's people and of the reliability of God's promises. In 1 Corinthians 11:25, "This cup is the new covenant in my blood," Paul means that Jesus' blood and sacrifice provide the means through which the renewed covenant between God and the people is ratified.[49] Christ's sacrifice "fulfills" the promises and meaning of God's covenant and testifies to the reliability of the divine promises.

Though Paul, generally writing to a Gentile audience less familiar with covenant language, did not often use the explicit word "covenant" (*diathekē*), he clearly functioned theologically within a covenant perspective. For example, "justification" is a covenant word since "just" (*dikaios*) and "justify" (*dikaioō*) are frequent terms that describe a person or action in conformity with covenant expectations, as in the case of Isaiah 53:11: "My righteous servant will justify many." David's prayer of Psalm 51 states God is "justified" when he judges David's sins (v. 4). Likewise, the term "reconciliation" (Eph. 2:16) is a covenant word used numerous times in the Old Testament, as in "to make reconciliation" (*kaphar*, the same root as "atonement," in Lev. 6:30; 8:15; 16:20; Ezek. 45:15, 17, 20; Dan. 9:24). Paul's use of covenant concepts such as "promise" (Gal. 3:17, 18), "fellow citizens" and "God's household" (Eph. 2:19), and the "two covenants" discussion of Hagar and Sarah (Gal. 4:21–31) all indicate his orientation to covenant community as the background to his contextual theology, even when he is using forensic language such as "justification."[50]

In Galatians 3:16–17, Paul does use the word *diathekē,* "covenant," and relates the covenant of Abraham to Christ. This covenant functions in a new way, through the agency of Christ rather than through the sacrificial ritual. The universal invitation of Christ's covenant establishes a covenant relationship with all who will accept it. This reflects Paul's concept of the community of believers as the "body of Christ." In the relationship of covenant faith, the community participates in the Christ event that brings in the new age of God's salvation (Rom. 6:4). As Robert Wall notes, "This is the great indicative of the Church's redemption: those who depend upon God's dependable work are reconciled with God and each other; it can 'now' experience a Christ-like life, characterized by freedom from sin, from death, from legalism, and from all that alienates humanity from God's love (Rom. 5–8)."[51]

It should also be noted that, as the concept of divine wrath in the Gospels does not seem to be the controlling factor in requiring the atonement, divine wrath is also carefully defined in Paul's epistles as being different from the pagan concept of the anger and hostility of their gods. God's wrath is the result of sinners receiving the consequences of their evil deeds (Rom. 2:5–9). It is important to see that God's redeeming love is at least as strong as his desire to pour out vindictive judgments on the whole of humanity. Here is where the forensic lens is often allowed to distort the covenant ideas of relationship and reconciliation.

The New Testament Covenant Community

In the same way that Israel's election by God expanded their sense of community beyond family relationships to view themselves as an entire nation and ethnic group, as expressed in Genesis 12:2–3, so those called into the covenant relationship with Christ as his body gained a new concept of their identity (Eph. 4:1–16; 2 Cor. 5:14–21). Although Christians, particularly evangelicals, tend to neglect the role of the community in favor of their emphasis on establishing a personal relationship with Christ, a covenant understanding of community underscores the importance of fellowship with each other as with Christ.[52] The New Testament community of the new covenant is both personal and interpersonal. In 1 John 1:7, John stresses the importance of remaining in community, particularly as the place where forgiveness occurs. He emphasizes the connection between light and fellowship and forgiveness of sin: "If we walk in the light as he himself is in the light, we have fellowship with one another, and the blood of Jesus his Son cleanses us from all sin" (NRSV).[53]

The New Testament Christian community finds, explains, and describes its identity—its being—as the covenant community of God. This community is a gathered community (Heb. 10:25, a unified community (Eph. 4), and a sacramental community (Acts 2:42–47). Stanley Grenz has expounded the theological and ontological character of the church as covenant community in his discussion of the New Testament metaphors for the church: church as a nation (covenant people of God), church as Christ's body, and church as the Spirit's temple (i.e., the corporate fellowship as God's dwelling place). The church is also seen in "a three-part delineation: mystical, universal, and local."[54] For each of these different manifestations of the community, covenant remains the thread uniting the people of God who are one in the Spirit, sacrament, and faith.[55]

The covenant-making God established not only the possibility of community but also its necessity; the covenant relationship entails the divine expectations of love of God and love of neighbor. The interdependence of the two may be most clearly expressed in 1 John 4:7–8: "Beloved, let us love one another, because love is from God; everyone who loves is born of God and knows God. Whoever does not love does not know God, for God is love" (NRSV).

The covenant theme establishes the Christian community in the history of the people of God. Willard Swartley writes: "Lines of continuity and major points of unity will also emerge in the biblical text, since ultimately the Bible testifies to the redemptive activity of one God. Some of the major points of unity and continuity are clearly the one God of the Old and New Testaments, the story of God's covenant peoplehood throughout the biblical history. . . ."[56] The covenanting of God in and with the Christian community establishes it as markedly his—the community *of* God.

This theology of God's covenanting atonement and its divine expectations answers the questions often raised by natural science: "How do living things, including human beings, exist in relation to one another in their common habitat?" The New Testament expressions of covenant community allow, and indeed require, the healing power of the atonement to reach beyond relations between God and humans and humans with humans to an ecological reconciliation and renewal of all things (Col. 15–20).[57]

Stanley Grenz has pointed out the destruction of community by sin, stating, "The fundamental result of sin is the loss of community."[58] The new creation in the atoning work of Christ is covenantal, expressing itself in reconciled community. As Howard Snyder puts it, "Christian community starts at the point of commitment and covenant. There is no genuine Christian community without a covenant. . . . Christian community cannot exist without commitment to Jesus as Lord and to each other as sister and brother."[59]

The expression of covenant in Christian community is to be a benefit of the atoning work of Christ. Walter Brueggemann notes the erroneous tendency to interpret the new covenant individualistically: "'The new covenant' is not a proposal for individualism, as Jeremiah 31:33 is often taken to be. Rather, it is in fact a powerful protest against the individualist autonomy of modernity, and an insistence that we are indeed members of one another."[60] Only through participation in the body of Christ—an image that permeates Paul's writings—do believers find liberty in their unity, being built up by one another (Rom. 12; 1 Cor. 12; Eph. 3:6). This image demonstrates how the benefits of community are based on covenant expectation.

The language of the new covenant pervades the book of Hebrews (8:8, 13; 9:15; 12:24) and provides the context for statements and admonitions regarding the Christian community. Hebrews 8:8–12—which displays the longest quotation of the Old Testament in the New, Jeremiah 31:31–34—not only speaks of the fulfillment of this prophecy but is replete with implications for the covenant community. This new covenant put in the midst of the corporate community sets apart the Christian community as the community of God.[61] Thus the community is both identified by and obligated to the expectations of the covenant.

It is important to note that this epistle, with its corporate exhortations, was intended for a corporate audience.[62] Therefore the author's exposition on the atonement of Christ rightfully leads to the exhortation for the community to hold fast to its corporate hope, spur one another on to love and good deeds, and be faithful to gather together (Heb. 10:23–25). Since Christ's atonement is both sufficient and superior to the old covenant, it fulfills the corporate hope of a real community of well-being and righteousness. The writing of the Law upon their hearts not only provides hope for a future but also potential for the present—through the "more excellent ministry" and the "better covenant" of Christ's reconciling covenant atonement (8:6 NAU).[63]

The description of the earliest church in Acts shows the fulfillment of covenant hope in the real devotion of their fellowship. The poor are not trampled on or oppressed (cf. Amos 2:7; 5:11; 8:4), but in stark contrast justice and mercy prevail as possessions and goods are distributed to all who have need. The covenant community is further realized in worship of God and growth of the community (Acts 2:42–47). The divine expectations of love have real effect individually and corporately, within the community and in the world.[64]

Eucharist and Baptism

The gathered community recalls and commemorates the "covenant event,"[65] established as a part of history but continuing into the present and future of the church. Thus Jesus' establishment of the sacrament of the Eucharist—"He took bread, gave thanks and broke it, and gave it to them, saying, 'This is my body given for you; do this in remembrance of me'" (Luke 22:19) and, "In the same way, after supper he took the cup, saying, 'This cup is the new covenant in my blood; do this, whenever you drink it, in remembrance of me'" (1 Cor. 11:25)—provided for the repeated gathering and eucharistic (i.e., thanksgiving) celebration of the "new covenant" and perfect atonement in Christ's blood. The narrative of Pentecost followed by the first New Testament description of the new church reveals a gathered covenant community sharing the Eucharist together frequently as an act of devotion (Acts 2:42–47; 20:7; 1 Cor. 11:17–34).

The Eucharist expresses a lasting and personal relationship between Christ and the church in a new and creative way. The Last Supper anticipated Jesus' death as the historical event upon which the covenant relationship with God would be based. With the cross we see clearly the faithfulness of Christ revealing in history God's righteousness that creates salvation (Rom. 3:21–26). The "new command" of love, "as I have loved you" (Jn. 13:34), stipulates the condition that binds Jesus and the church. The divine expectations for the church are to model the sacrificial love of Christ for others. This is participation in the covenantal relationship that is expressed in the Eucharist, as the anticipation, then, and the remembrance, now, of the cross, that becomes the most profound expression of the covenant relationship of interpersonal and sacrificial love.[66]

The participation of the community of faith in the Eucharist as a common act of worship and witness recalls the foundation of the covenant community (1 Cor. 10:14–22; 11:23–26).[67] The cup of faith takes the place of the sacrificial oath in confirming the new covenant relationship; Christ's person and work are God's offer, and the Eucharist and life of obedient faith are the church's response. The New Testament teaches that Jesus understood his death as the sacrifice by which a new and superior covenant would be enacted between God and the new Israel, notes Richardson. The Eucharist therefore takes the place of all the Old Testament sacrifices and feasts and becomes the "new Passover-memorial which commemorates the deliverance of the new Israel from sin and death."[68]

Similarly, baptism corresponds with circumcision as the initiatory rite of incorporation into the faith community. Circumcision was originally a sign of the covenant and served to identify the recipients of the covenant mercies as concrete proof of its existence.[69] It served as a symbol of regeneration and as an outward sign that sin had been removed (Lev. 26:41; Deut. 10:16). No longer a sacrament of salvation for the Christian church, in the new covenant its significance is transmuted into baptism, which includes both genders and incorporates all humanity who responds to the gospel in faith-obedience.[70] In the New Testament, baptism thus becomes the external sign of an interpersonal relationship with God in Christ.

The sacrament of baptism illustrates the union of the believer with Christ to participate in both his death and resurrection. This union not only takes place in history, but also is anticipatory of the complete and ultimate experience of salvation of God's people in the last day.[71] Romans 6 describes this identification of Christ with sinners and vice versa. In Romans 6:3–10. Paul shows that those who are baptized into Christ share his death as well as his resurrection-life and righteousness. That is the reason there is no condemnation for them (Rom. 8:1).[72] The Christ who died for our transgressions was also raised for our justification (Rom. 4:25). Thus the union with Christ in faith-obedience as expressed in baptism is based on the sharing in the totality of the incarnational life of Christ because he has first shared in the weakness of humanity (Phil. 2:5–11).

Law in the New Testament

Hartmut Gese addresses the controversial issue of the meaning of the Law in the New Testament in a very perceptive way. He shows that the Gospels see the Law "in terms of the proclamation and life of Jesus. Paul, with his theology of the cross, understands the law in terms of salvation history's goal—the death and resurrection of Jesus."[73] The apostle sees the Law as defining humanity's being in a state of alienation far from the glory of God. The wisdom of God is available to Gentiles through the revelation of nature (Rom. 1:18–23) and to the Jews through the Torah (Rom. 2:17–24). The Synoptics answer the question of Torah in relation to the role of Jesus. Gese says, "The Torah of Jesus is more than a simple and questionable freedom from Torah; it is the foundation of complete and perfect *shalom*, in which God's holiness penetrates the furthest depths of the world."[74]

Gese notes that by the references to the Decalogue of the original Torah, ("You have heard that it was said to the people long ago . . . But I tell you. . . ." Matt. 5:21–22, etc.), Matthew shows that the Torah of the new covenant completes the history of revelation. "The . . . Torah is not to be abolished, but to be 'fulfilled,' and this is absolutely correct," says Gese.[75] As Ezekiel and Jeremiah saw (Ezek. 36:25–27; Jer. 31:31–34), through the forgiveness of sins and the writing of the Torah on the heart of believers, a new spirit will be given that will bring total obedience to the Torah.[76]

In the transfiguration narrative (Matt. 17:1–8; Mark: 9:2–8; Luke 9:28–36), Jesus ascends the "high mountain" that is not further identified. The scene recalls the Old Testament: "Then the cloud covered the Tent of Meeting, and the glory of the LORD filled the tabernacle. Moses could not enter the Tent of Meeting because the cloud had settled upon it, and the glory of the LORD filled the tabernacle" (Ex. 40:34–35). At the transfiguration, Peter, James, and John were covered by the divine *doxa,* and they heard the revelation of the new covenant. "In the ancient event at Sinai," Gese concludes, "God revealed himself in the formula of self-introduction, 'I am Yahweh,' and then he gave the Decalogue. Here, however, God introduces his son, 'This is my beloved Son,' and then he continues, 'listen to him.' Jesus himself has become the revealed Word. The gospel writers could not present it more powerfully: Jesus himself is the Torah."[77]

In Paul's view, according to Gese's interpretation, the Law itself is the revelation of God and is not sinful (Rom. 7:7, 12). But the Law makes sin obvious and reveals how far humans are from God's glory and holiness (Rom. 7:13). The Law's purpose—fulfilled in Christ—is to overcome our lostness "by making peace through his blood, shed on the cross" (Col. 1:20). The Law leads to the cross because it was designed to provide guidelines for living when our world and inclinations are in rebellion against God (Gal. 3:24). Our failure to conform to these boundaries has resulted in our losing our moral compass bearings and has led humanity into a moral wilderness of alienation from God, the very source of life. And in our sin we are morally incapable of fulfilling God's covenant expectations for us as presented in the Law, for obedience is based on faith (Gal. 3:10–13). Therefore, in the disobedience of our rebellion against this Law, we have chosen the path of separation from God, which is death (Rom. 6:23). But through his identification with us, Jesus fulfills our faithful obedience to the Law, gives himself over to the elemental spirits of the world for us, and bears our death for us—the death which we inherited through Adam (Rom. 5:12). His atonement overcomes the distance between God and ourselves, for in him God is with us

(Rom. 3:25). The gospel of the Crucified One is thus the fulfilled goal of the Old Testament Law for Paul.[78]

N. T. Wright also emphasizes that in Christ the purpose of the Torah is fulfilled. Paul's theme in Romans is the covenant purposes of God, and he traces it from its inception with Abraham to its fulfillment in the Messiah. So now, Paul says, the Torah is fulfilled and the climax of the covenant is reached when anyone, Jew or Gentile, hears the gospel of Christ and believes it (Rom. 10:5–13). The "word of faith" (v. 8) is that "if you confess with your mouth, 'Jesus is Lord,' and believe in your heart that God raised him from the dead, you will be saved" (v. 9). Wright says this is the doing of the Torah of which Leviticus speaks, so that when Christ is preached and believed the Torah is being fulfilled.[79]

The purpose of the covenant all along was to remedy the sin that alienated Israel and all humankind from God. Now, in Christ, that has finally occurred. In place of these prescriptions of the Law, therefore, the church understands faith as the condition of entering into the covenant relationship with God based on God's work in Christ (2 Cor. 5:19; Rom. 3:25–26) to abolish the curse of the Law through the cross. "The righteousness of God has been revealed in Jesus Christ, who is the new Torah. Thus the mission of the church is to testify to the continuity of God's faithfulness to his covenant promises as they have finally come to fulfillment in Jesus the Messiah."[80]

McKenzie likewise points out that the covenant obligation in both the Old Testament and New Testament is to love God with all your being. Jesus' point in the Sermon on the Mount is that the intent of the Law in the Old Testament is the same as his own—obey the covenant Law by loving God and everyone else. Nevertheless, identification with Christ and the continued ministry of the Holy Spirit are necessary to enable one to live in conformity to that love. Jesus is not presenting instruction to replace that given by Moses, but clarifies, internalizes, and amplifies it. He is rejecting the distortions of those interpretations of the Law that limit the covenant principles to Israel alone. He makes clear that God is concerned for all people of all national and ethnic origins. The neighbor can be anyone. On that, both Jew and Gentile should agree.[81]

Finally, Paul says that while the old covenant was glorious, the new covenant is even greater because its Law is engraved on the heart rather than stone (2 Cor. 3:6–11). The former Law was temporary; the new law is eternal. The weakness of the old Law lay not in its integrity or its truth, but in the inability of the human heart to conform to its spirit without the indwelling empowerment of the Holy Spirit that was given after Christ's resurrection. Cranfield notes that "in the absence of the Spirit the law is misused and comes to be for those who misuse it simply 'letter.' . . . Not until Christ's resurrection and the gift of the Spirit could law come into its own as the law which is 'unto life' (Rom. 7:10)."[82] As the new Torah, then, the Spirit of Christ works within to restore and reconcile humanity and fulfills God's covenant goal by restoring the relationship with humanity that was lost by the fall.

7

Key New Testament Atonement Elements

How does the atonement work? While it is clear *that* Christ establishes this new covenant as the context in which forgiveness and reconciliation can occur, it is less clear in scripture just *how* Christ's action can cancel the effects of sin and reconcile humanity to God. A number of metaphors are used to depict the means of atonement. These metaphors include the ideas of sacrifice, ransom, redemption, reconciliation, justification, adoption, and regeneration. The common element in these metaphors is the concern to release the sinner from the alienating consequences of sin and restore the penitent to fellowship with God through forgiveness.[1] When interpreting these metaphors, they must all be understood against the background of the covenant with its personal and relational implications. The promises of the covenant require fulfillment of its obligations and conditions—its "divine expectations." Barr cautions against any facile attempt to render "covenant" as a unilateral sort of obligation.[2] Furthermore, the Abrahamic covenant is at least implicitly conditional and the Mosaic covenant is explicitly conditional and stresses Israel's responsibility: "Now if you obey me fully and keep my covenant, then out of all nations you will be my treasured possession" (Ex. 19:5).

The atonement originates in the character of God, whose nature is love. Love is God's holiness in relationship. Love, not wrath, initiates the atonement. Since love is an interpersonal reality, so is salvation. It is not an "it" that God offers, but a relationship he enters with believers. The concepts of atonement, salvation, and forgiveness are thus understood in terms of *hesed,* the covenant-love that brings together God and sinners. Forgiveness is a loving action that takes priority over all other principles. Jocz says, "In a sense God violates the principle of equity to practice mercy—and takes upon Himself the consequences in terms of suffering."[3]

This love does not limit itself to the laws of justice, although it is not in opposition to them.[4] It is not a legally accepted practice for one person to incur a penalty and for another person to pay the price. The failure to distinguish between God's righteousness and human justice significantly distorts the role of love in salvation. In the biblical context, God's righteousness means mercy, compassion, and pity. In the Old Testament it is used synonymously with salvation and redemption. If forgiveness is merely an impersonal principle or a legal act, salvation becomes simply a mechanical transaction. That is why the attempts to explain the atonement only as a legal transaction are unsatisfying. God's righteousness not only goes beyond, but may even contradict, legal justice in the sense of impersonal civil codes. God is a Father of love, not simply of legal justice. King David certainly did not get what he deserved, nor did he pay the equivalent ransom for what he did. Yet God forgave him. The atonement and salvation are not properly understood outside the context of the biblical covenant and the relational nature of covenant Law. New Testament salvation is the revelation of the loving faithfulness of a covenant-keeping God.[5]

The Wrath of God

God's wrath grows out of the divine love for creation and is an expression of the divine jealousy that seeks to protect the persons and creation within the covenant relationship. Like a parent that responds with a protective ferocity against threats to her/his offspring, God seeks to remove those whose actions pose a threat to the existence of the divine covenant purposes and bring destruction to the beloved covenant people, as in Deuteronomy 29 when God sought to protect the covenant by bringing curses on those whose idolatry threatened the community.

Although divine wrath is not the same thing as human anger, it is clearly a result of his people violating the divine covenant trust. In the Old Testament, the wrath of God is the divine anger focused against those who would destroy the covenant relationship between Israel and Yahweh. Deuteronomy 29:24–28 states: "All the nations will ask: 'Why has the LORD done this to this land? Why this fierce, burning anger?' And the answer will be: 'It is because this people abandoned the covenant of the LORD, the God of their fathers, the covenant he made with them when he brought them out of Egypt. . . . In furious anger and in great wrath the LORD uprooted them from their land and thrust them into another land, as it is now.'"

In Jeremiah 7:22–24, Yahweh says the divine wrath toward Israel is the result of their disobedience: "For when I brought your forefathers out of Egypt and spoke to them, I did not just give them commands about burnt offerings and sac-rifices, but I gave them this command: Obey me, and I will be your God and you will be my people. Walk in all the ways I command you, that it may go well with you. But they did not listen or pay attention; instead, they followed the stubborn inclinations of their evil hearts. They went backward and not forward."

Other examples of divine wrath are related to ceremonial and liturgical prac-tices such as the priests and Levites caring for the tabernacle and its functioning so that wrath will not fall on the Israelites (Num. 1:53; 18:5), or God striking the people with a plague because of their rebellion (Num. 16:46). In the Prophets, Yahweh's wrath is directed against Israel's enemies (e.g., Isa. 59:18; 63:3, 6), as well as against Judah and Israel for their sins (e.g., Amos 2:4, 6). In the Gospels, Jesus warns of God's wrath as he preaches to Israel (Lk. 21:23; John 3:36), as does John the Baptist (Matt. 3:7; Lk. 3:7). The wrath of judgment against the nations who reject God is prophesied in the Apocalypse (Rev. 6:16–17; 11:18; 14:10, 19; 15:1, 7; 16:1, 19; 19:15).

God's wrath is always in the context of justice and obedience. Paul teaches that wrath is unleashed upon those who reject the truth (Rom. 1:18). God's wrath is also based on accountability for one's actions and knowledge of moral expecta-tions. Sinners store up their own wrath (Rom. 2:5) by rejecting the truth (Rom. 2:8). God is impartial in his justice (Rom. 2:11), and bases justice and salvation on Christ's work and declares righteous those who obey what they know of God's revelation: "Indeed, when Gentiles, who do not have the law, do by nature things required by the law, they are a law for themselves, even though they do not have the law, since they show that the requirements of the law are written on their hearts, their consciences also bearing witness, and their thoughts now accusing, now even defending them." Rom. 2:14–15). In short, God's requirements to avoid his wrath are to be obedient to his divine expectations and to follow his laws of righteousness in order to avoid stockpiling our own wrath.

It is difficult to find any statements in Scripture that God's wrath needs to be appeased through the death of Christ in order for salvation to occur. Jesus calls Israel to avoid God's wrath by believing in him. In the New Testament, the phrase "wrath of God" occurs only in the Pauline writings and the Apocalypse: Romans 1:18; Eph. 5:6; Colossians 3:6; 1 Thessalonians 2:16; Revelation 15:7 and 19:15, although "wrath" is mentioned many times. In the Pauline material, the wrath of God is directed toward those who persist in rejecting God's love and justice. Nothing is said about that wrath being appeased, for it will certainly fall on those deserving of it. While believers are justified by Christ's blood and saved through him (Rom 5:9; Eph. 2:4–6), God's wrath will never cease to be focused on sin, evil, and corruption—Christ's atonement does not stop it. What Christ's atonement does is remove those united with him from the *consequences* of God's wrath. Paul says: "To those who by persistence in doing good seek glory, honor and immortality, he will give eternal life. But for those who are self-seeking and who reject the truth and follow evil, there will be wrath and anger" (Rom. 2:7–8).

Two of the Revelation passages (15:7; 16:1) speak of the bowls of wrath God will have poured out on the wicked. Paul proclaims, "The wrath of God is being revealed from heaven against all the godlessness and wickedness of men who suppress the truth by their wickedness, since what may be known about God is plain to them, because God has made it plain to them" (Rom. 1:18–19). Those who are repentant and seek to follow the way of truth are not the targets of divine wrath, but those who wickedly turn against the God of creation are "given over" to their own lustful and evil choices (Rom. 1:24, 26–27, 28). God's wrath clearly does exist, and it is directed against sin and unbelief.

But what is the "wrath of God," anyway? It certainly has to do with God's hatred of sin. God will never cease to hate sin, nor will he ever be pleased with those living in sin, although he loves them as his creation. Christ's death has not changed that. Neither is Christ without wrath, for he will administer the judgment of God's wrath upon sin when "God will judge men's secrets through Jesus Christ" (Rom. 2:16). "God and Christ are one, even in judgment," says Richardson.[6] It is Jesus who predicts the doom of Jerusalem and judgment upon Judaism (Mark 11:14, 20; Luke 13:34–35; 19:41–44). But this wrath is against sin and evil, not against the person, for God loves his creation. It is the devil, in contrast, who seeks to destroy persons (1 Peter 5:8). God's character is love. His wrath against sin and unbelief grows out of that love for his creation and the desire to maintain covenant integrity with his people. Wrath is relational in nature. Wrath is God's attitude and actions against that which alienates humanity and creation from him and his salvation and seeks to destroy life. Since God is the source of life, those entities alienated from him are in rebellion against him and are thus separated from life. Wrath is the destruction that comes from being disconnected from life. As Paul writes to the Colossians:

> Since, then, you have been raised with Christ, set your hearts on things above, where Christ is seated at the right hand of God. Set your minds on things above, not on earthly things. For you died, and your life is now hidden with Christ in God. When Christ, who is

your life, appears, then you also will appear with him in glory. Put
to death, therefore, whatever belongs to your earthly nature: sexual
immorality, impurity, lust, evil desires and greed, which is idolatry.
Because of these, the wrath of God is coming. (Col 3:1–6)

Although the death of Christ is the sacrifice that opens up salvation for sinners, his death does not diminish God's wrath against sin. In Ephesians 5:6, the
apostle says that "God's wrath comes on those who are disobedient." And the
warnings of the "coming wrath" (Matt. 3:7; Luke 3:7), the "day of God's wrath"
(Rom. 2:5), and the "wrath of the Lamb" (Rev. 6:16) are not limited to the days
prior to Christ's death. This wrath remains on sin and on everyone who lives in sin
and unbelief and rejects Christ. As John writes, "Whoever believes in the Son has
eternal life, but whoever rejects the Son will not see life, for God's wrath remains
on him" (John 3:36).

God does not intend, however, for those who live in faith to suffer the coming wrath, but to receive salvation from Christ who rescues those in him (1 Thess.
5:9). Believers are delivered from God's wrath *when they are restored to the
appropriate covenant relationship with God through faith in Christ.* And those
who through justification and reconciliation through faith in Christ have gained
access to God's grace shall be "saved from God's wrath through him" because
through Christ's death and resurrected life they have been reconciled to God
(Rom. 5:9–11) and reconnected to the source of life through union with Christ in
his death and resurrection (Rom. 6). Salvation from God's wrath is a result of having been justified and reconciled to God through the sacrifice of Christ's death.
But nothing in Scripture says that the way this has happened is that God's wrath
has been satiated by being poured out on Christ.[7] The Bible clearly says, instead,
that Christ, at God's initiative, saves humanity from being the targets of that wrath
of God, both in the present and in the future eschatological age.

> Therefore, if anyone is in Christ, he is a new creation; the old has
> gone, the new has come! All this is from God, who reconciled us to
> himself through Christ and gave us the ministry of reconciliation:
> that God was reconciling the world to himself in Christ, not count-
> ing men's sins against them. And he has committed to us the mes-
> sage of reconciliation. (2 Cor. 5:17–19)

God's retribution is directed at those whose sin threatens to destroy the community of faith and the creation. Wrath will certainly fall on those evildoers who
persist in rebellious ways.[8] Through Christ's atoning work, however, divine wrath
ceases against those who are brought into covenant relationship by union with

Christ. It is only the unrepentant against whom God's wrath is inevitable (2 Thess. 1:8–10). Gustav Aulén points out Luther's emphasis that the curse of sin brings God's anger upon sinners, but *the divine work of love opens up the path for the believer through the anger of God*.[9] That happens through his sacrifice on the cross as he fully participates in ("takes on") humanity's death resulting from sin,[10] so the sinner may participate in Christ's life resulting from resurrection. Thus, by identifying with Christ the sinner chooses to unsubscribe from the list of participants in God's wrath. This bases all aspects of salvation squarely in Christ's work, although divine wrath is not required to fall upon those who are obediently repentant and who participate in God's own provision of covenant obedience in Christ's sacrifice.[11]

The Righteousness (*dikaiosunē*) of God

Much controversy surrounds the interpretation of Paul's use of the phrase the "righteousness of God." The cultural nuance projected by the reader upon the term *dikaiosunē tou theou* in Romans 1:17 and 3:21 shapes its meaning. The modern Western reader tends to think of the term "righteousness," *dikaiosunē*, in the sense of the Greco-Roman idea of justice/righteousness as an ethical norm against which behavior or duties can be measured. But the reader needs to get behind Paul's use of the Greek language and understand his Jewish background as a rabbinical student.[12]

Old Testament Background for "Righteousness of God"

The biblical idea of righteousness is somewhat different from the Greco-Roman idea of an ethical norm. Rather than defining righteousness as a quality or virtue, the Hebrew community defines it in the covenant terms of right relationship. In the Old Testament, righteousness does include the judicial concept, but it also contains far more.

Dikaiosunē and its related Greek words are used over 460 times in the Septuagint (Greek Old Testament) to translate the words derived from the Hebrew root of *tsedeq*. The linguistic background of *tsedeq* can be seen in *Keret*, the fourteenth-century BC Ugaritic epic, where its root refers to right relationship to expectations. In the Phoenician tablets of Byblus from the twelfth century, the word appears with a different meaning when Yehimelek pleads for the prolonging of his life because he has been "a righteous and upright king." This seems to connote the quality of his rule, and that he has tried to accomplish what was expected of him,[13] thus conforming to the standards expected of a king. In Arabic, likewise, the concept of righteousness means that which is right, stable, and substantial. Thus the idea seems to be that of conformity to a norm.[14] It also means, "what is right, just, normal." It is the "rightness" or "justness" as of a perfect and just weight.[15] The Hebrew term is also used to refer to scales and weights (Lev. 19:36; Ezek. 45:10) and measures (Deut. 25:15), where it connotes conformity to proper standards.[16] The sacrifices of Deuteronomy 33:19, Psalm 4:5, and Psalm 51:19 are *tsedeq*—correct, conforming to a norm. However, this is not an absolute abstract standard of "rightness," but rather a "rightness" that is defined in each particular situation according to the context.[17]

Righteousness also governs the relationships within the community of Israel. That pattern of conduct that conforms to the demands of the community relationship and thus preserves society is regarded as *tsedeq*, or "righteousness."[18] Hermann Cremer, in his fundamental study, also emphasizes this relational aspect of *tsedeq*, describing the essence of its Old Testament usage as a relational concept referring to an actual relationship between two persons; *tsedeq* characterizes behavior that is faithful to the claims arising from the divine expectations of the covenant (covenant-faithfulness).[19]

Righteousness is thus not a quality possessed by a person, even God. Instead, it is the condition that characterizes a person's relationship to what is appropriately expected. For example, people are righteous when they act consistently with the expectations others have for them in a relationship.[20] From another perspective, it was the responsibility of the king to attend to the right ordering of Israel's life by seeing that the laws were obeyed and that well-being was enjoyed. Moreover, since the king was the representative of God's rule over the nation, the harmonious ordering of life was ultimately the concern of God. The norm by which *tsedeq* is determined for both God and the nation is the appropriate conformity to the covenant-relationship and its responsibilities, its divine expectations. When both Yahweh and the people are fulfilling their covenant-obligations to one another, things are ideally "as they should be," and the state of affairs that results is *tsedeq*.[21]

The Old Testament concept of the righteousness of God, therefore, refers to the right conduct of God in upholding the stipulations of the covenant, both for himself and for Israel. He never fails to fulfill his promises, in loyalty to his covenant (1 Sam. 2:2; Ezra 9:15; Deut. 32:4). God has taken on himself the obligations to rescue Israel and punish Israel's enemies. Thus righteousness is "covenant faithfulness." In the Psalms and Isaiah, this logic makes the ideas of salvation and righteousness virtually synonymous since God's righteousness is his acting to restore and sustain them within the covenant. The Lord says:

> I, the LORD, have called you in righteousness; I will take hold of your hand. I will keep you and will make you to be a covenant for the people and a light for the Gentiles, to open eyes that are blind, to free captives from prison and to release from the dungeon those who sit in darkness (Isa. 42:6–7).

The righteousness of God expresses the divine activity of grace in action for the vindication of his people. It is God's "putting things right" for them and in this sense bears the connotation of salvation.[22] Indeed, Isaiah expounds this aspect of *tsedeq* by making it the key to understanding the entire work of salvation. God reveals his righteousness in his redemptive acts by which he restored his covenant people: the Covenant, the Exodus, the provision of Canaan, the Law. On this point of God's righteousness providing the covenant salvation for Israel, Isaiah unites the concept of righteousness with God's lovingkindness, loyalty, and aid in distress (42:6, 21; 45:8, 13; 46:13; 51:6). Although this saving righteousness sometimes involved judgment for the heathen (41:2,10–12), its basic element was the gift of salvation, both to Israel and the Gentile world (51:5; cf. 45:24) through the establishment and maintenance of the covenant.[23] This salvation deliverance was for not only the weak and oppressed, but the Psalms, for example, show that it was available for any humble, trusting person who pleads a case against the wicked and whom God pronounces "in the right."[24] In line with this Old Testament background, Paul eloquently states the gospel is the "power of God for salvation" because it reveals God's righteousness as his saving activity that conforms to his covenant promises as the covenant community fulfills its expectations of obedient faith (Rom. 1:16, 17).[25]

God's righteousness has as its goal the restoring of relationships, not simply the legal task of matching punishments to crimes committed. From beginning to end, the righteousness of God seeks to restore covenant communion by bringing Israel back into the safety of covenant salvation. Thus the "righteousness of God" must be clearly understood as God's loving and holy character at work in his saving activity of salvation. The concept of "justice" may be involved in the sense that God's character has integrity and is consistent with his covenant expressions and promises, but "justice" understood exclusively as God's pouring out condemning and convicting wrath is not an accurate rendering of the full meaning of his righteousness.

The "Righteousness of God" in the New Testament

Even though Israel at times tended to rely on its election as the basis of its salvation, the New Testament exposed this fallacy. John the Baptist protested, "And do not think you can say to yourselves, 'We have Abraham as our father. . . .'" (Matt. 3:9; Luke 3:8). The Baptist showed that repentance was not only necessary, but that it must be based exclusively on faith in the Messiah (Matt. 3:8, 11). Jesus said, "I have not come to call the righteous, but sinners to repentance" (Luke 5:32). Jesus states in reference to the fulfillment of the Law and Prophets, "This is what is written: The Christ will suffer and rise from the dead on the third day, and repentance and forgiveness of sins will be preached in his name to all nations, beginning at Jerusalem"(Luke 24:46–47; see vv. 44–45). Luke also cites Peter preaching regarding Jesus, "God exalted him to his own right hand as Prince and Savior that he might give repentance and forgiveness of sins to Israel"(Acts 5:31). Likewise, Paul teaches, "I have declared to both Jews and Greeks that they must turn to God in repentance and have faith in our Lord Jesus" (Acts 20:21). Sanders says, "The heart of Paul's thought is . . . that one dies with Christ . . . which leads to resurrection and ultimate transformation, that one is a member of the body of Christ and one Spirit with him. . . ."[26]

In the New Testament, therefore, faith in God's atonement in Christ as the ground of covenant-maintenance replaced the atoning sacrifice of repentance that had come to be the basis of hope in the rabbinic theology of the day. Jesus' teaching of the saving righteousness of God negated the doctrine of salvation by repentance and works.[27] Parables such as the following emphasize God's forgiving grace and include a polemic against the atoning significance of the works-oriented repentance concept: the prodigal son (Luke 15:11–31), the Pharisee and the tax collector (Luke 18:9–14), the laborers in the vineyard (Matt. 20:1–16), and the great banquet (Luke 14:16–24). Jesus' primary purpose is to call to repentance those who place their trust in the forgiving grace of God rather than those who insist that their repentance in itself makes them righteous (Mark 2:17). Christ's work of salvation by God's righteousness in himself is also expressed by his acts of healing (Mark 1:14–2:12) and in his relationships with the sinful (Luke 19:1–10; 7:36–49). Therefore, salvation is not by works of law-keeping or by repentance as atonement, but by faith in the one of whom Isaiah prophesied, "by his knowledge my righteous servant will justify many, and he will bear their iniquities" (53:11).[28] The ground, or basis, of salvation was thus shifted to the work of Christ as the manifestation of the "righteousness of God" and the embodiment of the "divine expectations." This shift not only presents Christ as the continuation of the covenant hope, but maintains the unity of the Trinity in the cooperation of the Son and the Father and the Spirit, who energize and implement Christ's work, working together for the maintenance of the covenant relationship with humanity.

Among the New Testament writers, Paul alone clearly sees and develops the prophetic concept of the salvation function of the divine righteousness and its relationship to justification. The other New Testament writers seem to adopt the Septuagint usage of *dikaiosunē*, "righteousness," as conduct that is pleasing to God and harmonious to his will.[29] But for Paul, the "righteousness of God," *dikaiosunē tou theou*, is not so much conduct or an attribute as it is the saving activity of God. It is God's grace acting in order to vindicate his covenant people.[30] This righteousness is just in that it also addresses the relevance of Christ's sacrifice to cover God's forgiveness of sin in the past (Rom. 3:26).[31]

Paul always uses the phrase *dikaiosunē tou theou* in relationship to the atoning sacrifice of Christ (Rom. 1:17; 3:21–26; 2 Cor. 5:21).[32] It expresses God's intention freely and graciously to justify sinners. Legal justice operates on the concept of equity, of "this for that," or tit for tat. By contrast, the "righteousness of God" is not simply God's justice in operation for judgment, but his grace in operation for redemption. God does not offer "something" (salvation), but himself. Salvation means to accept God in the person of Jesus Christ. Love cannot be expressed in impersonal terms. We must distinguish between God's righteousness and human justice. The righteousness of God of which Paul speaks (Rom 3:21–26) "is not legal justice, but clemency, compassion, pity," Jocz reminds us.[33]

This distinctive interpretation of the "righteousness of God," coming as it does from a Jew whose inheritance was within the mainstream of Pharisaic Judaism, not only puts justification completely outside the ground of the "works of the law" (Gal. 2:15–16 NAU), but bases it upon faith in the atoning ministry of Christ.[34] This requires a fundamental reinterpretation of the concept of justification that to be "in the right" before God depends on one's achievement through obedience to the Law. Western distributive justice is based on what one deserves, in contrast to God's actions toward those who are undeserving.[35] It is "apart from the law" (Rom. 3:20–21). Instead, Paul shows that "righteousness" for the believer is a result of being "in Christ" through faith.[36] Thus righteousness is not a quality that is transmitted, or actually imparted, nor is it imputed as a moral fiction "as if" the believer possessed it. Instead, it is union with Christ, not the supposed imputation of righteousness, that is the basis for being "in the right" in relationship to God.[37]

This concept of receiving through faith the justifying effects of the outgoing "power of God for salvation" (Rom. 1:16, 17), which efficaciously reveals God's saving activity in Christ, is thoroughly and assuredly eschatological. However, through the life, death, and resurrection of Christ, the judgment and salvation that were formerly expected in the last days have been accomplished in the present.[38] As Quell and Schrenk say, "The justified, who have grasped the Now of forgiveness at the cross, can look forward with confidence to the final sentence. . . . It is declared in the light of history and grasped by faith as a present reality."[39] The "righteousness of God," his activity of saving mercy, has been revealed in the completed work of saving love demonstrated in the incarnational sacrificial gift of Christ's life through the cross and resurrection and made available to all those who in faith are united with him.

Justification

Perhaps the most hotly debated issue regarding the benefits of the atonement focuses on the doctrine of justification by faith and how it relates to other aspects of salvation. The traditional Reformed view stresses the primacy of justification and subordinates all other emphases to it. In contrast, the extreme view of Wrede, Davies, and Schweitzer claimed that the entire Pauline religion can be expounded with only a cursory reference to it.[40] Others such as James Stewart, without minimizing the significance of justification in Pauline theology, posit the concept of union with Christ as Paul's central message.[41] Others such as C. A. A. Scott and A. M. Hunter prefer to see justification as a part of the whole message of salvation, not the epitome of Paul's gospel. It is just the first step in Paul's whole teaching. Hunter understands "salvation" as a more comprehensive word to express the richness of Christianity according to Paul.[42]

George Ladd cautions against both an overemphasis on the subjective aspect of salvation—as in an exaggerated stress on the union with Christ—and against exclusive concerns with the objective, non-ethical, or legal aspects of salvation. One must properly balance the more objective themes of justification, reconciliation, and redemption in order to appreciate fully the complementary subjective doctrines of life "in Christ" and the indwelling Spirit of God.[43] Similarly, Ralph Martin insists that the *dikaios* words, including "righteousness" and "justification," are relational terms. When one is in the faithful relationship with God's divine covenant expectations, that person is righteous. The exclusively imputational "as if" nuance of forensic, legal acquittal tends to ignore the fact that Paul's terminology is couched in the context of interpersonal relationships that are *actually* restored through the process of moral transformation.[44] The believer does not act "as if" he/she is in right covenant relationship with God but has been *actually* restored to right relationship with God through Christ's covenant renewal activity in the incarnation, cross, and resurrection.

E. P. Sanders presents a balanced examination of Paul's thought on salvation. He says that when one takes the "righteousness by faith alone" position as the central theme of Paul's gospel, one misses the significance of the realism with which Paul thought of incorporation into the body of Christ, which Sanders sees as the heart of Paul's theology. Problems arise in interpreting Paul's writings, because Paul *does* emphasize both the "juristic" and "participatory" terms to reflect two conceptions of humanity's plight—transgression and bondage. Although these concepts use distinct terminology ("justification" is distinct from being "in Christ"), they are used *materially* together. The concepts provide different metaphors to say that apart from Christ humanity is condemned. "Justification" deals with acquittal of the sentence of condemnation and "union with Christ" deals with deliverance from the bondage and power of sin. Believers have both been acquitted of past sins and have died to the power of sin through union with Christ.[45] Sanders notes, "The forensic declaration of righteousness creates the sinner anew."[46] Although the two are different metaphors, they are parallel concepts. They are not events that happen successively, nor should they be prioritized. Therefore, in Paul's usage, justification by faith, union with Christ, and the ethical righteousness that God expects from believers should all be understood as consequences of biblical salvation. Paul's usage of the legal metaphor of justification describes release from sin's penalty and acquittal from God's condemnation. But for him this forensic metaphor involves more than a declaration of pardon. A faith-union with Christ, a "newness of life" that involves real moral change is also intended (Rom. 6:1–14).

The objective death of Christ accomplished a justification that, in union with Christ, the believer makes actual through subjective appropriation. Justification thus involves knowing Christ and being found "in Him" by faith (Phil. 3:8–9). "Righteousness," which Paul uses synonymously with "justification" (both words are translations of *dikaiosunē*), is thus not just a declaration at the beginning of new life in Christ; it is a state of existence. *Dikaiosunē*—God's righteousness/justification—both acquits the sinner and breaks the bondage of sin, making righteousness a reality in the life of the believer. It is both the pardoning of forensic justification *and* righteousness as the living power of right relationship to Christ's Spirit that overcomes sin.

This righteousness is the power that engages the entire life of the believer to overcome *adikia*, "unrighteousness," and *hamartia*, "missing the mark." No imputational moral fiction emphasis alone adequately deals with the reality of the newness of life in Christ. The justifying sentence leads to the righteous relationship of a new life in Christ.[47] The righteous covenant relationship is restored in reality. In this regard, James Denney says: "When a man believes in this [faith relationship] sense, he does the only thing which is right to do in the presence of Christ, and it puts him right with God. It really puts him right. . . . God justifies the ungodly man on the basis of his faith in Jesus, and there is nothing unreal about the justification."[48]

Thus Paul's usage integrates both forensic and relational concepts. To be justified involves acquittal for past sin, release from the bondage of sin, and incorporation into Christ by faith. The believer is declared to be righteous because God's judgment is also related to his/her being incorporated into Christ by faith. However, only because the believer is united with Christ does the righteous character of Christ become the character of the believer. Because the believer is transferred into the kingdom of righteousness and now participates in the life of Christ, the inheritance of Christ becomes the believer's own through the Holy Spirit.[49] Saving faith, justification, and union with Christ go together (Rom 3:21–26; 6:5–11; 8:1–4; Gal. 2:15–21; 3:26–29; Phil. 3:7–11). The gift of righteousness transfers one into fellowship with Christ. Quell and Schrenk say in regard to 2 Corinthians 5:21, "Because Christ representatively became *hamartia* [sin] for us, we can become *dikaiosunē en auto* [righteousness in him]."[50]

Paul Fiddes points out that "since all have sinned and fall short of the glory of God," if God were acting according to the strict letter of the civil law, he must condemn sinful humanity. But instead he justifies the unjust, which is contrary to all the laws of human justice and legality. How can this anomaly be explained? Fiddes suggests that the answer lies not in the penal theory solution that God has placed our sentence of death onto Jesus Christ so that God can carry out justice through a "transferred penalty," which is deduced from the legal element in the concept of "justification." This is *not* the meaning of "justification" in its biblical usage because Paul is not deriving the meaning of the term from the Roman law court, but from the Hebrew covenant setting, rooted in relationships. Because Hebrew covenant Law was concerned with the health of the community, the one justified or acquitted by the Jewish judge was then received back into the community by God's personal will, and the one condemned was shut out. The term "justification," then, should be understood as "accepted" by God, and not simply as "declared not guilty." "To be accepted" implies that a relationship is established, not simply that condemnation has been erased.[51]

God treats the justified person as righteous, not because he has transplanted perfect moral character into him/her nor because he *pretends* he/she is righteous by some kind of moral fiction. Instead, God puts us in right relationship with himself and we really *are* righteous in this relationship. This is not only a legal, but also an eschatological verdict in that the judgment that will be passed on us in the last days has already been anticipated and experienced here and now and is to be received in faith (Rom. 1:17; Gal. 5:5). The forensic aspects of justification must be understood in the context of the Hebrew covenant relationship and community model, rather than in the abstract civil justice sense of Roman law. Indeed, the tendency of Western Christianity to transform the ideas of righteousness and justification into exclusively legal categories seriously threatens to suppress the biblical covenantal relational aspects of salvation language. This is particularly ironic today when Christians are seeking to address a culture in which relational categories are becoming almost the exclusive linguistic currency of a postmodern society.

In Christ the believer actually is made righteous through faith-identification with the one who is the "righteousness of God." For Paul, then, "righteousness/ justification" is both a declaration that the believer is acquitted (forensic) and an affirmation that the believer is actually righteous by faith (incorporation or participation). Christ fulfills the divine expectations of the covenant, and the believer in him also actually fulfills them and enters into proper relationship with God, as well. All of this is accomplished in the context of the ministry of the Holy Spirit, who is the presence of Christ in the process of spiritual transformation and formation.

As a result of being justified by faith, then, in Paul's sense, the believer does not possess a quality or virtue of righteousness because, according to the biblical idea, righteousness is not an abstract quality that can be possessed or transferred. Rather, the believer is righteous because he/she has identified with Christ in faith-obedience and is thus living in a way that fulfills the covenant expectations required in order to be the recipient of the righteousness of God.[52] Justification, then, is conformity to an expected norm, in this case, to the divine expectations of faith and obedience. This relational harmony provides the foundation upon which the community of faith, the body of Christ, can be established.

Identification

The doctrine of the incarnation provides the basis of God's identification with sinful humanity. Christ must identify both with God and with humanity in order to be the connecting link that draws them together. The fulfillment of prophecy, the baptismal witness of John, the kingdom nature of Jesus' ministry in power over spiritual forces and nature, and his own self-witness of "I and the Father are one" all witness to the reality that he is one with God. But the identification with sinful humanity exhibits a cosmic level of condescension. In unequaled humility, he identifies himself with sinners, including experiencing the alienation from God because of their sin. His incarnation enables him to take human experiences onto himself, because he *is* humanity. Jakob Jocz shows that he does this not to satisfy an impersonal principle of justice, but rather to live the experience of sinners, even to the point of death. He is present for them in total identification. He is the "Man for others." Nevertheless, not only does he identify with humanity in his humiliation in dying with and for them once and for all, but he expresses humanity's new start in the power of the Holy Spirit in his resurrection.[53] Because he lives, we shall live also. *Thus in Christ's identification with humanity, the covenant is renewed and the loving family relationship with God is restored.* This becomes possible because, through the free grace of God, the Son of God becomes broken humanity so that humanity's brokenness may be restored to God's image again. In him, humanity obeys God and is reconciled.

Paul understood the atoning death of Jesus as not simply a removal of guilt and separation of the sinner from the disease of sin. It is to miss Paul's point to interpret his statements on the atonement to mean *only* that the crucified Jesus has taken the sin from the sinner and allowed the deadly consequences of sin to settle on himself to the exclusion of the sinner. Passages such as 2 Corinthians 5:21, "God made him who had no sin to be sin for us, so that in him we might become the righteousness of God," and Galatians 3:13, "Christ redeemed us from the curse of the law by becoming a curse for us," are often used to support such an exclusively penal substitutionary interpretation of Christ's death. However, these passages involve the concept of reciprocity that Paul so often emphasizes, as in Romans 6:5–11. They do not focus exclusively on Christ's objectively absorbing the judicial penalty which humanity has called down upon itself because of its sin. On the contrary, Paul sees the atoning death of Jesus as an example of what Gese describes as "inclusive substitution," in which the whole self of the sinful person is given to Christ as an offering of one's life, in response to Christ's giving his whole self as an offering of covenant restoration for humanity.[54]

As Sanders indicates, Christ's death provides acquittal for the sinner, and our participation in his death provides us victory over the power of sin—resulting in freedom from slavery and a transfer of lordship from uncleanness and sinful immorality to the lordship of Christ.[55] Thus justification and participation in Christ's death and resurrection cannot be characterized as two separate alternatives. Indeed, the participationist, union with Christ categories of salvation are at least as pervasive in Paul's theology as the forensic ones, such as in Romans 6:5: "If we have been united with him in his death, we will certainly also be united with him in his resurrection." Likewise, in 2 Corinthians 5:17: "Therefore, if anyone is in Christ, he is a new creation; the old has gone, the new has come!" He views the solution to sin not primarily in removing the guilt of transgression, but in the reality of the new life set free from the power of sin in which one participates through union with Christ.[56] Sin is not just an appendage transferred off the back of the sinner and onto a vicarious victim. Paul sees sin not merely as a person's actions, but also as his or her *very being*. Sin is not just something that a person carries, but something a person *is*.[57]

Parallel to the Old Testament sinner's identification with the sacrificial animal and participation in the animal's death as an act of surrender to God, so the sinner identifies with Christ in faith.[58] And this is effective because Christ has identified himself with sinful humanity and has united that sinful humanity with himself in the incarnation. Christ identifies with humanity in order to lead persons, through the sacrificial giving of his life, into union with God through sharing by faith in his death-resurrection (Rom. 6). In this way the sinner passes through the sentence of death and rises as a new person who has been reconciled to God. The death of all occurs in the atoning death of Jesus, and those who in faith participate in Christ's death-resurrection participate in the *new creation:* "the old has gone, the new has come" (2 Cor. 5:17). Through the grace of the covenant, God has opened the pathway to this new creation by identifying godless humanity with Christ, so that in this restoration of union with God, humanity becomes the "righteousness of God" (2 Cor. 5:21).[59] This revelation of grace totally redefines the moral order. As Jocz says, this revelation not only "violates the concept of equity, it abolishes it. No wonder that theologians have strained to interpret Christ's Atonement on the Cross in legal terms. . . . God's righteousness as we discover it in the gospel not only exceeds, but contradicts legal justice. . . . God ceases to be the guarantor of legal justice—He is seen as the Father who loves to the uttermost."[60]

The sinner is fallen, enslaved to sin and death—"a body that belongs to sin" (genitive of possession; Rom. 6:6), and ineligible for atonement under any of the conventional methods of sacrifice (Rom 1:18–3:20). Separation of the sinner from sin would be a separation from *oneself*. The sinner cannot be released from the bondage of sin except through death and resurrection—the crucifixion of the self (Rom 6:1–7:6). This is why the sinner cries out in despair in Romans 7:24: "Wretched man that I am! Who will rescue me from this body of death?" The sinner's own death will not accomplish deliverance, for death is the sentence for sin. Even if the sentence is paid, resurrection does not follow: "The wages of sin is death" (Rom 6:23), and this death is final. However, as an act of *inclusive substitution*, Jesus' death on the cross is the death of all who are identified with him. As Hofius states: "Because the Son of God has in this way [incarnational identity] *become one* with humanity who needs atonement, his death is therefore as such the death of the sinner, and his resurrection is as such the calling forth of the new person, who has been reconciled with God and has come to life by passing through the sentence of death."[61]

Christ has identified with the sinner in death in order to pass through the sentence of death and receive resurrection to a new identity, a new creation. Paul Fiddes notes that "Jesus so completely identifies himself with sinful human beings that he shares their experience of standing under God's verdict . . . [to] experience the consequences of human sinfulness."[62] This is not simply that God inflicts a divine penalty upon Christ, but that Christ fully experiences the consequences of human sinfulness and death, and creates in himself a new being.[63] Those who see the death of Christ as only a penal payment and transference of guilt to Christ, as if removal of guilt restores the image of God in which humanity was created, ironically are not taking sin seriously enough. Sin is not a thing to be removed, but a brokenness of self that must be recreated and healed through union with Christ in resurrection. It is a brokenness of the personal bond of fellowship with the God who offers salvation. The sinner's death does not atone because his/her death is only the just result of the alienation of sin. Sin cannot simply be paid for or justly transferred any more than death can be; the creature must be remade into the image of Christ. Only by coming through the judgment of death so that one's existence as a sinner is ended can one's life be given back as a new creature in Christ.

Christ's death constitutes identification with us at the deepest level (see Phil. 2:5–11). Herein lies the strength of Morna Hooker's emphasis on *place-taking* in the identification of the believer with Christ.[64] An incarnational exchange takes place in which God identifies godless humanity with Christ. This "interchange in Christ," Hooker says, "[takes place as] the one who is innocent shares the suffering and death which are deserved by Adam's descendents, and his vindication is shared by those who acknowledge him as Lord."[65] She uses 2 Corinthians 5:21 to illustrate the interchange. The balance in this verse is based on "sin" being a metonymy: "sin" is used in the sense of "sinner," and "righteousness of God" is used in the sense of "those justified in Christ."[66] Thus the verse literally means, "God made him [Christ] to be sin [all sinners] so that we [those identified with him] might be made the righteousness of God [those justified in Christ] in him" (2 Cor. 5:21). To understand this only as substitution is to seriously weaken the incarnational identification of Christ with humanity.

If one does not recognize this metonymy, one understands Paul to mean that God treats those who now are in reality *not* sinners (those justified in Christ) *as if* they were still sinners! The metonymy carries the much deeper sense that those who are "justified" through Christ's atonement are identified with him by the very nature of "righteousness," which is the prerequisite of atonement and reconciliation.[67] The metonymy here conveys the emphasis on Christ's identification with humanity; sin is not *transferred*, as seems to be indicated by Isaiah 53, but Christ *becomes sinful humanity.* In the incarnation he identifies with the sinner, and vice versa. This is a shift from the "exclusive place-taking" forensic idea to the "inclusive place-taking" participation idea of Gese and Hofius.[68] Christ was made humankind both at the incarnation and at the cross. He could only be "made sin" (2 Cor. 5:21) by participating in the human mode of existence. This does not contradict that Christ "knew no sin" (2 Cor. 5:21 NAU), but understands that Christ experienced sin not *ethically,* in terms of his behavior, but *cosmically,* in terms of his identification with human experience (Rom. 8:3).

The gnostic tendencies of Christian theology that have attempted to protect Jesus' sinlessness have also tended to diminish his participation in the humanness of the incarnation. As Bell points out, it is Christ's participation in human experience that illuminates the meaning of the Old Testament identification of the sinner with the sacrifice, and not vice versa.[69] And as Fiddes suggests, in this participation, "God the Father also participates directly in human estrangement."[70] Paul says that this is the redemptive exchange made possible by the incarnation. Christ is still the sacrifice "without blemish" because he is ethically without sin. The believer's righteousness consists of his or her being in the right covenant relationship with God, and therefore, is not an attribute of the believer that can be isolated from God. But through the work of the Holy Spirit, the believer is linked with Christ through the saving initiative of God's righteousness (1 Cor. 6:11).[71]

Because of our new relationship with God "in Christ," *we are in fact* "a new creation" (v. 17), and are qualified on the basis of our identification with Christ in his death-resurrection to be released from the bondage of sin and to live in communion with God.[72] The divine expectations of the covenant relationship are, therefore, not an impersonal transaction, but the establishment of a personal relationship between God and the transformed community.

Reconciliation

God's acts of salvation are directed toward humanity, for it is the creature that is fallen and alienated from God, not vice versa. The Bible does not say that God *becomes* merciful, or conciliated, reconciled, appeased, propitiated, etc., but that God *shows* himself *to be* merciful and gracious by sending Christ to do his work. It is *humanity* that is at war with God, not the other way around. Waldenström says it was the change in Adam's heart that made him believe God had changed. He quotes Luther as saying, "The evil spirit had snatched the true image of God from Adam, darkened it, and blotted it out of his heart."[73]

Many a parent whose wayward son or daughter has violated the parent's trust understands the phenomenon of the child then looking on the parent in anger and accusing the parent of being the offender when the parent has done nothing but love through all the disorder and alienation. The parent is not the one in need of reconciliation, for he/she has all along seen the child through eyes of love and intercession. James Dunn says in relation to 2 Corinthians 5:18–20 and Romans 5:6–11 that the state of hostility or estrangement communicates not the image that God is the angry enemy having to be begged, but that it is God as the injured Loved One who is initiating the search for reconciliation.[74] T. W. Manson notes in this regard that "Reconciliation is thus the keyword of Paul's Gospel so far as its working out in Christ is concerned. The driving-force behind the Gospel is the love of God. The *modus operandi* is reconciliation."[75]

The concept that God's wrath toward the sinner must be appeased before God can be moved to be reconciled with humanity is problematic from the covenant perspective. If Israel's relationship to God is to be understood as a demonstration of God's covenant salvation, then reconciliation (Greek *katallassein*) must be understood in covenantal terms rather than in the sense of the appeasement ideas often reflected in pagan worship and ritual. Furthermore, God is never the object of reconciliation in the Scriptures. It is humanity who needs to be reconciled. Paul says, "God was in Christ reconciling the world to Himself" (2 Cor. 5:19 NAU). Again, Paul notes in Romans 5:6–11 that the atonement saves us from God's wrath. And contrary to the propitiation of God view, sinners are the enemies of God—God is not the enemy of sinners.

> You see, at just the right time, when we were still powerless, Christ died for the ungodly. . . . God demonstrates his own love for us in this: While we were still sinners, Christ died for us. Since we have now been justified by his blood, how much more shall we be saved from God's wrath through him! For if, when we were God's enemies, we were reconciled to him through the death of his Son, how much more, having been reconciled, shall we be saved through his life! . . . We also rejoice in God through our Lord Jesus Christ, through whom we have now received reconciliation.

It is because Christ saves us from the sinful alienation from God that we are saved from God's wrath, not because Christ paid its penalty. Thus, in offering his life in obedience to God, we offer our lives to God—since we are in Christ. The reason for divine wrath is therefore removed.[76] In contrast, it is the heathen who try to appease God based on their belief that God is angry with *them*. Since God's disposition toward humanity had not changed and it was God who initiated the salvation process, then reconciliation proceeds from God to humanity, and not from humanity to God. The war between God and humanity is resolved by God's act of reconciliation through the atonement of Christ. He has made "peace through his blood, shed on the cross" (Col. 1:20). The enmity and estrangement of humanity from God is ended by God's sacrificial act in Christ that restores peace; humanity can fulfill its purpose to be in the proper covenant relationship. When this peace restores the relationship, humanity can fulfill its purpose to be in the proper covenant relationship.

As a work that proceeds from God's love and is thus directed toward humanity, reconciliation is an interpersonal word. It means, "to restore to right relationship."[77] What is it that needs restoration? Paul says again: "Once you were alienated from God and were enemies in your minds because of your evil behavior. But now he has reconciled you by Christ's physical body through death to present you holy in his sight without blemish and free from accusation" (Col. 1:21). The "evil behavior" is the cause of the alienation from God, and as that behavior is corrected by our transformation in Christ we are reconciled to God, because we are now able to relate to him out of a clear conscience. The removal of sinful behavior and the justification of the sinner are necessary in order to reconcile the sinner to God. Paul's exposition of this reality in 2 Corinthians 5:16–21, sheds much light on this phenomenon of human behavior:

> Therefore, if anyone is in Christ, he is a new creation; the old has gone, the new has come! All this is from God, who reconciled us to himself through Jesus Christ and gave us the ministry of reconciliation: that God was reconciling the world to himself in Christ, not counting men's sins against them. . . . We implore you on Christ's behalf: Be reconciled to God. God made him who had no sin to be sin for us, so that in him we might become the righteousness of God.

In clear words, Paul shows that God is the subject who initiates reconciliation, and humanity is the object who is reconciled. In fact, the imperative in 5:20 commands us to "be reconciled," or to set right our relationship with God. It is by participation in Christ that we are transformed so that we can see God through Christ's eyes and therefore see that we are reconciled.

Ralph P. Martin shows that this call to live in God's grace of justification is a call of perennial application. Furthermore, the present reality of living in the grace of God, he says, includes the sure confidence that the verdict of acceptance will be confirmed at the future judgment (Gal. 5:5; Phil. 1:6, 10; 3:9–11).[78] Martin goes on to say that reconciliation can be understood as the "interpretive key to Paul's theology." He affirms that Paul firmly anchors God's salvation process in the area of personal relationships both between humanity and God and with each other in society. Martin's further study of Paul's milieu and background indicates the apostle's familiarity with both the rabbinic and Greco-Roman philosophical worlds. However, he is first and foremost a product of the Jewish heritage, and understood the interpersonal covenant as the context for reconciliation and the renewal of relationship with God and humanity. As that covenant reconciliation is offered through Christ, our restoration begins.[79]

One cannot see God or understand his character until the reality of Christ's being formed in us and we in him recreates his eyes in our minds and souls (1 Jn. 3:2–3). We cannot be reconciled to him until Christ clears our vision as he reveals God's love in himself. Only as we become "new creatures" in Christ can we become reconciled to God. Our rebellion and alienation has not been excused or ignored, nor has God chosen to see us through the lens of Christ *as if* we were not really sinners. God does not count the sins of repentant sinners against them because in reconciliation their relationships with him are no longer the rebellious attitudes that caused the alienation in the first place. Now our alienation and hostility toward God have been healed and transformed through our identification with Christ, so that we are now really able to see God as he is and accept his invitation of love. Christ has shown us the way back to a proper relationship with God, which was God's original divine expectation for us. Again and again, the Bible identifies reconciliation as initiated by God and administered through Christ, so that sinners can be recreated in Christ's image through the ministry of the Holy Spirit.[80]

Union with Christ

The Old Testament covenant prescriptions made God's expectations clear and provided measurable standards by which one's behavior was judged. In the New Testament, Christ is the incarnation of God's will and the example of his covenant expectations. He is, in fact, the new Torah. Ritual obedience to the Law could not make a person like Christ. Only union with Christ in faith can make one righteous. James Stewart goes so far as to say, "The heart of Paul's religion is union with Christ."[81] For Stewart, and the many other sources he cites, union with Christ is the presupposition of everything that is important in salvation.[82] He believes that to fail to keep the union with Christ central is to endanger the entire doctrine of the atonement. Otherwise, the atonement tends to become something that operates "mechanically or almost magically . . . outside of us, independent of our attitude."[83] Furthermore, says Stewart, "the thought of sanctification, dissociated from union, loses all reality. . . . It becomes an 'extra'."[84] The essential relationship between faith and ethics is seen only when the "unfolding of Christ's own character within the believer's life" is truly a reflection in our behavior of the living and present Spirit of God.[85]

In the new covenant, the believer sacrifices his/her own life by an obedient faith-union with Christ (Rom. 6:5–11) through faith in and identification with Christ's sacrifice. Moreover, this sacrifice encompasses all of his life, death, and resurrection as the perfect expression of covenant obedience. The identification here is similar to the identification in the Old Testament of the sinner with the sacrificial animal by the laying on of hands. Christ, however, is not only a sin offering that expresses our repentance, he is also the entire covenant who expresses our thanksgiving and worship and pattern for covenant life. Identification with him in his death-resurrection does not just remove guilt; it also creates a new self in Christ. As Paul says, "If any person is in Christ, he/she is a new creature" (2 Cor. 5:17, my paraphrase). We identify with Christ's sacrifice through our own sacrifice so that his action on the cross is also our action in faith. And Christ as our sacrifice expresses a repentance so perfect and complete that it expiates fully the effects of sin for all those who in faith allow Christ to be the expression of their repentance. Because Christ has identified with us and chosen to participate in all our humanness (Phil. 2:5–11), he speaks for us and perfectly expresses our repentance and obedience, God's covenant expectations are met, and we are restored to covenant fellowship.

In Romans 6, as in numerous other Pauline passages,[86] Paul develops this incarnational concept that the union of the believer in the death and life of Christ as symbolized in baptism is a reflexive, or two-way, participation. The believer's participation responds to Christ's identification/participation in the life and death of sinful humanity. The faith-union with Christ internalizes obedience to God:

> If we have been united with him like this in his death, we will certainly also be united with him in his resurrection. (Rom. 6:5—see 6:6–11).

Paul thus shows that by participating in Christ's identification with humanity in death, humanity is enabled by faith to participate also in the resurrection to new life with Christ. The union with Christ is not a "mystical union," as it is sometimes called, but an actual one—effected through the believer's identification with the sacrifice, which is Christ. Through faith, by means of the Holy Spirit, the believer can participate in the experience of Christ, in both his death and resurrection. The actuality of the sinner's historical dying and rising again are separated in time from Christ's death and resurrection; they are not historically contemporary. But the death and resurrection are an actual death and resurrection for the believer because they are anticipated and empathically experienced in faith. They will be actually fulfilled eschatologically because all believers will eventually die and be resurrected with Christ at some point in history.

The union with Christ is made contemporary through the ministry of the Holy Spirit. In Kierkegaard's words, "Christ is our eternal contemporary." A believer's experience of faith as "Christ living in me" is not a purely subjective or mystical perception but is also real, objective truth. Jesus promised to send the Paraclete, who also is God even as Jesus is divine. And as Jesus and the Father are one, and as the Spirit is also in the Father and the Son, so all three are really in the believer through the indwelling presence of the Spirit (John 14:11–21). John remembers Jesus' words, "because I live, you also will live. . . . I am in my Father, and you are in me, and I am in you. . . . if anyone loves me, he will obey my teaching" (John 14:19–20, 23). To be in Christ requires death to the bondage of sin by participation through faith-obedience in the dying and rising with Christ, which leads to an ethically new life as the Holy Spirit creates an interpersonal bond between Christ and the believer. Also, if Christ is in believers, then his life is in them, working through the Holy Spirit to produce moral fruit (Gal. 2:20).[87]

Sanders notes that Paul does not make a primary causal connection between justification and ethical behavior. The foundation of ethics is rather in one's participation with Christ. Sanders says, "There should, however, be no doubt as to where the heart of Paul's theology lies. He is not primarily concerned with the juristic categories, although he works with them. The real bite of his theology lies in the participatory categories, *even though he himself did not distinguish them this way.*"[88] Though Paul does not see these categories as mutually exclusive, Sanders believes Paul is more concerned about participation in Christ than about repentance and guilt. His concern is not so much with violations of the law as it is with persons establishing unions that are mutually exclusive of the union with Christ. It is about idolatrous and enslaving loyalties, quite as much as the Old Testament prohibition to "have no other gods before me." This emphasis on participation, or incorporation into the body of Christ, has been minimized by much Protestant scholarship, particularly in German Protestantism by scholars such as Bultmann, Bornkamm, and Conzelmann because of their rejection of so-called "mystical" categories in favor of a forensically interpreted concept of the righteousness of God as it relates primarily to the individual. However, the incorporation into the body of Christ, says Sanders, is a more central theme than many of the German scholars have been willing to admit.[89]

The dilemma Paul addressed in Galatians is that the Law is incapable of salvation, and fulfilling the law will not save in itself. But we walk in "a new life" because Christ's life has become transplanted in us. We walk in his strength, not our own. This life of his contrasts with the impotency, expressed in Romans 7, that arises from seeking to justify ourselves by self-righteous obedience to the Law. Law-reliance is incapable of bringing new life, but—"thanks be to God" (v. 25)—new life in the Spirit results from our being united with Christ.

Given the New Testament's emphasis on the new life in Christ, why is justification—to be acquitted of one's transgressions against the law—so often seen as the central salvation metaphor? When one sees justification as the only thing, or even the main thing that happens, the participatory union with Christ and transformation into his image is often minimized, as in the case of the German scholars mentioned by Sanders. The lesser idea has become the greater. Justification understood as fulfilling the requirements of law and thus being the way to salvation is problematic because the fulfillment of the law itself cannot save—Paul was "blameless" (NAU) by the standards of the law, yet needed salvation by Christ

(Phil. 3:2–11; Rom. 7:7–25). To focus on justification alone sets up a forensic conundrum: the law condemns me, justification acquits me before the law, but how is this relevant to union with Christ, which really does save me and make me a new creature? The Old Testament covenantal system always required a penitent and faithful heart as well as obedience in order to remain in the covenant fellowship with God, and the salvation offered through Christ certainly expects as much.

The penal view sees the death of Christ as payment of a penalty, thereby enabling God to forgive. However, the statement, "Jesus paid the penalty for our sin," is not in the Bible.[90] Though Romans does speak of the "wages of sin," "the free gift of God" (NAU) is based on Christ's sacrifice. This gift carries a much broader significance than only a forensic payment of a penalty by Christ on our behalf. What God requires in order to be able to forgive with integrity is for humanity to demonstrate the will to remain in the covenant by obedience to its expectations. Since the humanity represented by Adam has not been able to demonstrate that obedience, the humanity represented by Christ must do so.

Through the incarnation, Christ has identified with humanity and, acting as its representative, *by his own life has offered the sacrifice that renews the covenant*. Because the death of Christ is the *ultimate manifestation of covenant obedience*—the criterion that puts the covenant in effect—Christ satisfies not the legal penalty for lawbreaking, but the covenant divine expectations for obedience. This is the implication behind Paul's exclamation in Romans 5:10, "For if, when we were God's enemies, we were reconciled to him through the death of his Son, how much more, having been reconciled, shall we be saved through his life!" In Romans 5:18 Paul says, "Just as the result of one trespass was condemnation for all men, so also the result of one act of righteousness was justification that brings life for all men." Gese also notes this theme of life: "To speak of atonement means to view death and resurrection together. In Jesus' death, his cross, we have life. This death, by breaking through to life, by reconciling us to God, has atoned for the entire cosmos. . . . [B]y his death we have union with God. And so his death is the victory over death, the dawn of a new creation."[91]

The Old Testament theme that "life is in the blood" is important here. The work of the cross was not to absorb death, but to conquer death and create new life—as a re-creation of creation and the purpose of the covenant. God's covenant with Abraham was a promise of life—a guarantee of the perpetuity of his seed. Adam's death stands in opposition to the purpose of creation; Christ's death recreates life in spite of all the damage death can do. Thus it vanquishes death and restores the life Adam lost (Rom. 4–5).

Being in Christ begins a new mode of existence. It completely changes the entire relationship to God, the world, and to sin. By humanity's being "in Christ," it may become reconciled to God and in right relationship to him. Life has been restored by the divine sacrifice of Christ in which God himself was working to reconcile the world to himself.[92] The loss of life incurred by disobedience and separation from the source of life has been replaced by the new life effected by reconnection to the source of life by faith-union with Christ. Such reconnected life must be included with any forensic declaration of justification. Without participation in Christ's death/resurrection through union with him, "justification" can remove one's guilt, but no life is restored. The legal metaphors relating to salvation can only be used biblically if we keep the balance of justification and union with Christ in the context of covenant relationship.

Regeneration

The exclusive focus on the forensic metaphor has often been allowed to distort the biblical message of regeneration and restoration of the image of God, which the New Testament calls for as a result of the atonement. In Romans 8:29, Paul writes, "For those God foreknew he also predestined to be conformed to the likeness [image] of his Son." Contrasting the earthly body with the resurrection body, Paul declares: "And just as we have borne the likeness [image] of the earthly man, so shall we bear the likeness [image] of the man from heaven" (1 Cor. 15:49). And in describing the glory of realizing the new covenant, he says, "And we, who with unveiled faces all reflect the Lord's glory, are being transformed into his likeness (image) with ever-increasing glory, which comes from the Lord, who is the Spirit" (2 Cor. 3:18). His use of the present tense indicates that this transformation into the restored image of God is going on now as a result of the atoning work of Christ.

This renewed relationship with the covenant God is a real restoration of the covenant union. It is not a moral fiction in which we are treated *as if* we were transformed into righteous persons by the work of Christ. Those united with Christ and participating in his death-resurrection are *really righteous* because righteousness is about being in the proper relationship of faith-obedience to the covenant God through our relationship with Christ. The identification of Christ with the sinner leads the sinner to be identified with Christ as a new creation—having a new identity, a restoration of the moral image of God, reflecting an appropriate relationship of sanctification, living an ethic of Christlikeness and obedience.

The Gospel of John stresses the idea of the new birth (3:3–8). "Regeneration" *(palingenesia),* a concept familiar in both Greek and Roman cultures, indicates a decisively new change in one's nature or personal life. The Old Testament prophets looked forward to a new birth for Israel (Isa. 65:17; 66:22; Ezek. 37) that would be related to the creation of a new heaven and earth in a cosmic regeneration (2 Pet. 3:13; Rev. 20:11; 21:1).[93] Christians, regenerated by the Spirit, already experience this eternal life of the Spirit (Eph. 4:22–24; 1 Tim. 6:12, 19), and look forward to its glorious consummation at Christ's return (1 John 3:2–3).[94]

This cosmic regeneration, say the New Testament writers, has been accomplished by God in Jesus Christ, although at present we see it only through the eyes of faith. The incarnation of Jesus Christ began the new creation, and his death and resurrection potentially re-create all humanity. The Spirit of God gives life to this new creation (John 20:22; cf. Ezek. 37:5–14), and the wind of Pentecost inaugurates it (Acts 2:2). As the Gospels indicate, the early Christians knew that the expected day of eschatological regeneration had arrived because of the gifts and work of the Spirit (Matt. 19:28; Mark 10:15; John 3:3). As Richardson points out, Christ had "taken all authority" by his resurrection (Matt 28:18), and by sitting at the right hand of the Father (Mark 16:19; Acts 2:33; et al.). Thus in order to enter the new age and participate in its regeneration life, one must become a new person by the Holy Spirit's work, and participate in the eschatological Kingdom of God.[95]

The Pauline literature emphasizes the real, though anticipatory, character of the new creation. The Christian is a new creation and walks in newness of life and spirit (Rom. 6:4; 7:6; 12:2; 2 Cor. 5:17; 4:16; Gal. 6:15; Col. 3:9–10). Christians are the "firstfruits" of the new age (Rom. 8:23; cf. James 1:18). While we do experience the life of the new age even now, its fullness will come with the eschatological age yet to arrive, as is seen in Titus 3:5–7:

> He saved us not on the basis of deeds which we have done in righteousness, but according to His mercy, by the washing of regeneration and renewing by the Holy Spirit, whom He poured out upon us richly through Jesus Christ our Savior, so that being justified by His grace we might be made heirs according to *the* hope of eternal life (NAU).

Therefore, one may become a new person who participates in the eschato-logical life of the new age through faith and by the power of the Holy Spirit—who breathes life into the new creation as at the original creation (Gen. 2:7; Ezek. 37:5–14; John 5:28–29). The eternal life *(zoē aionios)* of the age to come has been brought by Christ (John 3:16; 5:24–25; 10:10; 20:31).[96]

Sanctification

One of the key benefits coming from the atonement is the growth in spiritu-ality and Christlikeness known as sanctification. While often minimized or rel-egated to the period after death by those emphasizing the exclusively penal nature of Christ's atonement, sanctification is a central consequence of the covenantal understanding of grace, faith, and the atonement. Though much of the spiritual transformation described in sanctification is covered in the previous discussions on regeneration and union with Christ, Paul's emphasis on the new spiritual per-son created by the work of the Holy Spirit must not be ignored. He places this at the level of a moral imperative. His use of the indicative followed by the impera-tive admonishes the believer to hold fast to what has been received in justification and reconciliation (Rom. 6:5–14). "Our old self was crucified . . . " (Rom. 6:6 NAU), therefore, "Consider yourselves dead to sin, but alive to God" (Rom. 6:11 NAU). The relationship begun with justification and regeneration now moves to the deeper relationship of submission to the Holy Spirit's leadership (Gal. 5:16–26; Eph. 5:15–21).[97]

Thus, as one's relationship with God through identification and participation in the life of Christ occurs and matures, the restoration of Christlikeness contin-ues through grace to form the believer into the moral image of God as humanity was intended to be in creation. It is by this transformational participation in the life of the Spirit of Christ that the implications of Christ's work for covenant renewal bear fruit in the transformation of the community of faith into the shape of his body. William Greathouse points out that while the penal views virtually ignored the doctrine of sanctification, the Christus Victor view of the work of Christ clearly addresses the issue:

> Viewed positively, this act of God [union with Christ] is life in the Spirit (Romans 8). Christ reenacts in us the sanctification He ac-complished in the Atonement. . . . Thus Christ himself becomes our sanctification (1 Corinthians 1:30). . . . Meanwhile our sanctifica-tion has the character of spiritual warfare in which our victory over sin is assured as we permit Christ to live moment by moment in us

(John 15:16; Eph. 6:10–18; Philem. 6; Col. 1:18–23; Rom. 8:12–13, 26–39; Heb. 7:25).[98]

Christ as the Mercy Seat

In order to communicate effectively the meaning of atonement, justification, and sanctification in the New Testament, one must demonstrate how the grace of salvation is based on the work of Jesus Christ. In Romans 3:25, Paul refers to Jesus as the *hilasterion*. This Greek word has been translated "propitiation," "expiation," and "atonement cover" or "mercy seat." Since the etymology does not determine which nuance is intended here, it is necessary to look at the broader Old Testament context for clarification. The background for the meaning of the atonement concept lies in the Hebrew sacrificial system. The Hebrew term for the cover of the ark of the covenant is *kapporeth* (Ex. 25:17–22). It is based on the term for "atone," *kipper*. The *kapporeth* is the seat of God's presence where Yahweh appears at the sprinkling of the blood of the sacrifice on the Day of Atonement. If this term is translated as "propitiation," the sense is that human sin angers Yahweh, who then requires some penalty or sacrifice to appease his anger before the sinner can be forgiven. It is God who stands in the way of reconciliation. If the term is translated by "expiation," however, the relationship with God is hindered by sin, and the obstacle to right relationship must be overcome by a gracious action God provides. While the term has been translated either way depending on the context, the broad scope of the Old Testament theology of atonement does not support the propitiation usage here, for Yahweh is the one who provides the entire sacrificial system and is seen as the one who makes atonement (Deut. 21: 8; 2 Chron. 30:18; Ps. 78:38; and Isa. 6:7; Ezek. 16:63). It is Yahweh who consistently cancels sin and brings reconciliation. This is the point in the New Testament theology (particularly in the Book of Hebrews) which shows that Christ's sacrifice on the cross completes the fullness of the atonement theology of the Old Testament sacrificial system.[99] The "mercy seat" image of *hilasterion* helps us understand what Jesus actually did in according to Romans 3:23–25 where Christ is presented as an example of faith and obedience. Note the differences in the translations that follow (emphasis added):

> For all have sinned and fall short of the glory of God, and are justified freely by his grace through the redemption that came by Christ Jesus. God presented him as a **sacrifice of atonement**, through faith in his blood. (NIV)

. . . Whom God set forth *to be* a **propitiation** through faith in his blood. (KJV)

. . . whom God displayed publicly as a **propitiation** in His blood through faith. (NAU)

. . . whom God put forward as an **expiation** by his blood, to be received by faith. (RSV)

. . . whom God put forward as a **sacrifice of atonement** by his blood, effective through faith. (NRSV)]

. . .all have sinned and are deprived of God's glory; they are now justified by his grace as a gift through the redemption that occurred in Christ Jesus, whom God has set out openly in his blood (= death) as the **mercy seat** accessible through faith—a display of his saving righteousness. (Bailey's translation)[100]

In this passage, the phrase "sacrifice of atonement," is a questionable translation of the term *hilasterion*. Christ is the revelation of the mercy of God who offers the sacrifice. And there is no hint here that Christ is struggling to appease an angry Father, as indicated by the translation "propitiation." God's making a way of atonement for sin visible and accessible in Christ is the display of his divine righteousness.[101] The connection of *hilasterion* with the penal interpretation of "propitiation" is without support in the Greek Old Testament or other Pauline usage, say both Ziesler and Fitzmyer.[102]

On the contrary, God has taken the initiative in justifying the sinner, and has thus provided the ultimate paradigm of Christ as the witness of divine grace expressed in saving action. While in the Old Testament, blood had to be applied to the mercy seat by the priest, now God himself, in order to display his saving righteousness, has set out a new "mercy seat" in the person of Christ and has installed and dedicated it by Christ's own blood (Rom 3:25a).[103]

Dan Bailey has convincingly shown by painstaking exegesis and thorough historical and comparative literature analysis that Paul's usage of *hilasterion* without the definite article in this passage is correctly translated as "mercy seat." Furthermore, it is always used as a contract noun in the Bible. It is never used abstractly to describe theological ideas or functions, as Dodd, Morris, and many other scholars allege. The term refers to the covering of the ark, described in the Leviticus legislation, upon which the sacrificial blood was sprinkled for expiation of sins on the Day of Atonement and which was lost during the exile. Bailey shows that the Greek term never refers to an animal victim in any usage before the end of the Byzantine period. It does not refer to the means of accomplishing atonement, but rather to Jesus as the end in himself.[104] Identification with him *is* restoration to divine covenant relationship.

Like the mercy seat in the Old Testament, Jesus is now the location where God is present and where he may be safely approached, not just annually, but every day by everyone. As the mercy seat, Christ restores the relationship between God and humanity, becomes accessible to human needs, and demonstrates God's presence among us. Theologically, the mercy seat is not the sacrifice of atonement, which is slain, but the place where the atonement was effected by the sprinkling of the blood. Christ is thus portrayed as both the one effecting the atonement by the pouring out of his life (his blood) and the one receiving the sacrifice (i.e., mercy seat). This reflects the unified purposes of both God the Father and Christ the Son.[105]

Furthermore, the Jerusalem temple in Jesus' time did not contain the historic mercy seat: it had been lost when Solomon's temple was destroyed. Therefore, after the exile the ritual was performed *as if* the mercy seat were in place. In contrast, Jesus as the Mercy Seat is eternally available.

Referring to the *hilasterion* as the atonement slate (lid) over the Ark of the Covenant inside the Holy of Holies, John Hartley notes that God has set forth Jesus as that atonement slate. And while the original slate was hidden from view inside the Most Holy Place, Jesus died on the cross in full public view. He says, "This radical change in location of the Atonement Slate symbolizes that Jesus' death achieves expiation for everyone who has faith in him."[106] Thus Christ as the atonement slate becomes the boundary between the holy and the sinful. The Most Holy Place is now readily accessible to anyone who comes in faith. One may approach without preparation through fasting, ritual purity, or self-denial.

This movement of the blood ritual from inside the Most Holy Place to a hill outside the city is basic to understanding the shift between the old and new ways to God under the new covenant. "Jesus himself displaces the tabernacle and its entire sacrificial system, and he creates the new people of God without any barriers of race, social status, or gender. In making this radical change, God has revealed his righteousness . . . by providing redemption to everyone who has faith in Jesus."[107] As we have seen, then, God's righteousness is not judgment that must be exacted in the form of penalty, but salvation that is freely given out of God's loving desire to save out of wrath those who will obey in faith and put their trust in Christ, the Mercy Seat. Jesus as the new mercy seat supercedes the old one through his own death and resurrection.[108]

Even though he accepts the "mercy seat" interpretation of *hilasterion*, Gathercole's insistence on the penal understanding of this passage seems to go against the context.[109] Christ's public death on the cross is the demonstration of God's claim to be the "acquitter and savior of his people . . . [and] enables humanity to share by virtue of faith in the very uprightness that he manifests through the death of Christ."[110] A covenant understanding of Christ's work affirms that God's righteousness is incompatible with sin, but the issue is that punishment by death is not the only means by which God can act justly toward sin, as is seen in God's dealing with David. Contrary to Gathercole's assertion,[111] death is not the only way God deals with sin. Apart from gracious divine intervention, death is the result of sin. But God provided the sacrificial cultus to be used in the context of repentance and obedient faith, both for praise and celebration and for expiation of sin. As we have shown, these sacrifices, though slain, were not used as payments of appeasement, but gifts of obedient observance of the Law.

The crucified Christ thus represents God enthroned and unites us with God through the shedding of human blood. Union with God becomes possible because, in our present plight, in our suffering, in our existence in sin, Christ is identified with us. Gese says, "The curtain in front of the Holy of Holies has been rent in two, God is near to us, present with us in death, in suffering, in our dying. . . . Atonement is the sacrifice of life for the sake of making life whole. It brings the abyss of human life into union with the highest divine *doxa* [glory]."[112] The only appropriate response for the believer, then, is participation by faith in this union with Christ that he has initiated with his incarnation. In like manner, the believer, in faith, also becomes a "living sacrifice" through reconciliation and identification with the Mercy Seat (Rom. 12:1–2).

Christ as Sacrifice

As our Old Testament analysis has shown, a sacrifice is a gift of life and not a penalty.[113] This expression of obedience by the sinner, in identifying with the sacrifice, involves the person in the offering of the animal. But the offering is limited in its effectiveness and must be continually repeated. At best, however, even with the Day of Atonement ritual that covered all sins for all the people, the sacrificial system only *represented* the deliverance from sins; it did not actually eliminate them (Heb. 10:1–14). The purpose of the symbolic rituals of the sacrificial system was to teach Israel the proper attitudes and behavior with which to fulfill the covenant's divine expectations for their relationship with God. They were a shadow of the reality that was to come in Christ, says Paul (Col. 2:17).

While the law by continued repetition enabled the sinner by continued repentance and obedience to remain in the covenant community, it did not justify and set the sinner right with God. As Paul says, "We know that a person is justified not by the works of the law but through faith in Jesus Christ" (Gal. 2:16). The Law was given to function as a tutor to teach the nation of Israel how to serve God obediently (Gal. 4). It lacked the spiritual power to do so, however. That is where Christ fits in. As the perfect high priest, Jesus' unblemished sacrifice consummates the entire Old Testament sacrificial system.[114]

In the Old Testament, the covenant sacrifice was for establishing or renewing the covenant. The offerer identified with the sacrifice, so that covenant-breaking behavior could be forgiven. The sacrifice testified to the sincerity of the offerer's repentance and faith. Jesus' sacrifice, likewise, was for renewing the covenant with God after it had been broken by sin. When Jesus bears our sins, he is identifying with us in his incarnation so that our sins become his and his righteousness becomes ours by our faith identification with him. His sacrifice is his gift as our representative.

Christians need to give attention to the sacrificial metaphors in particular. Since the atoning work of Christ is frequently described with sacrificial terminology, it is tempting to understand terms such as "cross," "blood," "sacrifice," "lamb" as referring exclusively to Christ as a sin offering. However, when Paul speaks of Christ as a "Passover lamb" (1 Cor. 5:7), when John the Baptist speaks of the "Lamb of God" (John 1:29, 36), and when all four Gospel writers choose the Passover Feast of deliverance from Egypt to reveal Jesus as Messiah (Matt. 26; Mark 14; Luke 22; John 18–19), Christ is understood to be a sacrifice, but not exclusively a sin offering. The Passover lamb indicates celebration of deliverance from bondage rather than an appeasement for sin. Even when Jesus speaks of his blood being poured out for the forgiveness of sins at the Last Supper (Matthew 26:28), he is speaking in the context of the renewal of the covenant by his own sacrifice of his blood/life.

When the writer of Hebrews describes Jesus coming "to do away with sin by the sacrifice of himself" (9:26), the context makes abundantly clear that Christ is understood as the "mediator of a new covenant" who has set his people free from the sins committed under the first covenant as a "ransom" (9:15), not as a penalty. The entire passage dealing with the blood of Christ (Heb. 9:11–28) is a description of his work to establish a new covenant with humanity through his priestly work of self-sacrifice. When sacrifice is properly understood according to its Old Testament usage and applied to Christ in Hebrews, his sacrificial death is understood as a gift that renews the covenant relationship with God. In Christ, however, this is not a repetitive exercise, and it is not simply a proxy offering in place of the sinner, but it is a final covenant re-establishment based on his own identification with humanity as the divine priestly mediator who brings the alienated divine and human parties together in covenant fellowship.

Therefore, a sacrificial understanding of the atonement in the context of the covenant relationship emphasizes the need for participatory involvement in the "fellowship of sharing in his sufferings" (Phil. 3:10). Christ's work benefits me only as I experience it in faith-union with him. But the covenant emphasis stresses both the objective work of Christ before God and the subjective work of Christ in the believer and thus leads us to an appropriate faith response. Christ's sacrifice initiates and seals a new covenant relationship with God for all who will identify with that sacrifice in faith-obedience and be united with Christ and empowered by the Spirit.[115]

In the sacrificial cultus, blood symbolized the sinner's cleansing from sin, not God's appeasement. The sprinkling of the blood on the altar was to cleanse the sinners from ritual uncleanness so that they were acceptable to God. It was an expression of the repentance of the sinner through the life of the blood, because that is what the covenant required. The priestly function of the sacrifice, as seen in the sacrifice of Christ, was to remove the sins from the sinner and bring release from the bondage of sin. Blood was a synecdoche that represented the entire process of repentance, sin removal, forgiveness, and covenant restoration. It had no magical power in itself to remove or cover sin. The New Testament writers see the sacrifice of Jesus Christ, then, as bringing cleansing from the deathly sins that compromised the covenant community and restoring the covenant union with God through identification with that sacrifice.[116]

In today's culture, the common general understanding of the concept of sacrifice is that a gift of great value (not necessarily financial) is given out of love or a desire to help or protect others. The World Trade Center tragedies in 2001 provide examples of sacrificial behavior. One marvelous example is Franciscan Father Mychal Judge, the New York Fire Department chaplain who sacrificially ministered to the injured on September 11, until the collapse of the structure buried him as he cradled a fallen firefighter in his arms. It was not only that specific event that validates the sacrificial nature of Father Judge's actions, but his entire life of continual ministry to people in suffering and need.[117]

In a similar, though not identical way, in his incarnation Christ gives himself totally for our salvation by identifying and consecrating himself to the task of reconciling us to the covenant God. He identifies with everything human, including death, and the worst and most inhumane kind of death, so that no one stands beyond the reach of his oneness with us in the incarnation. By taking everything that is ours upon himself, he is able to give everything that is his to us in the grace of salvation. He cannot redeem that with which he does not identify "even unto death." His experience of separation from God on the cross ("My God, my God, why have you forsaken me?" Matt. 27:46 NRSV), which he experiences in his empathy with us, is necessary for his full identification with the sinful human race, lost as we are in our sin unto death. Thus his sacrifice is far deeper and more personal than simply settling accounts. The problem Christ confronts in his sacrifice is one of broken relationships that need healing, not simply a breach of contract that needs legal redress. His sacrifice is a passionate expression of his profound love for and identification with humanity.

Faith/Obedience

The term "obedience" occurs numerous times in the Bible. Christ's death was his highest act of obedience to God. In John 14:31, Jesus said, "The world must learn that I love the Father and that I do exactly what my Father has commanded me. Come now; let us leave." These words, spoken just before Jesus' arrest, indicate his firm resolve to give himself as an offering and sacrifice to God. Jesus therefore closes his earthly ministry with a priestly act of self-offering, which completes the mission God gave him. He is obedient unto death (Phil. 2:8). Jesus' entire sinless life portrays him facing suffering vicariously for us, and his final obedience on the cross accomplishes the atonement. He assumed our humanity, then offered it through his own self-sacrifice and became our righteousness before God by his obedience.[118]

Jesus' "sanctifying" himself affirms this priestly function. In the Old Testament, the use of "sanctify" often connotes the consecration of a sacrifice. In John 17:19, Jesus says, "For them I sanctify myself, that they too may be truly sanctified." He is performing a priestly work of sacrifice on our behalf; and by his identification with us, we, too, become sanctified and acceptable before God as we participate in his own self-sacrifice. Jesus' death ends the threat of eternal death for those who are in him. It establishes a new covenant between God and humanity. It creates the opportunity to start over in our relationship with God. And it brings new life to those in Christ. Jesus presents the Last Supper as the celebration meal of the new covenant by which we have become reconciled to God. We appropriate the atonement by our own faith-obedience in following the directions Christ gave us. It's not partaking of the elements of bread and wine that brings us into communion and fellowship with God, but obedience in following Christ's commands. Paul certainly sees the covenant promises as conditioned upon obedience. After recounting Israel's being "broken off" from the olive tree because of their unbelief (Rom. 11:17–20), he declares that only if they do not continue in their unbelief will they again be grafted in (Rom. 11:23). The community of the covenant are those who believe in Christ as "the children of the promise" (Rom. 9:8).[119] By obedient faith, then, we are brought into the new covenant and form the new community of the body of Christ.

Conclusion

Christ's atonement is vicarious not simply in that he became a sacrifice so that we would not have to be punished, but also in that by his life, death, and resurrection he modeled to us how we are to be "living sacrifices" (Rom. 12:1–2). Moreover, it is vicarious not in the sense of exclusive substitution understood only as representation, but as inclusive substitution understood as participation, as well. As such, sin is expiated only as our repentance and obedience are complete so that we are identified and united with Christ by faith in order to participate in the sacrifice of his total life (Rom. 6:1–10).

In the Old Testament, God in the Torah prescribed the sacrificial ritual for expressing repentance. In the New Testament, the proper sacrificial attitude is exemplified by obedient participation in Christ's life and death. Instead of a sacrificial ritual we have an incarnational sacrificial example. This example does not simply inspire the sinner to moral renewal, but requires that the sinner also express repentance for sin and personal surrender to God by identifying in faith with the dying and rising experience of Christ as expressed in baptism (Rom. 6:1–10). Thus obedient union by faith in Christ's sacrificial life and death enables the believer to conform to the covenant expectations. This is justification, since the believer is now actually brought into a relationship of righteousness in the covenant union.[120]

In fact, Romans 3:23–26 presents Christ as an example of faith and obedience:

> For all have sinned and fall short of the glory of God, and are justified freely by his grace through the redemption that came by Christ Jesus. God presented him as a *hilasterion* (mercy seat), through faith

in his blood. He did this to demonstrate his justice . . . , so as to be just and the one who justifies those who have faith in Jesus.

By becoming part of humanity, Christ, as the perfect expression of humanity in obedience to God, took the place of our weakness and rebellion and accomplished reconciliation with God for us. God "made Him who knew no sin to be sin on our behalf, so that we might become the righteousness of God in Him" (2 Cor. 5:21 NAU). Christ's sacrificial death gives us a perfect model of what obedience to God really is. Peter said that God finds favor with our obedience to him in the face of unjust suffering:

> It is commendable if a man bears up under the pain of unjust suffering because he is conscious of God. But how is it to your credit if you receive a beating for doing wrong and endure it? But if you suffer for doing good and you endure it, this is commendable before God. To this you were called, because Christ suffered for you, leaving you an *example,* that you should follow in his steps. . . . He himself bore our sins in his body on the tree, so that we might die to sins and live for righteousness; by his wounds you have been healed. (1 Peter 2:19–21, 24; emphasis added)

The kind of obedience God desires is the kind Christ showed when he obeyed to the point of death. The writer of Hebrews expresses a similar emphasis on this prototypical example in calling Christ the "pioneer (*archégos*) of [our] salvation" (2:10 NRSV) and "the pioneer (*archégos*) and perfecter of our faith" (12:2 NRSV).[121]

Understanding atonement in terms of covenant is thus the predominant biblical background for salvation, and it emphasizes a relationship that expresses expectations to which a penitent may respond. Such an understanding avoids the difficulties of other theories and is consistent with the spiritual formation emphasis on internal moral transformation and subjective holiness of life, also properly understood in covenant terms.[122] Through its emphasis on union with Christ in obedient faith, the covenant paradigm of God's grace in the story of redemption also opens up a valuable resource for spirituality by removing the concepts of righteousness and holiness from imputational interpretations of salvation. And through obedience in following Christ's model, the gracious work of the Holy Spirit enables the believer to be restored into the moral image of God through the empowerment and character transformation that results from identification with Christ and from walking in the Spirit (Rom 8:1–17).

8

Divine Expectations in Christian History

In the history of Christian theology, the efforts to explain how the death of Jesus Christ results in atonement and reconciliation between God and sinful humanity have taken many directions. Numerous theories have attempted to explain the atonement in particular historical and cultural contexts. H. D. McDonald catalogs at least seventeen different theories or sub-theories of the meaning of atonement.[1] Such diversity is an indication of the complexity of the concept of atonement. While all of these concepts may contain valid emphases, we must still provide clear guidelines about what is essential in establishing a comprehensive biblical understanding of atonement. There has never been, however, a particular theory singled out in the history of theology as the only valid orthodox theory to the exclusion of all other theories. That is, not until the present period in the twentieth and twenty-first centuries among evangelicals. Based not on any common agreement among theological traditions, but on popular usage by preachers, teachers, and theologians who are concerned to maintain an orthodox, evangelical, and biblical explanation of the atonement, the penal substitutionary theory has by default become elevated in popular evangelical Christianity, not only as the dominant and preferred theory, but as virtually the only theory that is compatible with the biblical understanding of salvation.[2] Whether this choice of theory is useful and adequate to communicate the atonement concept to persons in the twenty-first-century culture with its cultural diversity and pluralistic aversion to exclusivism remains open to question. It needs to be evaluated for effectiveness in comparison to other theories that have been used in the church at various times in its history and analyzed for its faithfulness in unpacking the meaning of the biblical claim that "Christ died for the ungodly" (Rom. 5:6).

We will assess several theories that attempt to explain the atonement, as well as present a mediating position that may have the advantage of representing more clearly and faithfully the biblical orientation of Christ's atonement and which may be more useful in communicating the atonement meaningfully to twenty-first-century society. Given its central place in the Bible's presentation of the message of salvation, the concept of the covenant may provide a useful hermeneutical lens through which to view the various atonement theories proposed in different historical and cultural periods and locations in the process of Christian history. The fact that no one theory that has been proposed in the history of the church has proven universally acceptable and useful in all cultures and historical periods suggests that a different perspective on Christ's work needs to be examined for its effectiveness in communicating the biblical message of the atonement for the salvation of humanity in this contemporary postmodern cultural climate.

The thesis of this study is that the covenant interpersonal perspective incorporates all the biblically based motifs within itself as the central salvation model or integrative motif of the Bible in regard to salvation history. Indeed, the point of seeing the atonement in the covenant framework is to provide a biblical focus that brings each of the theories into perspective as a part of a unified picture of the atonement narrative so that they are not viewed in competition with each other. Within the integrative motif, each theory becomes a complementary part of the whole collage of biblical metaphors that give insight into the work of Christ.

Issues That Challenge Biblical Concepts of Atonement

Obviously, none of the images for the atonement in and of itself is capable of carrying the entire meaning of the atonement. However, the rationalism of Western Christianity has tended to present the various theories of atonement in juxtaposition to each other or has sought to fit as many of them as possible into a rational theory according to various and often competing visions of theology in order to isolate the "correct" or "orthodox" dogmatic principles. Such an approach, called propositionalism, has often reduced the rich diversity of metaphors used in Scripture to a monochromatic statement of abstract propositions.

An inductive and truly biblical analysis of all of the metaphors and images used by the biblical writers regarding the atonement is essential to understanding the fullness of its meaning. All the metaphors used in Scripture have canonical authority and have been useful in the church in different historical and cultural situations.[3] Though complementary within the context of covenant community, certain historical and intellectual shifts in the history of the church have tended to skew the biblical meanings of these concepts. In adapting biblical terminology to their particular historical situations, the various theologians of the church may have contributed to the understanding of the atonement for their particular situation, but obscured it for others. This phenomenon, which may be called a "paradigm slip," has proven quite mischievous in removing some of the concepts from their biblical settings and redefining them according to criteria from other cultural settings, or in assigning specific theories a priority not biblically substantiated. I am not describing the interpretive process known as contextualization, in which the core meaning of a term is painstakingly retained. On the contrary, with a paradigm slip some of the terms become accommodated to cultural situations that are alien to the biblical context altogether. The rest of this chapter will analyze some of these tendencies that have removed the biblical atonement concept from its biblical covenant context and created theological problems.

The Rise of Christendom

As early as the second century, the church theology began to shift its perspective from the Palestinian context of biblical covenant community to a more philosophical perspective, in order to be more intelligible to the Greek and Roman mind. This shift, motivated by a desire to communicate the gospel more effectively to a different culture, was understandable and necessary from the church's perspective; but we must not lose sight of its significance for later theological developments. It meant that Christian revelation would now be recast from the concrete, interpersonal biblical forms of speech to the philosophical thought forms of the Greek categories.[4]

During the fourth and fifth centuries, the Christian church changed from a decentralized movement of charismatic missionaries who were generally despised and persecuted into a centralized and politically established institution endorsed by the emperor Constantine and most of his successors. After the church gained official toleration and then endorsement as the religion of the empire by Constantine in the early fourth century, a process that some have called "Constantinianism" began.[5] From a persecuted minority, the church became a persecuting majority, with the power of a now-Christian emperor behind it and the will to proselytize vast areas of Europe under ecclesiastical control. During this period from roughly the fourth to the twelfth centuries, in which the church's alliance with the empire is also sometimes called "Christendom," the church became a formal institution united around the pope, the bishop of Rome, confessing the Apostles' Creed, and organized according to an episcopal form of church government ultimately controlled by the pope.[6]

This institutionalizing of the church resulted in a corresponding institution-alizing of the process of salvation. A sacramental system was implemented that objectified the benefits of Christ's atonement into a series of sacraments and me-diated it through the priests for forgiveness of sins and the dispensing of grace. The sacrament of penance, in particular, was developed to deal with the issues of guilt by applying a series of penitential activities prescribed by the priests. The sacrament of the Mass became the focus of worship as a kind of mystical reenact-ment of the atoning death of Christ.

Using a vocabulary originally developed by Tertullian and Cyprian in the third century, this quantifying of the process of salvation became known as the "penitential system." In this system, a concept of merits became a sort of account-ing system for tracking the dispensing of grace through the church's sacraments and the assignment of penance for sin and guilt.[7] Because the effectiveness of the sacraments was related to a system of merits, the repetition of sacraments and penitential exercises led to various practices intended to increase the merits accumulated through these works. Although there are always pious persons who rise above any historical or cultural situation to develop a personal relationship with God, the majority of the members of a society in which Christianity was the mandatory state religion lost all vision of a covenant relationship of faith and obedience in fellowship with God and his community.

The Reconceptualizing of the the Law

As the discussions of the Old and New Testaments have shown, the bibli-cal concepts of the Law were covenantal in nature and based on the righteous and holy character of the covenant God. The context of the Old Testament Law within the "I-Thou" relationship of the covenant ultimately led to Christ as the new Torah. Through interpersonal union with him in faith and growth through the ministry of the Holy Spirit, the faith community grew into the likeness of Christ through faith. The Old Testament Law covenant relationship led to the people's forgiveness and reconciliation with God and each other.[8]

In later Judaism, that concept of the Law began to be developed in the direc-tion Sanders calls "covenant nomism."[9] Later Christianity interpreted the cov-enantal obligations as legalism and externalism in the church after the third cen-tury. As the covenant background of the concept of the Law faded further and further into the background in the Roman society, the church allowed the para-digm for understanding the judicial and legal metaphors to slip from that of the biblical covenant to the model of Roman civil law. The prominence of the Roman legal practices and the role of the sixth-century Justinian Code in formalizing the Western concept of retributive justice influenced the church's interpretation of the New Testament forensic imagery and led to a focus in the doctrine of salvation on the legal categories of guilt, punishment, satisfaction, and acquittal. The biblical juridical metaphors that presupposed a relational basis to the God of the covenant were reinterpreted into secular and abstract legal categories.[10] While we can understand this shift in the light of subtle social pressures, it resulted in a not-so-subtle theological metamorphosis of the concepts of atonement and salvation. Rather than the Law reflecting God's directions for maintaining right covenant relationships within the community of faith, it became a system of penitential accounting tables of just and meritorious rewards and equivalent retributions and penalties.

Even before the era of Constantine, the theologians of the church, in their concern to clarify the church's theology in the Latin culture, began to transfer the church's theology into the concepts of Roman law. The theology of salvation thus assumed the legal concepts of guilt and punishment. Viewed from within the covenant community of faith, Israel saw sin as a violation of covenant trust, and God's wrath was his jealous response to protect the covenant relationship. But as this relational understanding was lost, the church increasingly viewed God in the context of the ancient Greek and Roman gods. For these deities, who had no loving relationship with human creatures, no interest in protecting the divine image in creatures, and no nature of love as the ultimate goal of reconciliation, their wrath called for appeasement and propitiation by religious rituals.[11]

In this changing context, Tertullian (A.D. 160–230?), a lawyer who is often called the "father of Latin theology," developed a vocabulary to reframe the language of salvation in legal terms. His treatises "On Penitence" and "On Purity" provided the basis for a shift in the dynamics of theology and salvation from covenant renewal by faith-obedience to that of a satisfaction of legal guilt by paying the appropriate penalty. This Latin view of atonement interprets the death of Christ in legalistic or forensic terms. Tertullian introduced this legal perspective into Christian theology as a motif for understanding salvation, which involves the ideas of merit and penance, or repentance. God honors good deeds, he said:

> God, we may be sure, will not sanction the reprobation of good deeds, for they are His. Since He initiates and preserves them, so also must He needs approve them; since He approves them, so also must He reward them. . . . Now since God presides as judge in order to exact and safeguard justice, something so precious in His sight,

and since it is for this that He establishes every single precept of His moral law, can it be doubted that, just as in all our actions, so, too, in the case of repentance, justice must be rendered to God?[12]

Faith thus leads to salvation based on the merits of keeping the rule of law, although God does assist humanity to do good deeds.[13] This idea of salvation by the merits of keeping the rule of law became associated in Tertullian's mind with the idea of satisfaction. He says:

> What folly it is, what perversity, to practice an imperfect penitence and then to expect a pardon for sin! This is to stretch forth one's hand for and not pay the price. And the price which the Lord has set on the purchase of pardon is this—*He offers impunity to be bought in exchange for penitence.* If, then, merchants first examine a coin, which they have stipulated as their price, to see that it be not dipped or plated or counterfeit, do we not believe that the Lord, also, pre-examines our penitence, seeing that He is going to give us so great a reward, to wit, to life everlasting.[14]

This penitence, or penance, as a satisfaction, is the payment of a temporal penalty in order to escape an eternal consequence. In this reinterpretation, sin becomes indebtedness rather than an interpersonal violation of the covenant relationship with God. The compensatory work of satisfaction therefore propitiates, or satisfies, God's claim against the accused. Tertullian notes: "Herein [in some eternal act] we confess our sin to the Lord, not as though He were ignorant of it, but because satisfaction receives its proper determination through confession, confession gives birth to penitence and by penitence God is appeased."[15]

Although Tertullian did not apply the term "satisfaction" to the death of Christ, his use of these legalistic concepts and language prepared the way for them to later be applied to Christ's death by Cyprian in the third century. The first Christian writer to interpret Christ's death as a satisfaction in payment for sin, Cyprian also began to apply the term "merit" to the work of Christ. Tertullian had defined "merit" as going beyond what was strictly obligatory in observing God's "law."[16] Persons are often unable to counterbalance their bad deeds with good ones, and therefore wind up with indebtedness to God for underachieving his "law." Some exceptional persons, however, are able to amass merits beyond their own personal needs by performing meritorious deeds such as voluntary celibacy, fasting, martyrdom, and other heroic deeds—and thus earned an overplus of merits. These were considered supererogatory, or beyond what is required. Cyprian also began to apply the idea that the surplus of merit earned by Christ could be transferred to other people. He also added that merits can be transferred from one person to another, an idea that one would be hard-pressed to find in Scripture. In addition, he described the work of Christ as a "satisfaction."[17]

Bringing these ideas together, the Latin theory of the atonement came to view salvation in terms of a legal relationship between two parties in which humanity is now indebted to God. Since Christ and the church have collected a surplus of merits, these may be transferred through the sacraments of the church to those who need them and therefore satisfy or compensate God for the indebtedness of those unfortunate sinners who are short of merits. Christ's work, then, is to make an offering or payment to satisfy God's justice and pay off the claims of indemnity against humanity. Thus the Latin view sees the atonement as a legalistic transaction that involves the transfer of the merits of Christ *as humanity* to pay the indebtedness of the sinner to God. This differs significantly from the identification and participation emphasis of Irenaeus and the classic idea of ransom or recapitulation,[18] which we will examine in the next chapter.

As this alliance of church and state continued to develop, one result of the Constantinian identification with the state was that the concept of covenant Law based on grace and the *ḥesed* of a loving God was largely lost. In its place, the penitential theme developed throughout the medieval period, coming to full expression with the debt of honor "satisfaction" concepts of Anselm in the eleventh century. Thus the forensic, judicial paradigm based on repayment of legal or moral debts became the central framework of Christian theology during this time, rather than the biblical concept of moral renewal through reconciliation with God in covenant community. Jocz notes that without recognizing this gracious difference between God's righteousness and willingness to forgive and human systems of legal justice, there is no answer to the ethical issue of equity. In the exclusively forensic view of salvation, Christ's death violates even the human laws of justice, because for one person to incur a penalty and someone else to pay the price is considered immoral since justice is served only when the guilty are required to pay.

Up to the present day, these and other changes in the concept of "law" have hindered our seeing clearly the biblical meaning of the atonement as the loving restoration of the covenant community in the image of God, for which humanity was created. Understanding "law" as the rational emphasis on absolute, impersonal ethical standards, rather than moral obedience to and restoration of the interpersonal commitments of the divine expectations of God's covenant, has resulted in a devaluing of the relational benefits of the atonement in union with

Christ and the restoration of the image of God through Christ's regenerating and sanctifying grace.

The Focus on Guilt Rather Than Obedience

The quantification of the concepts of guilt and punishment in the Western church, particularly from Augustine in the fourth century through medieval Scholasticism in the sixteenth century, became the central focus for the church's understanding of the atonement.[19] The preoccupation of the medieval church with assessing and addressing the problem of guilt and the complex penitential system of merits and penance became a source of spiritual oppression and defeat until the Reformation. The medieval theological concept of the "treasury of merits" pictured the church as the dispensary of grace, understood as merits or "infused grace," and justification as an accounting process in which the excess merits of saints and Christ could be transferred to the account of the sinner through the sacraments and the performance of penitential works in order to gain salvation. Thus the means of salvation became primarily sacramental. In medieval Catholic theology, guilt was understood as legal or moral indebtedness and could be removed by a penitential process of attrition, confession, satisfaction, and absolution. This required total submission to the church episcopal hierarchy for salvation, and resulted in vast numbers of persons having little understanding of the reality of a relationship with Christ or a sense of assurance from the Holy Spirit of forgiveness of sins.

This system may have accounted for more spiritual casualties than victories. Augustine and Luther, for example, experienced the pathological guilt and fear of damnation that it placed on sensitive Christians who sincerely sought peace with God. This false guilt and unnecessary fear resulted in the kinds of excessive penitential morbidity to overcome guilt such as that seen in their own tortured pilgrimages to faith. There is little wonder that such grotesque distortions of the biblical, covenantal, relational gospel called forth the reaction of the Protestant Reformation in the sixteenth century.

Since the medieval church hierarchy mediated salvation, individuals had no means of directly evaluating their relationship with God. Furthermore, in a feudal society people became accustomed to submitting to the directions of those in power over them. Consequently, although the church gave absolution to those who confessed, this did not satisfy the spiritual uneasiness of introspective, and possibly neurotic, persons such as Martin Luther. Born the son of a coal miner, this precocious young man became an Augustinian monk whose life became a pilgrimage of seeking relief from a sense of guilt over sins that might have been overlooked in confession, and thus not forgiven. His superhuman penitential exercises nearly destroyed his health while leaving his soul unsatisfied. To him, God was a vengeful, wrathful, distant being whose horrible threats of judgment echoed through Luther's mind unceasingly. John Wesley was also such a man. Quite conscientious, Wesley grew up in a pious Puritan-Anglican environment where he was schooled in a disciplined form of faith. Throughout his development into adulthood and even as an Anglican priest, he was unable to satisfy his spiritual hunger and find release from guilt by any of his pious exercises. Both he and Luther found spiritual transformation and healing only after realizing that faith in the work of Christ brought freedom from all condemnation without the assistance of zealous works of merit.[20]

Though these stories are well known, they are sadly still being repeated in different forms in the spiritual lives of many persons today who have been subjected to similar forms of legalistic, guilt-oriented interpretations of a God whose wrath must first be placated before he can love and forgive sinners. They see God as a dispenser of justice who loathes lawbreakers and keeps accounts of their guilt and sin. For such people in the twenty-first century, the recovery of the biblical concept of atonement in the covenant context of the spiritual transformation available through identification in faith with Jesus Christ and the empowering work of the Holy Spirit promises hope.

The Reinterpretation of Biblical Concepts

This cultural and contextual shift from the Hebrew covenant community context of righteous relationship with Yahweh to the Western Christendom world of sophisticated, rational philosophy and Greco-Roman legal patterns led to a very legitimate need to recontextualize the Christian message. The church's fathers and apologists took on this task with sincere intentions and utilized neo-Platonic and other conceptual frameworks to legitimize Christianity in the pagan Greco-Roman world. Theirs was a monumental task and one that for centuries served the church well in shaping its message for its ministry context. To bring the story of salvation from the context of a tribal culture of nomadic Jews punctuated by the reinterpretation of that story through the ministry and sacrificial death of a backcountry Galilean Jew and expect to communicate it to a society of sophisticated and cultured Romans and Greeks was indeed a daunting task. Their work was providential and foundational for the church's mission.

That said, however, this reinterpretation did bring into Christianity some material changes that have been problematic ever since. The theology of the atonement and salvation is a key example. While Paul and the New Testament writers were Jews steeped in the tradition of the biblical covenant faith and community, and while they could use terms out of the Roman culture such as "justification" without evacuating from them the background of covenant love and forgiveness and the interpersonal nature of covenant Law, not all the later writers had this balance in their cultural and conceptual frameworks. Sin, for example, was often seen in the light of neo-Platonic views of the material body. Since matter, according to this system, was inherently evil, and the human body was made of matter, the physical body was an inherently sinful entity and would continue to be so throughout this life on earth. Augustine struggled with this problem of the flesh for his entire life. Ultimately, the Western church attempted to resolve this issue by denial of the body through ascetic, monastic, and celibacy practices in an attempt to separate the spirit from the contamination of the body in order to focus on God's work more effectively.

This concept of sin's connection to physical matter and to the body was unknown in the Hebrew tradition. The Nazirites certainly followed a lifestyle of privation, but out of a sense of calling, not as an attempt to deny the reality of their physical bodies. The concept of sin as violation of covenant trust and relationship with God, which could be forgiven and restored, was replaced with the complex sacramental and penitential system. And the Hebrew understanding of a God who could be angry with sin, but who implemented a system of sacrificial rituals to restore the sinner to covenant fellowship and who ultimately brought eternal reconciliation with himself through Jesus Christ was taken over by the pagan idea of gods who must be propitiated and bribed to withhold their wrath from sinful creatures. Atonement thus became a system for repaying indebtedness through legal sentences. Ultimately this deteriorated into the practice of the penitential accumulation of merits in order to earn justification, or the substitution of the excess merits of saints and Christ for one's demerits of sin. This was the distortion of the penitential system that the Reformation sought to correct with its emphasis on faith alone for salvation.

The Preservation of Tradition at the Expense of Relevance

In addition to the biblical metaphors for atonement, other theological theories have been set forth throughout the history of doctrine, primarily since the eleventh century. The church has never endorsed any of these theories as tests of faith, although some of them—particularly the penal view, have enjoyed wide acceptance. While these theories have been useful within their cultural contexts, the very fact that they have arisen out of specific cultural/historical settings tends to limit their universal relevance. Theological creativity in expressing the gospel in relevant cultural terms is necessary, but the freezing of some of these theories into creedal and dogmatic forms diminishes their effectiveness when the cultural and historical milieu changes. The wisdom of the apocryphal quotation attributed to Karl Barth certainly speaks to this dilemma of tying theological categories to cultural hitching posts: "A faith that is wed to the spirit of the age will become a widow in the next." While the church's theology cannot redefine itself in terms of every shift of the intellectual and cultural landscape, it certainly cannot continue the error of becoming more attached to the landscape than to the universe of revelational truth communicated to us through the biblical narrative.

Although it is arguable whether the worldview of modernism with its rational, scientific, and technological foundations has, in fact, succumbed to the acids of postmodern intuitive and subjective relativism, it is certainly true that the allegiance and imaginations of twenty-first-century generations have made radical shifts of perspective. It would be unwise for Christianity to attempt to reinvent itself now as a postmodern movement and jettison two thousand years of history and reliance upon revelation, sound concepts of truth, and the development of modern technology which has effectively addressed so many challenges of suffering and brokenness. On the other hand, it would be equally unwise to refuse to see that Christians have tended to become "rootless immigrants," to use Bruce Shelley's phrase,[21] whose culture has moved away and left them in isolation, and whose message has lost its voice to the next generations. In its concern for preserving tradition, the church has become less than effective in proclaiming the newness of the gospel to much of the culture of today. The essential biblical message must now be voiced in a translation that is understandable to a new millennium.

The theological systems and ecclesiastical institutions devised in the past should not define the Christian tradition. Rather, it should be defined by its radical passion that sacrificially steps out into the mainstream of the world and with all its might uses every technique at its disposal to fulfill the Great Commission in every age. The legitimate tradition of the Christian faith is its willingness to move beyond every comfortable expression of familiarity into the unknown abyss of the principalities and powers of this age with the proclamation of the love of God in Christ in the power of the Holy Spirit. That is the Spirit who has motivated the church's theologians and missionaries who have developed these various interpretations of the meaning of the atonement. Their legacy to us is not to freeze-frame their proclamations into theories and propositions, but to continue to reframe the gospel message in the language patterns of the uttermost parts of the earth—which now are often right in front of us.

The Need to Recover the Covenant Perspective

The concern of this study is that Christianity recover the biblical, interpersonal covenant understanding of the nature of God, salvation, atonement, and reconciliation. This ancient concept of covenant has great relevance to the culture focused on experience, relationship, and community that has developed in the twenty-first century. The essential characteristics of the covenant are as relevant to the world of today as to ancient Israel. We need to move away from models and images that alienate the present cultures, unless those images and ideas are inseparable from the core of the gospel. In a world of alienation, multicultural diversity, distrust of institutions, and uncertainty of the future, the message of a God who is approachable and who desires to establish relationships with humanity is sorely needed.

The forensic reinterpretations of the biblical models of salvation tend to be perceived by many in the postmodern culture as relics from the Western modernist establishment of religious authoritarianism. A return to biblical covenant understandings of relational faith will help the church regain a voice in its mission to this millennium. In our contemporary age that distrusts absolutes in language and that sees rational argumentation as self-serving and intent upon asserting power and control, the tendency of Christian theology to define itself in terms of rationally valid propositions and theories endangers its credibility, to say the least. On the other hand, in a world defined by images and metaphors and diverse communities, the radical image of a covenant community that gives symbolic and narrative expression to its realities, and that finds its identity in its relationship to a personal God who is defined by his sacrificial love for his followers, has a fundamental appeal.[22]

Seeing the covenant image as the core expression or integrating motif of the concept of salvation can be very effective in this diverse cultural setting. We need to ask how the concept of covenant with its stories, narrative, and rituals, and its personal incarnation in Jesus Christ and his sacrifice and resurrection, can be presented to this contemporary culture in as effective a way as some of the historical theories have been when they were developed. To this end we will analyze a representative selection of the historical theories of Christ's atonement. What made them useful in their context? How can the metaphors expressed in these theories be shaped by the covenant narrative?

Conformity to traditional dogmatic and ecclesiastical formulations are not inherently attractive to the diverse and relational postmodern culture. In other words, God's gospel invitation to salvation based on the divine righteous character and the saving initiative of Christ's sacrificial atonement is more effective than are threats of eternal damnation because of guilt and sin.[23] In fact, the relevance of a covenant relational community model is not only more attractive, it also seems much more in line with the biblical context of Micah 6:6–8 (justice and mercy) and Romans 12:1–2 (obedient response to God's saving love.)

In communicating the atonement, one must first understand the difference between an image, such as a metaphor or metonymy, and a theory. An image is a word picture or figure of speech that is used to communicate the meaning of a reality that goes beyond the image itself. It communicates the reality of a concept without requiring an extended systematic, logical analysis. We are familiar with images such as C. S. Lewis's Aslan, the lion who communicates divine characteristics, or a national flag, which communicates in a symbol the values of a nation—as was seen in New York City after the 9/11 tragedies. Images have meanings associated with them that can communicate to the very deepest psychological and spiritual levels.

On the other hand, a theory is a structured attempt to develop a satisfactory explanation of an idea that accounts for all the meanings, implications, and logical consistencies that go into forming a comprehensive and verifiable conclusion that is coherent with reality. A theory may include images, metaphors, and other figures of speech, but it goes further in attempting to explain the abstract ideas that can be formulated into logically consistent descriptions of an idea.[24] When the theological concern to make the images fit the nuances of the theory becomes more important than allowing the images to reflect the diversity of meanings in an extremely complex concept, that concept is usually distorted. The church desperately needs to find more effective and culturally relevant images with which to communicate the Christian message to a postmodern world.

A Historical Survey of Atonement Theories:
Three Classic Theories

For the early church, the doctrine of the atonement was central to all others. The doctrines of creation, incarnation, Trinity, and Christology, for example, were developed with a view toward safeguarding the hope of salvation. Whenever these doctrines were challenged, the church fathers rebutted them with statements such as the following: If Christ were not truly human, or not fully equal to the Father, then humanity cannot be saved. Christ became human that we might become restored to the divine image. It is through Christ's incarnation, life, and resurrection, and by means of the work of the Holy Spirit, that salvation has been accomplished.[1] The early church's responses to heresies were rooted in its concern to protect the doctrine of salvation from being undercut by either an underemphasis or an overemphasis on Christ's flesh, since salvation is based on the bodily identification of the Son of God with humanity. The church theologians responded to this danger by attempting further explanations of the nature of Christ's atoning work in the form of several theories that built upon certain metaphors that developed in the course of the discussion. We will assess three major categories of atonement theories in relationship to the characteristics of the covenant understanding of the theology of salvation.

Retrieving the Classic Views

The church's earliest theological conceptions of the death of Christ consist of several related ideas generally described as the "classic" or "dramatic" ideas of the atonement. These concepts became less popular in the late medieval era with the rise of the rationalism of Scholasticism beginning in the eleventh century. They have also been generally relegated to antiquity by the Western rationalism of Enlightenment modernism, including Protestantism, which in the Western world took upon itself more of the rationalistic methods of modernism than is often acknowledged. However, the "classic" narrative or story presentation of the nature of Christ's atonement deserves closer analysis by Christians who desire to communicate to the postmodern world.

The classic, or dramatic, theories work from the basic idea that God is carrying out in Christ a victorious conflict against the powers of evil that are hostile to his will. The release of humanity from bondage to these powers brings about a new relationship, one of reconciliation between God and the world. This is a continuous cosmic drama and is initiated by God himself. There is thus a change in God's attitude toward the world that is demonstrated in his initiating this cosmic drama of the world's salvation.

The three classic views—recapitulation, ransom, and Christus Victor—understand sin primarily as enslavement under evil powers. This has a corporate as well as a personal dimension. In contrast to the objective theories, which see sin as primarily transgression of law, or the subjective views, which focus on spiritual and moral immaturity, the classic view understands the effects of salvation less individualistically than either.[2] Salvation is a deliverance of humanity from bondage through participation in the death and resurrection of the incarnate Christ. Aulén sees this as the dominant idea of the atonement throughout the early church period from the New Testament era on for the first thousand years of Christian history.[3] In the fourth century, Athanasius offered a summary of this view. He says the Word takes on a human body capable of death so that he could die for all and enable all to be saved from corruption by the grace of the resurrection. By participation in his death and life, humanity has overcome death and received incorruption.[4]

In the late medieval era, the classic ideas fell out of fashion in favor of Anselm's satisfaction approach for rather complex reasons. The rise of Scholasticism included a rationalist concern to authenticate the truths of revelation with the proofs of reason, a process known as the Medieval Synthesis. The recovery of the Platonic and Aristotelian ideas during the encounters with Arabic scholars during the Crusades led to this renewal of Greek rational categories as the framework of the medieval epistemology known as Realism (Anselm) or Moderate Realism (Aquinas). With this rise, the dramatic nature of the classic articulation of the atonement came to be considered irrelevant. Since it was not easily expressed through syllogistic deductive reasoning and had never been reduced to a formal systematic formula, it fell into disuse in the theological/philosophical teachings of the church in favor of the later Anselmian views.[5]

In the eighteenth and nineteenth centuries, the theological struggles between the liberal Enlightenment theologians and the conservative orthodox Protestant theologians largely ignored the classic views of the atonement. Locked in controversy over orthodoxy, the conservative theologians were critical of the primitive expressions of Christian theology that were not expressed formally as rational doctrines. The classic views were therefore perceived as representing a lower and more primitive theological level since they used primarily metaphorical images and symbolic expressions to communicate the atonement. They lacked the sophistication of the more rational doctrines. Meanwhile, the liberal theologians intensely disliked the "mythological" language of the early church that described Christ's redemptive work through the grotesque imagery of Christ's victory over and deception of the devil. The entire dramatic view was thus labeled "mythological" and summarily rejected as inferior.

Aulén is sharply critical of both of these evaluations. He alleges that both of them underestimated the depth of the biblical narratives and failed to see the relationship between the dramatic views and the New Testament presentations of Christ. These views are not simply primitive expressions of a doctrine that came to full development in the medieval Scholastic theologians such as Anselm, but they present a fundamentally different perspective than the Latin understandings of the atonement.[6] These often-ignored views therefore warrant a sympathetic overview at this point.

The Recapitulation Theory

Writing scarcely a hundred years after the Apostolic Age, Irenaeus (120–203) established the earliest framework for Christian theology through his exposition of the central ideas of the Christian faith. He did not follow the more philosophical approach developed by some of the later church fathers, nor did he fall into the more bizarre ransom imagery of the later preachers. Furthermore, the doctrine of the atonement was central to his writing and set the tone for the communication of this doctrine for several hundred years. His whole theology rests on the answer to the question, "For what purpose did Christ come down from heaven?" His answer states, "That He might destroy sin, overcome death, and give life to man."[7]

The manner in which Irenaeus developed this answer has given his approach to the atonement the label of the "recapitulation theory." In Latin, the term *recapitulatio* literally means "reheading," or "providing a new head," in the sense of providing a new source or origin. Irenaeus takes the idea from Paul's concept of Christ as the "second Adam," who becomes the new head of the human race in the place of the "first Adam" who sinned and fell (Rom. 5). Through his identification with humanity in his incarnation, Christ recapitulated, or "summed up in himself," all of humanity, so that what humanity had lost in Adam (the perfect image of God) could be recovered in himself. Motivated by his desire to refute the teachings of the Gnostics of his day who were denying that Jesus was a heavenly redeemer who actually took on human flesh, Irenaeus showed how every aspect of the life and work of Christ is necessary for salvation.[8]

Participation in the experience of humanity through the incarnation is the basis of Christ's redemptive work, which includes not only his death but his teaching, resurrection, ascension, and triumphal reign with God. Jesus entered into our death, so that as he was raised from death we would be alive in him (Rom. 6:6–7; 2 Cor. 5:14; Eph. 2:4–5). But not only was his death our death, his resurrection was also our resurrection (Rom. 6:5; 2 Cor. 5:15; Eph. 2:6). He was identified with us in our death resulting from sin in order that we might become identified with him in his resurrection to new life (Rom. 6:1–14). Irenaeus says, in other words, *he became like us that we might become like him.*[9] Irenaeus saw redemption as a divine cosmic drama that involved the whole of world history and which had as its central moment the life, death, and resurrection of Jesus Christ. Redemption is the restoration of creation to what God had intended. This world was created by God, but was subjected to destitution and decay by the evil work of Satan in Adam. Sin had also divided humanity from itself. Now through the identification of Christ with humanity as the new Adam, he recapitulates the process of re-creation—gathering together all creation, including humanity, in himself in order to reverse the fallen direction of Adam that ended in corruption and to undo in himself all the devil's work of destruction. In restoring humanity's innocence as the image of God, humanity's relationship of adoption as sons and daughters of God, and humanity's future immortality and incorruption, Christ recovers the destiny of God's plan and our communion with him.[10] This provides the foundation for Christian fellowship and community as God brings redeemed humanity together in reconciliation with each other as well as with God.

This salvation drama involves victory over the dominion of evil and the eschatological transformation of all creation back into God's pure, irreproachable, blameless image in which it was created. Christ's work is primarily a victory over the powers that hold humanity in bondage to sin, death, and the devil. This recapitulation does not end with the triumph of Christ over his enemies, but continues with the Spirit's work in the church. The complete recapitulation of creation is eschatological. It is not completed in this life but is part of the gift of the Spirit of

God that is the earnest of future glory and the crucial point that begins the process of restoration of creation in the victory of Christ over these hostile powers.[11]

Irenaeus is often criticized, along with other Eastern Fathers, for viewing salvation as a bestowal of life while placing little emphasis on sin. Salvation and the atonement basically are seen, according to this criticism, as the bestowal of life and a victory over mortality even before they involve forgiveness of sins and victory over sin. This is a somewhat misleading criticism because the Eastern theologians do not see a separation between sin and subsequent death as its result. Where sin is, death is also, and vice versa. The goal of Eastern theology, which Irenaeus represents (even though he served much of his life in Gaul), is to answer the question, "Why salvation?" with the reply, "To be free from sin and death, in order to break down the wall of partition between God and humanity, to enter into inner and complete communion with God, to be at one with Him."[12]

The recovery of this communion with God is accomplished not only through the cosmic triumph over the powers that have kept humanity in bondage, but also through Christ's incarnational identification with humanity. God in Christ is united with humanity in new life. In Irenaeus' view, Christ's death is not to be separated from his incarnation, resurrection, and ascension. By his obedience to God, Christ recapitulates the experience of human fallenness and annuls the disobedience of Adam. The resurrection becomes the first manifestation of this decisive victory over the powers of evil that was won at the cross and is the starting point for the bestowal of the Holy Spirit and the continuation of the work of God in the hearts of humanity.

Irenaeus stresses the Trinitarian focus of redemption, basing the atonement on the incarnation:

> Since the Lord thus has redeemed us through His own blood, giving His soul for our souls, and His flesh for our flesh, and has also poured out the Spirit of the Father for the union and communion of God and man, imparting indeed God to men by means of the Spirit, and, on the other hand, attaching man to God by His own incarnation, and bestowing upon us at His coming immortality durably and truly, by means of communion with God, all the doctrines of the heretics fall to ruin.[13]

Thus God himself, in the Word Jesus Christ, has entered into the experience of sin and death in the incarnation to take up the conflict with the powers of evil and bring it to a decisive victory. *His identification with humanity is so complete that it even includes the experience of death.* God has mercifully delivered humanity, through its participation in the death and life of Christ from the doom of death that had been its sentence. Those who in faith participate in his obedient experience as their new head may enter into a new humanity, with the ultimate hope of sharing in the immortal nature of God. In contrast to the Gnostic view of salvation as escaping creation and its physical limitations, for Irenaeus, redemption is a process of restoring creation. Ultimately, this restored life will be characterized by the transformation and recovery of the image of God to become partakers of the divine nature (2 Pet. 1:4). This is the beginning of the idea of redemption known as "deification," or *theosis.*[14]

Again, in contrast to the later doctrines, Irenaeus does not see the atonement as an offering made to God by Christ as humanity, because *God remains the effective agent of the work of redemption throughout.* Whereas the Latin theory of atonement sees Christ as man who offers an acceptable offering from man's side to God, Irenaeus sees the Word of God as the Creator of all who overcomes the devil through man. No other power could have accomplished this deliverance; therefore God himself accomplished it *through* the humanity of Christ as his instrument. The obedience of Christ is not a human offering made to God from humanity's side. Rather, the divine will "wholly dominated" the human life of the Word of God, who perfectly expressed God's will in his incarnate life of obedient sacrifice.[15] The Word's incarnate life is thus the recapitulation of the way humanity was intended to respond before it went astray in Adam. Irenaeus differs here from the Latin view in emphasizing that the work of atonement is not simply authorized, sanctioned, or initiated by God, but that from beginning to end God himself is the effective agent who, through the Word of God incarnate, enters into the world and human experience in order to reconcile it to himself.

Atonement and incarnation are inseparably linked, as are the Father and Son, in this process. There is no sense of an antithesis between Father and Son in the work of redemption, for God's love in the Father and Son, and ultimately in the work of the Spirit in the church, creates a new relation between humanity and God. This unified work of redemption victoriously confronts the hostile forces of evil that have dominated the human experience and dramatically vanquishes them, thereby reclaiming the world and reconciling it unto God.[16] Thus, the recapitulation view lays the groundwork for the restoration of all creation in the last day, although the process begins with the indwelling presence of Christ's Spirit in this age. The restoration of all creation and its deliverance from the evil powers of chaos and destruction provide the basis for a Christian theology of ecological responsibility, as well as human healing and wholeness.

Variations of the Irenaean view appear in the tradition of the Greek Fathers from Irenaeus (120–203) to John of Damascus (c. 675–c. 749). With all their diverse terms and images, Origen (185–254), Athanasius (296–373), Basil the Great (329–379), Cyril of Alexandria (376–444), Cyril of Jerusalem (c. 315–386), Gregory of Nazianzus (325–389), Gregory of Nyssa (?–386), and John Chrysostom (c. 347–407) all express the same dramatic understanding of Christ's redemptive work. Even though they represent different schools of theology and express different attitudes toward Greek philosophy and other theological perspectives, they share a profound agreement on the nature of Christ's work.[17]

Among the Western Fathers, says Aulén, the dominant view for many centuries was also the classical dramatic understanding of the atonement. Even though Tertullian, Cyprian, and Gregory the Great laid down and developed the foundations of the Latin forensic view, this view was not fully dominant until the work of Anselm in the eleventh century. Many Western theologians accepted the classical dramatic view, including Ambrose (340–397), Augustine (354–386), Leo the Great (d. 461), Caesarius of Arles (470–543), and Gregory the Great (540–604). In the case of Gregory the Great, although he developed some of the most vivid, even lurid, images of the dramatic theme and popularized it in his preaching so that it was assured a place in medieval theology for centuries, paradoxically, he also expressed the Latin view with a thoroughness almost rivaling Anselm's later theory. Moreover, his development of the idea that human guilt necessitated a sacrifice grew into the Latin understanding of the Mass, which he was instrumental in forming into the central liturgy of the Catholic tradition.[18]

The Ransom Theory

The most controversial aspect of the dramatic theory is its use of images such as the ransom price to portray Christ's dealings with Satan to negotiate the release of humans from Satan's domain of sin and death. The religious motive for using such images is the desire to communicate humanity's guilt and God's judgment, and to show how God himself overcame the bondage to Satan resulting from this judgment. Despite the many versions of the story, the basic idea in the ransom concept is that the devil (and death) had gained a rightful claim on humanity because of the fall and its curse. Since God's love leads him to seek the deliverance of enslaved humanity, and since it is not lawful to use violence to wrest control of the slave from the rightful owner, how can God negotiate a release? The image of ransom supplies the means to negotiate the release. Origen suggested that the ransom cannot be paid to God but to Satan, since he has humanity in his power. The ransom payment Satan seeks is the life of Christ. Christ gives himself in exchange for the life of humanity; but Satan then finds that Christ cannot be contained by death—as he breaks free from Satan's control, thus vanquishing death and rendering it no longer the master of humanity.[19]

Other theologians object to the picture of God paying a ransom of his Son to Satan; the devil is an evil robber and a tyrant with whom it is not fitting for God to negotiate. Gregory Nazianzus refers to Christ as a sacrifice rather than a ransom, and Chrysostom characterizes Satan as a tyrant who unjustly murders the innocent Christ and therefore is justly dethroned and forced to give up those under his power.

Nevertheless, the idea of the deception of the devil generated some of the most vivid imagery, such as the bait and the fishhook, a drug mixed with food, a mousetrap, and so on. While a literal interpretation of such images obviously raises the specter of distorted ideas of God, the underlying concept that God is not aloof from the process of redemption, but rather deeply involved in it, is profoundly biblical.[20] The ideas that humanity is responsible for its sin and that the judgment of death on that sin is a righteous one are also sound. And crude as the ransom-price image may be, it reflects the classic idea that the payment of the debt to release humanity from bondage is God's own act effected through the sacrifice of Christ. That sacrifice is in no way understood as a means of placating or propitiating God's wrath, but is initiated by God himself. This image contains no sense of a difference or conflict between the Father and the Son, as in the Latin view.

Aulén says that Augustine directly repudiates the idea that the Father can in any way be placated by the death of the Son, because that would imply some sort of difference or conflict.[21] He also provides a variation in the ransom idea by noting that death was Satan's dominion, but by inflicting death on one who was sinless Satan forfeited his control over it.[22]

Thus the ransom theory version of the classical dramatic view, in spite of some of its fantastic and lurid imagery, particularly in the writings of Origen, is grounded in the orthodox understanding that the atonement portrays God as both the Reconciler and the Reconciled. Through the work of Christ, God corrects the relationship between humanity and the divine Creator. The atonement involves not just something God objectively does to humanity, but in which humanity is involved as well through its incarnational identification with the Son of God. Christ fully represents both God and humanity in the process of the dramatic redemption of humanity.[23]

The Christus Victor Theory

A prominent view of the atonement which has its roots in ancient orthodox tradition but has more recently gained attention is the dramatic, or classic, Christus Victor theory of Gustaf Aulén. His concern is to vindicate Luther's interpretation of the atonement, as well as to rescue the patristic interpretations of the atonement from the distortions to which they had been subjected in subsequent theological evaluations, such as the attacks by the liberal schools of Harnack and Ritschl.[24]

Aulén desires to show the distinction between Luther and later Lutheran orthodoxy. He wants to show how the Reformation was not merely a protest against abuses but a movement to deliver Western Christendom, or Constantinianism, from the domination of an ecclesiastical system that had reduced the gospel of salvation to a rationalized theology and a moralistic ethic. Medieval Catholicism had turned the gospel into a system in which the way to God was through justification by works and human merit, in opposition to Paul's clear teaching to the Galatians. Luther believed God had given him a message of deliverance, so was later sharply critical of the systematizing of Protestant orthodoxy—which he felt led the church back into slavery, since Protestantism had become as legalistic as medieval Scholasticism and Christendom had been hopelessly divided. Aulén's hope is that this divided Christianity could find a way to reconcile through a common return to the old evangelical and catholic "classic" faith that all Christian traditions share in common.[25]

Modifying the earlier ransom motif, Aulén sees Christ in cosmic combat with the powers of darkness. He claims to present the dominant approach of the New Testament and early church, which, he argues, sees the atonement not as a legal transaction or juristic sentence, as in the Latin and Swiss/German Reformed and Lutheran traditions. Neither does this view see Christ as merely an inspiring example of love, as in Abelard's theory. Instead, Christ is the cosmic champion who overcomes the evil forces that hold humanity in bondage. Christ has met the cosmic forces of evil on their own ground, in history where they were entrenched, in order to break their power. Through his work we may sing, "In all these we are more than conquerors" (Rom. 8:37).[26] "Having disarmed the powers and authorities, [God] made a public spectacle of them, triumphing over them by the cross" (Col. 2:15). Church of the Nazarene theologian William M. Greathouse calls this theory "one of the most influential treatments of the atonement to appear in our time." He says further, "Aulén has done the church a service in rescuing the dramatic view of Christ's work and restoring it to its rightful place as a New Testament representation of the atonement."[27]

Aulén's concern is to recover the genius of the classical idea of the atonement that it is primarily a movement of God to humanity, not of humanity to God. He says the classical understanding is not a theory which requires the resolution of the evidence into a systematic set of principles that are logically consistent and which explain the data. Instead, the classical approach allows the biblical paradoxes regarding salvation to stand: the infinite God accepts the humility of the incarnation; the victory over the dark forces of evil is accomplished by divine self-sacrifice; God is both the Reconciler and the Reconciled; his love prevails over his wrath, and yet love's condemnation of sin is absolute. All attempts to resolve these paradoxes and force them into purely rational systems have either failed or have robbed the concepts of their religious depth. Many of the patristic attempts to reconcile the doctrines of the incarnation and redemption were unsuccessful because they "sought to transform theology into a speculative metaphysic or an idealistic philosophy."[28]

The classic idea of atonement has never been formalized as a rounded and finished theological doctrine. Instead it is a motif, a theme expressed in many variations. Aulén admits that many of the forms in which this idea has been expressed have sometimes used crude and realistic images that have suffered the disgust of later theologians. He notes, however, that these images are only popular helps for understanding the primary idea, which is the important issue.[29]

In contrast to the movement of God to humanity that he sees characterized in the classic view, Aulén criticizes the Latin forensic theory because it subjects the idea of atonement to the systematizations and abstractions of the law courts. This leads to the consideration of justice as the key issue in atonement. God seems to be more distant and the satisfaction for divine justice must be paid by humanity to God in the person of Christ. This makes humanity, not God, the agent in the work of atonement, since it is God to whom satisfaction must be paid. This minimizes the incarnation and obscures its relationship to the atonement because God is no longer the direct agent in the atoning work. This views Christ as a human making atonement on humanity's behalf, which raises the specter of Docetism, the heretical view that Jesus did not actually have a human body and only appeared to die on the cross; and that raises difficulties regarding the two natures of Christ that are not easily resolved.

In addition, if Christ is acting as God to placate God, this also raises serious difficulties for the oneness of the Trinity. Furthermore, it presents the issue that God requires a compensation, or satisfaction, so that his mercy can be free to act on humanity's behalf. This sets the Father and Son at odds until God's wrath is satisfied. The Latin view is thus a rational attempt to explain how divine love and divine justice can be reconciled. It postulates that love is regulated by justice and is only free to act according to the limits set by justice. This is the scholastic approach that allows the dialectical method to take precedence over issues of faith. It attempts to provide a comprehensive explanation of God's government of the world, to solve all questions and riddles in this world and that to come.[30]

Aulén also sees the Latin view as diminishing the idea of sin by viewing it as an objective power of evil and as less than personal. When the Latin view claims that the justice of God is preserved by the payment of a compensation for sin, even though that may be by Christ, this lessens the reality of God's personal demands on humanity—his divine expectations. The Latin view, with its penitential system, has allowed sin to become substantialized, or materialized. *Salvation is thus reduced to the removal of guilt, rather than understood as the transformation of the person in Christ.* God's claim on humanity and the restoration of his image in humanity can never be accomplished by obedience to any law or the satisfaction of any balancing of merits that neutralizes one's offenses toward God.[31]

Sin is objective, personal, and existential, and it cannot be removed by a legal transaction or imputation of Christ's righteousness that does not require the participation of humanity in the atoning work of the incarnate Christ. Effective atonement must fully include humanity in the process of death to sin and resurrection to new life in him. The Christus Victor idea focuses not primarily on the removal of the punishment and consequences of sin, such as guilt, but on overcoming sin itself in the form of victory over the evil powers of Satan. Moreover, it continues the classic idea that the victory of Christ is gained once for all and is carried on in the work of the Holy Spirit in the community of faith.[32]

Finally, Aulén also critiques the subjective moral influence theory as a rationalized view of love that tends to lose the idea that divine love is hostile to evil. Salvation, in turn, is little more than humanity's gaining a new attitude toward the world: harmony, peace of mind, and self-realization. Such a theory preserves the idea of divine love and of Christ as the true image of God but rejects the realities of sin and justice that require an atonement between God and humanity in any profound sense.[33]

In contrast, the Christus Victor view understands that death is the greatest and most objective barrier to salvation. It is death that cosmically separates humanity from God. Death had to be defeated, and the purely objective theories of atonement do not seem to take this matter seriously because they are focused exclusively on the issue of propitiation for human sins. It is because of the fallenness resulting from humanity's action that death entered human history through a man, Adam. Therefore, so the reasoning goes, death has to be removed by a man, the God-man Jesus Christ (1 Cor. 15:21–22). The forensic theories thus see sin as the primary problem and death as a secondary problem, since it is the penalty of sin. They focus, therefore, on how to pay the penalty. In the classic motifs, on the other hand, the focus is on the life that overcomes death, because death is the primary problem in that humanity sins because it is in a relationship of death before God (Rom. 5:12). It is this cosmic power (i.e., death) which held humanity in bondage that Christ overcame in his victorious combat.[34] Release from its bondage allows humanity to be restored to its relationship with the Creator. The focus is thus on the core issue of restoration to oneness with God, not on the compensation for the symptom of the core issue, which is sin.

The Classic Views in Relation to the Covenant Interpersonal Understanding

After this analysis of the classic views of the atonement, how does this perspective measure up to the criteria of the covenant interpersonal concept of the atonement? Interestingly, given the tendency of late medieval, Reformation, and modern theologians of both liberal and conservative perspectives to dismiss the classic views as fanciful imagery, these views rate rather well in relationship to the characteristics of covenant teaching. They maintain a central focus on the love of God: love is the beginning and end of the classic idea of the conflict between good and evil and the final liberation in Christ. These traditions place a stronger emphasis on incarnation than do the penal and moral example theories. The goal of reconciliation is seen universally as the outcome of the atonement in the classic view's focus on overcoming the enslavement of humanity to the forces of evil, allowing persons in Christ to recover their relationship to God. The work of Christ in giving himself as a ransom for the deliverance of humanity is a clear self-sacrificial motif. It is a giving of oneself for the sake of love.

In addition, forgiveness and healing through a restoration of the image of God in the humanity that shares in the incarnation with Christ is a key feature of the classic view. Here the classic position speaks to the need for spiritual renewal and becoming like Christ evident in the New Testament emphasis on discipleship and spiritual formation. In implementing the healing of salvation, the Spirit brings together the humanity that was divided from itself and from God and forms the community of those in Christ. The nature of this reconciliation with God is interpersonal, as is the understanding of the incarnation and the role of divine love in the entire process of redemption. The victory over the powers of disorder also addresses the concern for the renewal of creation—ecological issues—since the cosmos has been set free from the dominion of darkness and death. And the classic view is profoundly Trinitarian, as we have seen.

The dramatic theories make the incarnation foundational for salvation. Christ's work in overcoming death as a result of his victory over sin becomes the basis for his present work in the world where he continues, through the Holy Spirit, to break down the power of sin and restore humanity to God's image. In these views the devil had rights over humanity, but this element does not develop into a rational demonstration of the logic of the atonement as in Anselm. Instead, they show that God sympathizes with the desperate plight of humanity, loves them, and is motivated by divine love to liberate them. Augustine, for example, depicts humanity as delivered into the power of the devil on account of its sin, and guilt rests on the entire race. Yet God does not cease to love them, and the incarnation is the proof of the greatness of this love. God's plan of sending the Son to enter into fellowship with humanity, to take upon himself our sufferings and the evil and death of our human experience, is born of this love. Christ takes on the tyrants as the representative human and overcomes them, releasing humanity from their bondage to death and reconciling them to God, thus effecting their atonement through his love.

The emphasis of Christ's atonement lies not just on his death, but also on his life. The Word becomes human that he may restore the life that had been lost, and he does this by bringing the life of God into the world to identify with humanity and prevail over sin and death. Christ's victory, his passage from death to life, establishes a new relationship between God and humanity. The later Fathers show that death and the devil are the executors of God's judgment on sinful humanity. In Christ's victory over these evil powers, humanity's deliverance from the power of death and the devil is at the same time humanity's deliverance from God's judgment. By his own act in Christ, God reconciles the world to himself. Thus God is not only the Reconciler, but the Reconciled.[35]

All in all, apart from some of the fanciful and grotesque imagery used to communicate the classic ideas, and notwithstanding the difficulties in determining to whom the ransom is paid—if indeed that is even central to the concept—the classic views, particularly as presented by Irenaeus and Gustaf Aulén, show significant consistency with the characteristics of the biblical covenant understanding of salvation. Indeed, the dramatic narrative motif provides rich resources for creative communication of the atonement to a postmodern audience sensitized to the reality of spiritual forces.

Thus we see that the dominant view of atonement during the first millennium of the church's theological development was the classical dramatic perspective. Even though the Latin view was growing in influence among some in the Western church, the dramatic view was certainly the most widely understood popular expression of the work of Christ among the most influential theologians of this entire era. To dismiss this body of Eastern and Western theologians as primitive, fanciful, and mythological, as some modern theologies have done, is simply theologically and historically irresponsible.

10

A Historical Survey of Atonement Theories:
Three Forensic Theories

The forensic imagery of the law courts as a template for organizing the biblical data on atonement and salvation seems like a legitimate motif. The Old Testament role of the covenant Law as a central organizing structure for Israel's life is clear. The Pauline metaphors from the legal realm are well known. The descriptions of the trial and crucifixion of Jesus in terms of legal charges of blasphemy and sedition, declarations of innocence, and an opportunistic sentence of capital punishment by a Roman court are all part of the Christian tradition.

A cautionary note is sounded, however, when the perspectives of Jewish and Roman law are applied to Jesus' situation. The Gospel writers raise questions about the very assumptions of the legal system that condemned Jesus. The Jewish covenant Law could never be reduced to a code of rules because it was based on Israel's relationship to God, and that is where Jesus ran afoul of the literalistic legalism of his day. And neither do these Gospel writers accept Roman law as the ultimate authority; the will of God is absolute. Jesus' teachings and lifestyle, in fact, challenged the absolute demands of both religious and secular law. His focus was on living out the purpose of God for his life. And although the New Testament uses legal language to describe the atonement,[1] this legal language must be understood in its biblical context of covenant relationships in which "justification" means setting relationships right for the health of the covenant community.[2]

The forensic models of salvation grew out of the Latin theology of Tertullian, Cyprian, and others who developed the theology of the penitential system of merits to which the Protestant Reformers such as Martin Luther and John Calvin objected so strenuously.[3] It was from the categories of Roman law that Western theology drew the conceptual categories of the sacrament of penance and the ideas of justice in terms of punishment, merit, satisfaction, and absolution. Roman legal theory and practice provided the vocabulary of the Latin penitential system.

It is ironic that in spite of their rejection of penitential theology and works righteousness, the Reformers succeeded in removing only the liturgical expressions of the penitential system. The Reformation theologies retained the central forensic conception of justification with God being based upon the transfer of merits and the satisfaction of a penalty. This is a concept drawn directly from the secular Western legal systems.[4] Apparently the Western European legal tradition and Latin theological orientation had become so deeply rooted by the time of the Reformation that the Protestant theologians were unable to reconceive theology in any other way than the forensic understanding. Driver says in this regard, "Protestantism has often proceeded more in the spirit of Western law than in the gracious spirit of biblical covenant which is revealed most fully in the saving work of Christ."[5] The conception of merits of righteousness offsetting the demerits of sin in humankind made it necessary for the Reformers, and particularly later Protestant orthodoxy, to formulate their conceptions of salvation around the idea of a substitutionary payment of penalties for transgressions against God based on the merits of Christ.

Even though, in the Protestant understanding, Christ alone, not the believer, presented those merits, the satisfaction of a divine accounting process still underlies the penal substitutionary understanding of Christ's atonement. The forensic theories of atonement have interpreted the acquittal of the sinner through the cross of Christ either in terms of the transfer of the penalty of death leveled by God against sinners or as a payment of satisfaction to God to restore his divine honor. Since justice is served only when the accounts balance, the doctrine of limited atonement was submitted to allow justice to quantify the amount of merit needed to balance the celestial books with the merits contributed by the death of Christ. The other alternative to a limited atonement doctrine was universalism, since Christ's merits were infinite. Therefore, if Christ's merits were deposited to the account of humanity, all of humanity's penalties would be paid.[6]

Such an accounting of merits or payment of satisfaction seems radically out of step with the Old Testament system of sacrifice offered as a gift of obedience to make atonement to maintain the covenant community in relationship to God.[7] The Old Testament sacrifices were not construed as payments of penalty for sin, since an animal sacrifice was certainly not the equivalent in value of a transgression against the God of the covenant. Furthermore, the forensic tradition overlooks the interpersonal covenant accountability in the Hebrew covenant Law, the rabbinic tradition, and the theology of Paul. This oversight leaves the way open for the development of an atmosphere of ecclesiastical and theological legalism which, in fact, has appeared in various nuances of legalistic and guilt-oriented Protestant theologies.

To their credit, however, these forensic expressions of atonement theory have been seriously concerned with contextualizing the meaning of the atonement for their particular historical and cultural situations. Three main expressions of the legal theories are found in the satisfaction, penal substitution, and governmental versions of the forensic theory of atonement.

Satisfaction Theory

The term "satisfaction," as Tertullian used it, means the discharge of an obligation by a method acceptable to the debtor. It is not a legal equivalent of punishment, but God takes it as an expression of genuine contrition, which makes it appropriate grounds for annulling the real penalty—which, in our case, is death. In the medieval feudal society of Anselm, justice was based on the honor of the overlord; any offense was considered an affront to the overlord, since justice was embodied in his person and dignity. When this dignity, or honor, was transgressed, the offender had to make restitution to the overlord either by direct punishment or by the alternative of satisfaction through payment of money, service, or some other acceptable substitute gift.[8]

This concept formed the basis for the penitential system of supplementing faith with meritorious works of penance. Also, in the feudal cultural context, Christ's death is not punishment *per se*, but something God accepts *in place of* the punishment due humanity for sin. However, later medieval theologians came to understand satisfaction as a true alternative or equivalent of the punishment due for sin. Thus Christ suffered the pain of death, but not the total punishment for sin. But the pain of the cross was accepted by God as satisfaction, or the equivalent substitute for punishment.[9] This provided for the role of penance as a continuing expression of repentance on the part of the sinner to maintain the payment of his/her indebtedness to God and the church.

Anselm of Canterbury

Anselm of Canterbury (1033–1109) developed the first substantially different approach to the doctrine of the atonement after the first millennium of Christianity's existence. Known as the "Father of Scholasticism," he led the way in shifting theology from its traditional basis in exegesis of Scripture and tradition to philosophical categories. This Scholastic system, utilizing the categories of reason to substantiate the truths of faith, led to a dialectical methodology that dominated late medieval thought and which came to be known as the Medieval Synthesis of faith and reason. This rational approach to faith issues was an attempt to make theology relevant to the intellectual world and to free it, as least to some extent, from papal authoritarianism.[10]

In response to a series of discussions with a group of Jews about the necessity of the incarnation of Jesus Christ, Anselm, who was the Archbishop of Canterbury from 1093 to 1109, began his treatise *Cur Deus Homo?* ("Why the God-Man?"). In short, his answer was that God needs to be satisfied by the payment of humanity's debt of sin against him in order justly to forgive humanity. Anselm defines sin as stealing from God the honor that is due him by not having a will that desires to please God; thus to sin is to dishonor God.[11] God's justice cannot condone sin or ignore it; and humanity can do nothing to make restitution or reconcile itself to God and restore his honor, because of the infinite nature of the offense. And since humanity ought to make the payment, as should be expected of someone who has stolen another's property, but cannot, the solution must come from God. Furthermore, God's will and purpose in creating humanity of necessity cannot be frustrated because of his omnipotence and justice. Therefore, God must find a way to reconcile himself to humanity while still maintaining his honor. That is accomplished by the incarnation and the death of Christ, the God-Man, as the only adequate satisfaction for human sin that maintains God's justice.[12]

The satisfaction theory advanced by Anselm in the late eleventh century reflected the understanding of honor and satisfaction found in the feudal code of chivalry when "knighthood was in flower." God is presented as a feudal overlord, with humanity—as his vassals—arranged in a socially stratified hierarchical system. This vassal humanity had offended the honor of the overlord by disobedience in not fulfilling their obligations to him.[13] Anselm saw the atonement as a restoration of God's offended honor by the meritorious and supererogatory obedience offered by Christ on behalf of humanity. The obedience of Christ's life had merit to make amends for the infinite dishonor brought upon God's name by sinful humanity.[14]

Anselm defined sin in terms of a debt toward God. By this he did not mean simply a commercial indebtedness, but a kind of moral and religious obligation or "ought." God is not free to leave sin unpunished because his justice requires its punishment. Anselm said that for God to forgive sins out of compassion without satisfaction or punishment is impossible: "To remit sin in this manner is nothing else than not to punish; and since it is not right to cancel sin without compensation or punishment, if he is not punished, then is it passed by undischarged. . . . It is not fitting for God to pass over anything in his kingdom undischarged. . . . It is therefore, not proper for God thus to pass over sin unpunished."[15]

Anselm goes on to say that justice is regulated by law; and if sin is neither paid for nor punished, it is subject to no law and justice is unsatisfied.[16] Since there is nothing greater than supreme justice that maintains God's honor, which is tantamount to God himself, God maintains nothing with more justice than his own honor and dignity. The honor that has been taken away from God must be repaid, or punishment must follow, in order for God to be just to himself.[17]

Anselm insisted that the sin that had dishonored God must either be punished or satisfaction paid, although there is no concept here of a payment to Satan, for Anselm rejects the idea that Satan has any rights whatsoever. Neither does he stress the vicarious suffering of the penalty of sin, but rather that the dishonor perpetrated upon God must be restored by the compensation of Christ's obedience, which is propitiatory and meritorious: "Does it seem to you that he wholly preserve it [honor], if he allows himself to be defrauded of it as that he should neither receive satisfaction nor punish the one defrauding him? Therefore the honor taken away must be repaid, or punishment must follow; otherwise, either God will not be just to himself, or he will be weak in respect to both parties; and this is impious to think of."[18]

It is problematic whether Anselm unduly restricts God by his rationalism and avoids considering God's freedom to express his grace. However, it is here that Anselm argues that Jesus, the God-Man, is compelled by his own love to offer his life to the Father in satisfaction for the debt of humanity. As God, Christ's merits are infinite and therefore more than sufficient to offer as satisfaction. As humanity, Christ represents the party from whom the satisfaction must come. "None therefore can make this satisfaction except God, and none ought to make it except man. . . . Then necessarily one must make it who is both God and man."[19] Since in the feudal economy one's honor was one's identity, estate, and personal worth, the restoration of honor to God restores the order of the universe that had been disrupted by humanity's sin. Anselm thus rejects the idea of penal substitution, since Christ is not actually punished in our place. However, God releases humanity from punishment since Christ's death satisfies the divine honor. This solution speaks to the culture that operated in the context of feudal law that did allow alternatives to punishment, such as the practice of the duel or joust, which enabled a champion, or representative, to face a challenge of honor on someone else's behalf.[20]

Analysis of Anselm's Satisfaction Theory

Colin Gunton points out that there is a difference between the Latin concepts of *satisfactio* ("satisfaction") and *poena* ("punishment"). God is faced with the dilemma of either directly punishing sin (*poena*) or accepting a compensatory satisfaction from another source (*satisfactio*), in this case from Christ. This is a substitutionary exchange, says Gunton, although he says it is not primarily penal in character. Therefore, he says, Anselm is not presenting a penal substitutionary view of atonement. But this attempt to separate the idea of satisfaction with Christ's payment by death from the idea of penalty resulting in the sinner's death is a distinction that appears to be only technical and not a real difference, since the end result of death is the same in both cases.[21] Gunton further comments that the sacrifice of Jesus is not a punitive substitution because his death was a "free and voluntary human act." It is not the required death of an animal, but the voluntary self-giving of a man; and at the same time also the gift of God.[22] However, it is difficult to see how Anselm avoids presenting the atonement as a legal, transactional event based on a *quid pro quo* ("this therefore that") exchange of merits, in which the life of the Son of God is of such value that it outweighs the accumulated debt of human sin.[23]

Anselm pushes at the edge of Trinitarian orthodoxy in assigning to the members of the Trinity the process of negotiation for a proper satisfaction. Viewing atonement as the making of a transaction or commercial agreement between the Father and Son threatens the oneness of the Trinity, although he attempts to present it not as a legal transaction but as an act of grace. To view the Father, Son, and Spirit as having separate wills and identities which are able to negotiate and make transactions with each other has no basis either in the New Testament or in Christian orthodoxy.[24] Moreover, the whole transactional image carries more overtones of power than of love, says Gunton, and precludes any understanding of God's love entering into a relationship with humanity.[25] Even though Anselm adds a boilerplate statement at the end of his thesis to affirm the Trinity, his theory is still weak at this point. He says that Christ offered himself for his own honor to himself, as well as to the Father and the Holy Spirit. He also suggests that Christ offers his human nature to his divine nature, which raises serious questions about his Christology as well.[26]

Also, this arrangement does not involve sinners at all in the process, unlike the Old Testament identification of the sinner with the animal sacrifice and the New Testament concept of faith-union with Christ in his death and resurrection. A transaction that docs not involve sinners also goes against Irenaeus' view of recapitulation in which humanity participates in the renewal of the relationship with God, and which is the earliest expression of a Christian understanding of the atonement—central to Christian teaching for over one thousand years. In the focus on the objectivity of the honor of God, Anselm overlooks the subjectivity of the restoration of relationships between humanity and God.[27] His view tends to equate salvation with the remission of a debt of corporate humanity, and overlooks both individual as well as corporate participation in the experience of Christ. Anselm is therefore in danger of ignoring the subjective incorporation of believers into Christ altogether with his exclusively objective orientation. His view also insufficiently emphasizes the love of God in forgiveness by treating atonement as a rational cause rather than as the restoration of relationships.

Instead, Anselm's approach deduces the rational necessity of the death of Christ, since logical necessity requires that God be reconciled with creation. This rationale belongs to the world of metaphysics more than to theology, says James Denney.[28] Furthermore, his focus on restoration of the honor of God, though an important consideration in any atonement theory, tends to diminish his consideration of the role of Christ's resurrection and ascension and the work of the Holy Spirit, which are also essential to the redemptive value of the atonement.[29]

Anselm's is not a theory that lovingly appeals to the hearts of sinners, nor is it seen as a free movement of divine mercy, nor is it useful in presenting Christ as a moral example that motivates the response of love and obedience. It is a legal formula growing out of the penitential system that nevertheless did have appeal to a feudal society that understood the issues of honor and satisfaction prominent in their culture.[30] But it reversed the biblical emphasis on the atonement being first and last an initiative of God that seeks to reconcile humanity back to himself. Instead, Anselm places humanity, albeit in the form of Christ, in the role of devising a scheme to reconcile God back to an attitude of grace through an act of satisfaction. Christ as the representative of humanity offers the satisfaction in place of humanity, even though God through Christ initiated it. Although the incarnation motivates Anselm's attempt to resolve the atonement puzzle, he does not successfully demonstrate that Christ fully shares and identifies with the sinfulness of humanity. Rather Anselm presents Christ as compensating for that sin with his own infinite merit.

In addition, even though many scholars emphasize that Anselm takes sin quite seriously, he sees it as indebtedness and a basis for the exchange of satisfaction, which is an insufficiently personal or dynamic understanding of sin from a biblical perspective. Anselm offers a law-based theory, but the law is the Roman forensic system infused with feudal power and hierarchy rather than the biblical covenant understanding of Law based in the relationship of faith-obedience between the covenant community and God.

Even with these shortcomings, Anselm's satisfaction theory became immensely popular in the later medieval period, and with some modifications became the main theory advanced by the Protestant Reformers in the form of the penal substitutionary theory of atonement. However, once Protestantism discounted the idea of the treasury of merits, it minimized the relevance of Anselm's theory; the theory's influence and feudal model went the way of chivalry. The rejection of rationalistic Scholasticism by the Reformers and their emphasis on salvation by faith alone called for another articulation of the atonement.[31]

Penal Substitution Theory

Though rooted in Anselm's satisfaction theory, the idea of atonement as the substitutionary payment of penalty by the death of Christ found its fullest development in the Reformation and post-Reformation eras. With the Reformers' rejection of the treasury of merits idea, the satisfaction of debt metaphor was replaced by the forensic metaphor of sin and guilt as deserving capital punishment. This view argues that since sin has brought the penalty of death upon humanity, the only way sinners can be saved is by Christ's suffering on their behalf and absorbing the penalty of God's wrath within himself.

Martin Luther

The indulgence controversies had exposed the medieval concept of merits and the penitential system as unbiblical. Martin Luther (1483–1546) was obsessed with demonstrating the sole sufficiency of Christ for salvation. With his conviction about the inadequacy of the works of believers and his Augustinian view of sin as depravity, he could not be content with Anselm's emphasis on sin as taking honor from God. Luther's understanding of the "righteousness of God" placed salvation beyond the level of human participation. In his tract "On the Bondage of the Will," he denied every human response toward righteousness apart from God's grace alone. This raised the question of how humanity could be saved in view of its radical moral corruption and helplessness.

The development of political theory throughout the feudal period had redefined the ideal of justice in terms of abstract law rather than in terms of personal dignity as in Anselm's age of chivalry. In this revised view, justice was served when the offender against the law had been punished. The concern was not to restore interpersonal relationships, or to restore the master's honor, but to satisfy the penalties required by justice. While Anselm drew his view of law from the penitential system, Luther used these newer views of retributive justice to describe death as the legal penalty for sin against an infinite God. Since the law of society demanded punishment for sin, someone must endure that punishment; and since Christ was "made to be sin for us" (2 Cor. 5:21), Luther saw Christ as the legal substitute to bear the legal penalty for sin.

McDonald contends that Luther rejected the term "satisfaction" because it is associated with the concept of merit. He says that Luther thought it should be abolished from the theology of the church and returned to the law courts and jurists from which the Roman Catholics had derived it. He understood satisfaction as so connected to the penitential system that it concealed the truth of the gospel.[32] However, Althaus demonstrates convincingly that Luther used the term extensively.[33] For Luther, Christ did not just make satisfaction by paying respect to the offended honor of God, but he really accepted the actual punishment of humanity's sinfulness in his own body to accomplish reconciliation with God.[34] Yet Christ not only suffered the punishment due the transgressors, he also satisfied God by taking humanity upon himself in all its brokenness and by obeying the divine law in loving God and carrying out all the Father gave him to do. This is where Luther differs from Anselm who sees the option as *either* punishment of the sin or satisfaction for it. Luther saw Christ's suffering, then, as the way he satisfied God *and* reconciled us to him: "Christ, the Son of God stands in our place and has taken all Our sins upon his shoulders. . . . He is the eternal satisfaction for Our sin and reconciles us with God, the Father."[35]

In his sufferings, Christ entered into the deepest experiences of sinners in the hopelessness and forsakenness of our situation before God. He literally identifies with the full human experience of death by descending into hell to gain victory over it, as well. Christ thus overcomes wrath and destroys hell and the power of judgment. Luther shares this interpretation with Calvin, and against Melanchthon and the view of Lutheran orthodoxy, that the descent was a triumphal victory march to terrify and damn the devils through his power.[36] Lutheran theologian Gerhard O. Forde says Luther's theology of the cross is not simply about Jesus becoming our substitute to pay the bill we could not pay. Rather, God comes into human experience, in Christ, to share in the meaninglessness of death. Without the resurrection, Christ's death is without significance. The hope lies through the cross, because there is no cure for the old Adam. The cross is God's way of getting the point across that humanity cannot avoid death. Christ dies "ahead of us" in identification so that his death is our death, and the newness of his resurrection life is our life as well.[37]

Finally, Luther does emphasize Christ's battle with sin personified as the demonic powers of death and hell. In Aulén's interpretation of Luther, through the power of God working in Christ, through Christ, God swallowed up the powers of Satan and hell. Christ's deity is indispensable, for without it he could not have survived the battle against these mighty enemies. Through the divine power of his incarnation Christ annihilates sin and death and overcomes their power. God victoriously raised Christ from the dead, making his death and resurrection inseparable. While his death satisfies God's wrath, his resurrection reconciles us with God.[38]

Luther makes the point that while Christ's work is done outside us on our behalf, it is of no use to us without faith. It is helpful to us only as we identify with Christ through faith. Christ has become one with humanity through his love, and humanity must become one with him in faith. Only through faith does this "wonderful exchange," this wedding ring uniting Christ with our souls, have any effect. Through faith the believer can appropriate Christ's work of the cross and be drawn into his suffering and death. This is Paul's idea of union with Christ in faith through being crucified with him and sharing his sufferings by faith (Rom.6; Gal. 2:19–20).[39] This union and impartation emphasis in Luther's theology of spirituality has also been identified by the Finnish School of Lutheran interpretation as a form of *theosis*.[40] Thus in his incarnation, death, and resurrection, Christ identifies with humanity and reconciles creation with its Creator. We are able to face the sufferings and battles of life through Christ's presence in us and in the community of faith. It is therefore clear that Luther did not view Christ's work as exclusively penal, but also as a incarnational participation in humanity's experience of alienation from God.

Philip Melanchthon

Luther's associate, Philip Melanchthon (1497–1560), formulated the penal theory in a more rigid forensic way by emphasizing the objectivity of Christ's work so that it is only God who is appeased and reconciled to humanity. Thus God's righteousness is only *imputed*; the sinner is not *made righteous* in justification.[41] As Grensted notes, Melanchthon redefined the sacrificial metaphor: sacrifice is no longer just a supreme act of worship done to God, but an offering to turn aside the wrath of an angry Deity.[42] Such an interpretation scarcely does justice to the Old Testament understanding of sacrifice, which included several forms of offerings that did not involve the shedding of blood. It also overlooks the fact that the most serious forms of sin had no means of sacrificial expiation. For these intentional sins, God's forgiving grace formed the exclusive basis for forgiveness. Thus the offering of sacrifices was an act of obedient and faithful worship. Melanchthon began the process of reducing the doctrine of the atonement to a virtually exclusively penal understanding that moved Lutheranism away from the more balanced perspective of Luther, who saw the breadth and complexity of the atonement motif, particularly in the classic forms of the victorious Christ as expressed in his great hymn, "A Mighty Fortress Is Our God."

John Calvin

John Calvin (1509–1564) led the reform in Geneva and authored the principal systematic theology of the Reformation, *The Institutes of the Christian Religion.* Strongly influenced by the theology of Augustine, Calvin took the doctrine of sin very seriously. While some might view Calvin's concern for the problem of sin as the starting point of his theology, Robert Peterson shows that the "free love of God in Jesus Christ" is his actual starting point.[43] While this may surprise those who respond negatively to Calvin's doctrine of predestination for salvation, his commentaries and sermons clearly indicate that he saw God's love as central to the whole concept of redemption. In his commentary on Ephesians 3:17–18, on knowing the vastness of the love of Christ, he wrote: "By these dimensions Paul means nothing other than the love of Christ, of which he speaks afterwards. . . . As if he had said, 'In whatever direction men may look, they will find nothing in the doctrine of salvation that should not be related to this.' The love of Christ contains within itself every aspect of wisdom."[44]

Calvin's commentary on 1 John 4:9 likewise states, "Christ is such a shining and remarkable proof of the divine love towards us, that, whenever we look to Him, He clearly confirms to us the doctrine that God is love."[45] Calvin continued to emphasize the connection between God's love and the person of Christ. He presented a view virtually identical to that of Irenaeus when he points out that God became a man and took what was ours (humanity) in order to impart to us what was his (salvation). The Father manifests this love through him.[46] Indeed, Calvin founds the whole doctrine of election not only on the will of God but on God's love, mercy, and grace. A key focus in his commentaries is that God's eternal predestination of his people for salvation is inseparable from his love.[47] Although neither the popular understandings of predestination nor many of the subsequent Protestant theologians maintained this unity of love and election, it was clearly Calvin's intention to do so.

Furthermore, Calvin saw the incarnation as the prerequisite for the atonement. Unless Christ is fully God and fully human, salvation is forfeited. It was for our salvation that God in Christ became a human, to show his love for us. Calvin treats the incarnation, Christology, and the Trinity extensively in the *Institutes* and elsewhere.[48] In order to be the Savior, the eternal God became a real human in Jesus of Nazareth. Had he not been genuinely human, he could not have saved us. Many passages in his commentaries affirm the sinless humanity of Jesus Christ.[49] Thus, the exclusive purpose of the incarnation was for Christ to function as Mediator and reconcile God and humanity.

Calvin described the offices, or roles, of Christ with the traditional categories of "prophet, king, and priest." The prophetic office of Christ is as the teacher of doctrine. As the greatest of prophets, Christ comes endowed by the anointing of the Holy Spirit to give us the perfect doctrine to end all prophecies. . . [and] continues his prophetic ministry through the present ministry of the Holy Spirit to bring the "inner" teaching of the Word, applying the gospel to sinners' hearts.[50]

The office of king has to do with the spiritual nature of his reign. The kingly ministry through the Holy Spirit brings salvation to the souls of Christians and initiates and preserves the church. Christ's ministry on behalf of his people against the assaults of spiritual enemies makes victory possible.[51]

In the office of priest, Christ fulfills the Old Testament predictions and types as the high priest. In his commentary on Hebrews, Calvin shows how Christ and his work constitute the reality of which the Old Testament priesthood and ceremonies were only shadows. In Christ these have come to an end.[52] Their significance was temporary, while Christ's is eternal and unique in that he is the only one to be both priest and sacrifice for sin. Calvin says, "This was because no other satisfaction adequate for our sins, and no other man worthy to offer to God the only-begotten Son, could be found."[53]

The role of the priestly office was reconciliation and intercession. This priestly work reconciles us to God, appeases God's wrath by propitiation, presents a sacrifice to remove our guilt, makes satisfaction for our sins, obtains grace for us, and gives us access to God.[54] Because he has opened the way to God by his work of reconciliation, Christ now intercedes constantly for us before the Father for our salvation.[55]

After clearly establishing God's love and the incarnation of Jesus Christ as the ground of the atonement, Calvin explains how he understands the atonement to work. He is the primary originator of the theory known as the penal substitutionary view.[56] However, it must be noted that though Calvin emphasized the penal view, he also expressed most of the other views as well. As the obedient second Adam who overcame the sin of Adam by his righteousness, Christ overcame the death that came from Adam. This work of obedience involved the entire life of Christ, not just his death. It is through this obedience that Christ obtained reconciliation for us.[57] While not using the imagery of the classic theory, Calvin expresses here some of the aspects of the recapitulation view of Irenaeus. He also emphasized the Christus Victor theme. Viewing sin as the adversary who preys upon the human race, Calvin pictured Christ as the champion who overcame the enemies of humanity: "Thus also Christ as a valiant and illustrious general, triumphed over the enemies whom he had vanquished. . . . For us Christ subdued death, the world, and the devil."[58] He summarizes his position in the *Institutes*: "Clothed with our flesh he vanquished death and sin together that the victory and triumph might be ours."[59] Calvin developed this victor theme extensively in his commentaries and preaching, effectively presenting Christ as the divine-human victor who finally defeats Satan through his death and resurrection.

In a more legally oriented perspective, Calvin depicted Christ in his atoning role as our legal substitute, our sacrifice, and our merit. The common theme in these motifs is the underlying framework of the Law as the context for understanding Christ's atonement. Calvin taught that Christ both fulfilled the Law on behalf of believers during his life and took the condemnation sinners deserve in his death. He defined the Law as the expression of God's character as "a perfect pattern of righteousness" and notes that the Law contains the "knowledge of the divine will."[60] Calvin does not understand the Law to be an abstract, impersonal code, but an instrument to learn of God's will. Although he says that the Law promises a conditional salvation, in reality perfect obedience to the Law is found in no one; and we therefore are excluded from the promises of life and fall under the Law's curse. For example, the Ten Commandments, which are given to reveal God's will and the way to salvation, become for sinners a means of condemnation because the Law exposes their sins, as Paul teaches in Galatians.[61] Since none can fulfill the Law's expectations, all are condemned. Sinners therefore need another to keep the Law in their place. God must be appeased, and this requires a satisfaction. Calvin writes: "No common assurance is required, for God's wrath and curse always lie upon sinners until they are absolved of guilt. Since he is a righteous

Judge, he does not allow his law to be broken without punishment but is equipped to avenge it."[62]

Calvin says Christ totally fulfilled the divine Law as the legal substitute for humanity. He submitted to the Law and kept it in every part, thus showing himself as a type of complete submission and obedience. He argues that Jesus fulfilled the Law even down to its smallest detail. Calvin sees Christ's perfect law-keeping as what qualifies him to be his people's legal substitute. Jesus submitted himself to the bondage of the Law and chose to become liable to keep the Law so he could obtain an exemption for us.[63] Calvin says, "For if righteousness consists in the observance of the law, who will deny that Christ merited favor for us when, by taking that burden upon himself, he reconciled us to God as if we had kept the law?"[64] He says that since we could not escape God's judgment, the penalty that we deserved was imposed on Christ in Pilate's condemnation of this righteous man. In order to deliver us from that judgment, Christ allowed himself to be condemned before a wicked and profane man like Pilate.[65]

Thus Calvin sees Christ's obedience to the Law as the basis of justification. God can declare sinners righteous not on the basis of their obedience, but on the basis of Christ's obedience, which Calvin defines as righteousness. But where is the obedience of the penitent sinner that is described in the Old Testament sacrificial cultus? Calvin states that Christ performs the obedience for us, not in participation with us, but objectively outside of and apart from us.

Not only does Calvin express the work of Christ negatively as absorbing the penalty of sinful humanity, but also positively as meriting grace and salvation for them. He does not intend to portray Christ's merit in obeying the Law in opposition to God's mercy, for God initiated salvation. But he presents Christ's merit of law-keeping as the means of God's sending his love to believers. Christ's work of appeasing God's wrath with his sacrifice and overcoming our transgressions with his obedience is ordained as the means of gaining our salvation.[66] He says: "By his obedience, however, Christ truly acquired and merited grace for us with his Father. . . . I take it to be commonplace that if Christ made satisfaction for our sins, if he paid the penalty owed by us, if he appeased God by his obedience—in short, if as a righteous man he suffered for un-righteous men—then he acquired salvation for us by his righteousness, which is tantamount to deserving it."[67]

Christ's death on the cross merits grace for believers. Calvin says, "The apostles clearly state that he paid the price to redeem us from the penalty of death. . . . The Son of God was crucified as the price of our righteousness."[68]

Although Calvin means to distinguish between the medieval concept of salvation as an exchange of merits in the penitential context and Christ's substitutionary death for us, the distinction seems insufficient. The penitential idea of merit as a commercial exchange does not appear genuinely different from the substitution of Christ's merits for our salvation. Furthermore, Paul points out that law-keeping is not the basis of justification anyway. The Law brings knowledge of sin. In fact, the righteousness of God is "apart from" the Law. It is through faith, not merit (Rom. 3:20–22). That is why Abraham's faith was "considered" righteousness (Rom. 4:3)—it was the *same thing*. Merit is not the basis for righteousness, even Christ's. The actual relationship of righteous covenant fellowship is the basis for salvation. That comes from union with Christ, not the substitution of his merits for our lack of them.

Contrary to some popular interpretations of Calvin, he does see the union with the Father and Son through the presence of the Holy Spirit as beginning the restoration of the divine image. As "partakers of the divine nature" (2 Pet. 1:4 NAU), Christ's essence is infused in us at justification. Thus he shares elements of the *theosis* emphasis seen in Augustine, Aquinas, and the Eastern theologians, and does not limit his understanding of Christ's work to objective forensic categories.[69]

Governmental Theory

In response to the penal substitutionary views of atonement, the Socinians, a sixteenth-century group of unitarian intellectuals, presented criticisms that shook the very foundation of the penal views. They pointed out that satisfaction and pardon are incompatible. If a creditor has been satisfied by a payment of a debt, there is no need to forgive the debt. They also questioned the justice of penal satisfaction. If, as Anselm had said, the one who makes satisfaction is seen as identified with the offender in the God-Man, then it is unjust to impose the penalty of the guilty on the innocent. In addition, they said, Christ's suffering does not meet the demand of satisfaction because sinners deserve eternal death, yet Christ did not suffer eternal death, but temporal death.[70] Anselm would have rejected the latter critique particularly because even temporal death for the divine Son of God more than compensates for the eternal death of all humanity. Nevertheless, the criticisms were felt with force.

Hugo Grotius and the Arminians

Not only were the Socinians' attacks on the penal theory becoming increasingly effective, but other questions were being raised by orthodox thinkers. Hugo

Grotius (1583–1645), a Dutch legal scholar, was troubled by the assumption of the penal substitutionary view that punishing an innocent person (Christ) in the place of guilty humanity served the cause of justice. The anthropomorphic nature of the descriptions of God's wrath also concerned him. However, as a lawyer, he did have a deep appreciation for the deterrent role of just punishment for crimes and for upholding law and order in the universe. Grotius saw that humanity's best interests would be served by God's upholding the moral order, thus the purpose of divine punishment was the restoration of humanity's obedience, not the satisfaction of the divine wrath.[71] He therefore altered the penal theory by defining justice as a need for orderly government in a moral universe rather than as the internal need for God to administer retributive penalties upon the offending parties. Sin is an offense against public order; and punishment involves only the restoration of order, not retributive compensation for injury.

The governmental view reflects an Arminian[72] concern to understand the atonement in a way that does not require a limited atonement, as in Calvin's penal substitutionary model, nor require a penitential maintenance of spiritual graces, as in Anselm's version. However, the governmental view maintains the need for a previous satisfaction of God's wrath as a prerequisite for the forgiveness of sins, although not as a response to retributive justice.[73] As Maddox explains, "Christ did not take our place in punishment; his death took the place of our punishment, fulfilling its governmental purpose as a deterrent."[74] The divine goal was obedience, not to seek retribution. For Grotius, Christ's suffering was penal, but voluntary; and the example of Christ's passion serves as a deterrent of fear to discourage sinners from continuing in a path that disrupts the moral order.[75] Therefore his position is a sort of reverse moral influence emphasis: Christ's death is a warning against sin.

With some changes, the Arminian and Wesleyan theologians tended to follow Grotius' governmental theory. The Arminian theologian Stephanus Curcellaeus (1586–1659) emphasized the idea of sacrifice rather than satisfaction of wrath through punishment, describing the priestly work of Christ as propitiatory, but not penal:

> Christ did not therefore . . . make satisfaction by suffering all the punishments which we had deserved for our sins. For, firstly, that does not pertain to the nature of a sacrifice, and has nothing in common with it. For sacrifices are not payments of debts, as is evident from those of the law. The beasts which were slain for sinners did not pay the penalties which they had deserved, nor was their blood a

sufficient ransom for the souls of men. But they were simply offerings by which men sought to turn God to compassion, and to obtain
from him remission of sins.[76]

Curcellaeus therefore reinterpreted the penal substitutionary and satisfaction
concepts in favor of a sacrificial basis for justification. This modified the strict
governmental approach and emphasized the priestly work of Christ as propitiatory, but in the sense of a sacrificial gift.[77]

Wesleyan Theologians

John Wesley's followers generally developed some form of the governmental theory of atonement in which the atonement is a satisfaction to uphold the
rectitude of a moral government rather than to propitiate the offense against the
personal dignity and righteousness of God. While quite ambivalent about how to
characterize the penal substitutionary concept, they were clearly opposed to the
imputational elements of salvation that simply consider the believer "as if" he/she
were righteous, while not being really such in the sense of moral transformation.

English Methodists Richard Watson (1737–1816) and William Burt Pope
(1822–1903), American Methodists John Miley (1813–1895) and Wilbur F.
Tillett (1854–1936), and twentieth-century Church of the Nazarene theologian H.
Orton Wiley (1877–1961) developed various alternative expressions of governmental ideas.[78]

For example, Wiley has cautioned against failing to distinguish between the
fact of the atonement and theories about it. He warns against stating the idea of
Christ's substitution as a penalty for sin in such a way as to make Christ a sinner
or to make atonement merely a commercial transaction. However, like Wesley,
Wiley seems to vacillate between describing Christ's sacrificial work as a "representation of the pure life which the sinner should have" and saying that his
sufferings "were penal inflictions for our sins."[79] He understands "propitiation"
to mean that "the substitute endures the punishment which otherwise would fall
upon the guilty themselves," while stating on the same page, "It is on this basis of
representation that the idea of substitution must be considered."[80]

Furthermore, while affirming a penal understanding of the cross, Wiley clearly rejects the "penal satisfaction theory"[81] as a Calvinistic theory. The danger of
this theory, he contends, is that our sin is only imputed to Christ and therefore
only an external transfer of merits results, without clearly expressing the internal union of the believer with Christ. The penal substitutionary theory also leads
either to unconditional election or universalism, he says: on the one hand, the

nature of a penal atonement cancels all punitive claims against the elect, thereby predestining them to salvation; on the other hand, if Christ's penal death was for all, then all will universally be saved.[82]

Wiley seeks a middle ground in describing Christ's sufferings as "a provisory substitute for penalty in the interest of moral government."[83] He believes the atonement is grounded in a governmental necessity that makes it impossible for God to dispense with the sanctions of his immutable laws. Since God cannot set aside the execution of the penalty, he must either inflict his retributive justice on the sinner or provide a substitute. Thus God "makes prominent the sacrifice of Christ as a substitute for penalty."[84]

However, it seems obvious that if Wiley and other governmentalists see Christ's sacrifice as only a substitute for penalty, they cannot avoid describing his work as penal in some way. It appears that while the governmental theory rejects the logical implications of penal substitution and unconditional election of orthodox Calvinism, it has not totally separated itself from the liabilities of a penal understanding of the atonement. Most of the governmentalists sought to avoid the penal substitutionary emphasis of Calvin and its imputational implications by understanding Christ's death not so much as a penalty to propitiate God's wrath as a necessity to uphold the moral character of God in maintaining the integrity of the moral government of creation. Nevertheless, even as they sought to portray the death of Christ as a "distinguished example" of the punishment that sin deserved and a deterrent to sinfulness, they still understood the cross as in some way a penalty, although not in the more commercial sense seen in the doctrine of limited atonement.[85]

John Wesley: Modified Penal Satisfaction Theory

John Wesley (1703–1791), the founder of Methodism, approached atonement in a way that retained a penal theory but also included a basis for spiritual growth. He saw the need for a moral government of the universe being consistent with the character of God.[86] Christ is the second Adam who represents all humanity, makes himself an offering for sin, bears the iniquities of the human race, and makes satisfaction for the sins of the whole world. Wesley's *Notes on the New Testament* shows that he understood Christ's death as a punishment due to us because of our sins.[87] Since there had been no ecumenically approved doctrine developed on the atonement, Wesley took a somewhat eclectic approach that drew from the metaphors of several perspectives on the issue, preaching the sufficiency of Christ in his evangelistic appeals.[88] He often seemed to reflect Anselm's idea that since sin is a violation of God's honor it deserves infinite punishment. Yet his understanding of the atonement differed substantially from both the Anselmic and Calvinistic penal views. He saw Christ's work as universal in extent and conditional upon faith. While he did not systematically develop an atonement theory, he was much concerned with the practical and evangelistic applications of the doctrine.

Wesley's thrust in his sermon, "Salvation By Faith," emphasizes that the faith through which we are saved involves "a full reliance on the blood of Christ, a trust in the merits of his life, death, and resurrection; a recumbency upon him as our atonement and our life, as given for us, and living in us."[89] His emphases on the believer's response of faith and the life of sanctification and the universal nature of Christ's work differ greatly from any consistent form of a penal substitution theory as developed by Reformed and Lutheran theology.

Death is the penalty for violating the old covenant for all humankind. Wesley speaks of Christ purchasing humanity's redemption and of his life and death involving a "full, perfect, and sufficient sacrifice, oblation, and satisfaction" for the sins of all humanity. Additionally, says Collins, Wesley interprets the *hilasterion* (mercy seat) language in Romans 3:25 as "propitiation," rather than "expiation"; and he took issue with William Law for the latter's use of "expiation" and his claim that God does not have wrath or anger toward humanity that must be appeased.[90]

Although Wesley did not equate divine anger with human wrath or vengeance, he did see God's anger as being motivated by love for the sinner and as a foil that enables humanity to more fully appreciate God's love.[91] He wrote to Mary Bishop:

> But it is certain, had God never been angry, he could never have been reconciled. . . . I do not term God . . . "a wrathful Being," which conveys a wrong idea; yet I firmly believe he was angry with all mankind, and that he was reconciled to them by the death of his Son. And I know he was angry with me, till I believed in the Son of his love; and yet this is no impeachment to his mercy. But he is just, as well as merciful.[92]

And while Wesley did believe that humanity has contracted a debt to God that it is unable to pay, he rejected the implication that satisfaction was made to the divine law, because he objected to the personification of law as a "person injured and to be satisfied."[93] Wesley emphasizes the complete and ongoing nature of Christ's work in his stress on the totality of salvation in Christ's roles as prophet, priest, and king.[94]

Wesley's understanding of salvation as involving not only the justification of the sinner, but the regeneration and sanctification of the believer—as well as the radical expression of one's faith in ethical behavior—did find support in other aspects of atonement theology from the Fathers. Wesley incorporated aspects of Irenaeus' recapitulation theory in his mix of expressions of the atonement. He wrote: "When he [Christ] was incarnate and became man, he recapitulated in himself all Generations of mankind, making himself the centre of our salvation, that what we lost in Adam, even the image and likeness of God, we might receive in Jesus Christ."[95]

Wesley sees that Paul's theology of union with Christ involves participation in the "newness of life" (Rom. 6:4; 2 Cor. 5:14–15). Christ's incarnational identification with the human race eternally changed its possibilities, notes Leon Hynson. Christ shares with humanity in all of its experiences, death and life, and by his resurrection brings it into fellowship with the Godhead. Wesley sees that in our identification and participation of union with Christ through faith, we are both *enabled* and *obligated* to walk in the ethical application of "newness of life."[96] This emphasis on a Christological recapitulation as a basis for an ethic of transformational love is a central covenantal understanding. However, the Irenaean elements in Wesley's atonement theology were not clearly developed and tended to be submerged in the Anselmian satisfaction emphases.

Analysis of Wesley

A. S. Wood agrees with William R. Cannon and Albert Outler in noting that while Wesley held a penal view of atonement, he did not set the atonement inside a legal framework "in which God is made subject to an eternal, unalterable order of justice."[97] This is what makes Wesley's view problematic, for the penal theories by definition set the atonement within a legal framework of "unalterable justice." That is also why these theories are in tension with the biblical covenant understanding of the Law within the interpersonal, loving, framework of God's covenant fellowship, reconciliation, and accountability. The Western, abstract, forensic justice views of "law," as has been shown, tended to obscure how God's wrath toward sin is based on his loving desire to protect the covenant community and to prevent his creatures from violating its divine expectations expressed in the covenant Law.

Neither the penal models presented by Anselm and the Reformers nor the governmental model provide an adequate basis in the atonement for the transformation of the image of God in the believer and growth in sanctification and holiness in this life that Wesley envisioned. This was part of Wesley's frustration concerning the adequacy of the forensic atonement models as foundations for a biblical soteriology. The forensic models seek to remove guilt and restore the order of justice, not to transform the relationship and restore the moral likeness to God. The forensic tradition, with its substitutionary understanding of sacrifice, invariably expresses the outcome of Christ's saving sacrifice in imputational terms. This leads its proponents, Wesley thinks, to minimize attention to holiness, which involves conformity to the Law of God.[98] It is at this point that the substitutionary and transference understanding of the sacrifice of Christ falls short of Wesley's soteriological goals. Had Wesley also developed the recapitulation and identification emphases of Irenaeus, he might have avoided the theological dilemma he faced in failing to resolve the imputation/impartation issue. This is an essential issue to be considered in any further examinations of the connections between his view of atonement and his social ethics.

Wesley's understanding of the atonement was eclectic and functional, and certainly leaves room for further analysis of this concept by those who follow in his spirit. In fact, as Dunning and others have pointed out, Wesley was never able to resolve the tension between the implications of the penal satisfaction or substitution theories and his understanding of the biblical call to holiness and spiritual formation. Precisely at this point Wesleyan scholars have noted how he constantly struggled with the implications of the penal concepts for his own theological commitments such as an unlimited atonement, prevenient grace, the possibilities of inward spiritual development and sanctification in this life, and the need for faith and accountability in one's assurance of salvation.[99] An atonement theology that is consistent with Wesley's biblical emphases on both justification and sanctification of heart and life by faith should provide an adequate basis for these benefits of the work of Christ.

A covenant-based understanding of the sacrifice of Christ as sacrificial *identification* with humanity in absorbing the effects of the deadly results of sin avoids the liability of the imputational penal models that depict Christ as obeying the Law as a substitute for humanity and imputing his own merits to them for their salvation. A covenant matrix that demonstrates the relationships between the Trinity and human beings, the roles of the entire Trinity in the atonement, the interpersonal union aspects of Christ's incarnation, and his sacrificial work on the cross brings resolution to the complex dynamics of the forensic, substitutionary, incarnational, participatory, and sacrificial aspects of Christ's atonement. This provides a strong basis for a view of salvation that understands Christ's work as a sacrificial atonement of covenant renewal in which the entire Trinity participates. This renewal likewise involves the believer in a vital union with Christ and in the process of restoration of the divine image. This restored covenant relationship *is* righteousness. The imputation-impartation debate becomes irrelevant when we return to the biblical model of salvation as renewed covenant relationship and see the Western, Latin penitential forensic model appropriately as only *one* Western cultural contextualization which may not effectively communicate the entirety of the meaning and relevance of the atonement in all cultural and historical contexts.

Assessment of the Forensic Theories

With some variations, the penal theory has been adopted almost universally by the churches in the tradition of Reformed Calvinism and Lutheranism, as well as by other conservative traditions that have adopted the theological categories of Protestant orthodoxy, such as Pentecostalism and numerous denominations in the nineteenth and twentieth century revivalist, holiness, and evangelical traditions. There is certainly value in the traditional view. The idea that human sin has corrupted God's moral order in the universe and disrupted his creative intentions so that the Creator is disappointed and his wrath is revealed against this chaos has validity. The sending of Jesus to mediate the deadly division between Creator and creation as humanity's substitute presents a profound message of what God is willing to do to give humanity eternal life. However, the exclusive use of the penal view tends to omit other critical issues that require the portrayal of a bigger picture than just to insure entrance into heaven. The atoning work of Christ must provide the foundation for the therapeutic transformation of humanity for living out the kingdom of God here and now.[100] The penal understanding of atonement with its imputational emphasis does not by itself adequately provide the foundation for spiritual transformation and intimacy and the renewal of the divine image in sanctification, because *imputed* relationship does not easily translate into *actual* relationship which is basic to righteousness and spiritual formation.

It is significant that John Calvin, in his teaching and preaching, included several other emphases of atonement along with his penal theory. His understanding of these views is consistent with the covenant characteristics that we have induced from the biblical material as criteria for assessing atonement theories. In Calvin's understanding of Christ as the example, victor, second Adam, and prophet, king, and priest, he certainly is thinking in terms of covenant characteristics and interpersonal spiritual concepts. His emphasis on the Holy Spirit in the Christian life is also focused on union with Christ. His approach stresses forgiveness, healing, community, spirituality, and a Trinitarian understanding of salvation, although in focusing primarily on the penal aspects of Christ's death he shifts his emphasis to appeasement and justice. Calvin's inclusion of such themes as the classic recapitulation and ransom, moral influence, obedient sacrifice, and cosmic victor reflects his desire to maintain balance in his atonement views. Nevertheless, his articulation of penal themes was so potent that it virtually eclipsed these other emphases, prompting scholars of Protestant orthodoxy who followed the Reformers to overlook the balancing of these perspectives.[101] Accordingly, they appealed almost exclusively to penal emphases. Justice came to be seen as completely retributive and transactional, with its demands being met only on penal terms.[102] Some of these emphases call for our critique.

Righteousness as a Moral Quality

One faulty assumption that arises out of an exclusively penal view of atonement is the view that righteousness is a moral quality rather than a relationship. Calvin says that, since a righteous God cannot love iniquity, his wrath must therefore fall on our sin. He can show his love to humanity only after his avenging justice is satisfied. Christ must therefore be our substitute and take the pain and penalties of sin upon himself. Only after this is done can God transfer the merits of righteousness from our substitute to us and by a legal fiction impute Christ's perfect obedience to the sinner. Calvin seems to be defining "righteousness" here as "obedience." Calvin says, "The word righteousness often has the same effect in Scripture as observance of the law, and so this passage may be expounded thus: It is necessary for Christ, from his free submission to the law, to keep it in every part."[103]

Paul, in contrast, treats the concept of the righteousness of God as God's saving activity on our behalf, as has been previously shown, and he sees righteousness for the believer as right relationship with God. Furthermore, he sees law-keeping as in no way able to merit salvation (Rom. 3:28; 4:2; Gal. 2:16; 3:11; 5:4). Nowhere in Scripture is righteousness used as a property that belongs to someone. It is not a thing; it is a relationship. And God's acting consistently with his character of holy love is properly righteousness. But Calvin depicts righteousness as a quality or thing that God imputes or acts *as if* a person actually has. He writes:

"Justified by faith is he who, excluded from the righteousness of works, grasps the righteousness of Christ by faith, and clothed in it, appears in God's sight not as a sinner but as a righteous man. Therefore, we explain justification simply as the acceptance with which God receives us into his favor as righteous men. And we say that it consists in the remission of sins and the imputation of Christ's righteousness."[104]

If the individual is treated only *as if* he or she were righteous ("appears in God's sight . . . as righteous"), how is the corruption of the soul healed? In addition, Calvin points out that God's wrath does not really rest on Christ, for this would be unjust. But God treats Christ *as if* he were angry. Christ does not actually bear God's hostility, but merely something exactly like it! Calvin says:

> Yet we do not suggest that God was ever inimical or angry toward him. How could he be angry toward his beloved Son, "in whom his heart reposed" [cf. Matt. 3:17]? How could Christ by his intercession appease the Father toward others, if he were himself hateful to God? This is what we are saying: he bore the weight of divine severity, since he was "stricken and afflicted" [cf. Isa. 53:5] by God's hand, and experienced all the signs of a wrathful and avenging God.[105]

Note the exegesis of Isaiah 53:5 that Christ was "stricken and afflicted," as Calvin adds, "by God's hand." His insistence on interpreting atonement as a penal act forces him to see Christ's suffering as punishment by God, but his sense of justice refuses to allow him to interpret this supposedly divine punishment on Christ as wrath. Therefore, Christ suffers not wrath, but punishment like it. And humanity does not really have righteousness, but is treated as if it did. The participatory aspect of the incarnational identification of Christ with humanity and vice-versa is given inadequate emphasis.

Calvin presupposes the legal model of atonement along with the idea of Christ's merit as the framework for the atonement. This understanding of righteousness as a moral quality rather than a relationship requires an exclusively objective view of the atonement and an imputation of the merits of Christ to God's children in a way Grensted describes as "a mere legal fiction."[106] Righteousness is thus something acquired by the merits earned by Christ through his obedience to the Law. Calvin says, "What was the purpose of this subjection of Christ to the law but to acquire righteousness for us, undertaking to pay what we could not pay?"[107]

This understanding of righteousness as a commodity or value that can be transferred from person to person is inconsistent with Paul's understanding of righteousness as the consistency between expectations and performance. It is not a substance or virtue, but a relationship that either does or does not exist. When Christ acts consistently within the expectations of the relationship of the Trinity, he is being "righteous." When Christ's relationship with God becomes our relationship with God through Christ's incarnation in humanity and in his bringing humanity in obedience to God, humanity is really righteous in relationship to God—not just imputed, or fictionally regarded, as righteous. This is what Paul means by union with Christ (Rom. 6). The obedience called for by the imperatives in Romans 6:11–13 is not just imputed, as might be inferred from verse 11, "Consider yourselves dead to sin" (NAU). However, the imperatives in the context (verses 12–13) call for behavioral action, not moral fiction, in response to being united with Christ in his death and resurrection (see Rom. 6:5–10): "Therefore do not let sin reign in your mortal body so that you obey its lusts, and do not go on presenting the members of your body to sin *as* instruments of unrighteousness; but present yourselves to God as those alive from the dead, and your members *as* instruments of righteousness to God (NAU—italics in original).

If the incarnation means that Christ is really human, rather than simply making an imputed or docetic appearance as human, then the righteousness he shares with us is really righteousness and not merely an imputed appearance *as if* we were righteous. When Calvin understands righteousness as a thing rather than a relationship, he creates extreme difficulty for avoiding implications that weaken the meaning of the incarnation. If Christ really takes on the full experience of humanity, then humanity, in faith, takes on the full experience of a reconciled relationship with God—which really *is* righteousness. The penal explanation alone does not carry this weight.

Ethical Tension within Penal Theory. In the context of the biblical covenant, forgiveness and covenant righteousness were based on God's grace in response to repentance and obedience. In contrast, the imputational view of righteousness resulting from the penal view of the atonement is in tension with the biblical call to holiness, since the believer can never, in this view, be considered really righteous, much less holy. Calvin saw the problem in part, but scarcely improved the situation. His doctrine of imputation led him to say that God's wrath does not really rest on Christ, but God treats him *as if* he were angry. Likewise, the believer does not become righteous, but God treats him *as if* he were righteous. This diminishes any practical understanding of sanctification because by a moral fiction God treats the believer only *as if* he/she were righteous.[108] The irony of this attempted solution is that the foundation of the penal theory is its insistence on the integrity and absolute justice of God, not a presumption that God only acts *as if* he were just.

In addition, down through history the penal views have retained the legal and penitential vocabulary of "merit," "satisfaction," "substitution," and "penalty." Not only have popular applications of this view expressed the passive cheap grace idea that everything has been done for us and thus no moral good works are necessary for the Christian, but it has also been expressed by the opposite extreme of legalism and works righteousness. In a twenty-first-century cultural context filled with an endless array of religious alternatives that focus on earning one's way to heaven through good works, the terms and accompanying ideas of the penitential system raise problems for communicating a salvation of faith that does not rely on works righteousness.

The personal faith relationship essential to a biblical covenant—which both Calvin and Luther clearly saw—tended to be replaced by a Lutheran sacramentalism and a Calvinistic predestinarianism that understood covenant as a unilateral, deterministic, and juristic set of divine decrees. In terms of "law" (not covenant Law), still modeled after the Latin and Western civil codes, the believer was considered righteous, even though this was a legal fiction. He/she was not actually righteous because righteousness was not understood in the covenant sense of "right relation" but only in the legal sense of payment of penalty, so that guilt is removed only through the fulfillment of the stipulations of the legal sentence.

Note that technically this transaction is not forgiveness, but justice fulfilled on the grounds of a payment recognized by the "law"—the substitution of another victim. Indeed, when a legal sentence is fulfilled by payment of penalty, there is no basis or need for forgiveness. Gracious forgiveness on the basis of legal payment is an oxymoron. The biblical idea of forgiveness resulting from obedient and faithful response to the covenant stipulations of God's relationship to humanity is thus replaced by the forensic emphases of justice, guilt, penalty, and legal satisfaction by carrying out the terms of the legal sentence. One may either serve a sentence to satisfy the "law," or be pardoned and forgiven, but not both. This dilemma is hardly solved by positing Christ as the vicarious payment for our sins. Forgiveness is still antithetical to penal payment.

Calvin uses the term "merit" with regard to Christ's death. Although he attempts to define "merit" as being based on God's grace,[109] the term is so deeply associated with the penitential system that it is doubtful whether it can be used without giving Christ's atonement the flavor of commercial exchange. This is certainly the predominant popular understanding of penal substitution. It is also the reason Luther refused to use the concepts of merit and satisfaction. He wanted to abolish them from the church's theology and return them to the jurists from whom the Catholic Church got them in the first place because he thought they concealed the truth of the gospel.[110]

Extent of the Atonement. A final issue in the forensic theories relates to the extent of the atonement. While the Lutherans affirmed that Christ died for all, but only those who believe may access these benefits, the Reformed view, at least since the Synod of Dordt in 1618–1619, insisted on limited atonement, in part to protect the doctrine of salvation from universalism. As a result, however, the principle of love became subordinated to the principle of justice in Reformed theologians such as Francis Turretin, Johannes Quenstedt, and Charles Hodge. In Hodge's theology, the concern is more that justice is satisfied in its demand for punishment of sin. His son, A. A. Hodge, who strengthened this view, says that the exact penalty of the "law" was executed on Christ as the sinner's substitute. God's justice is therefore primarily punitive and vindicatory.[111] Only when justice is fully satisfied can sin be pardoned.

Again, the question must be raised as to how pardon or forgiveness can be applied when sin's penalty has already been paid by Christ's vicarious death. Numerous theologians have addressed the concern that the payment of all penalties for sin by Christ leads logically to universalism because if Christ took the penalty of all, then justice requires the pardon of all. The only logical way to address this problem is by setting forth the doctrine of a limited atonement by which the merit of Christ's sacrifice applies only to the elect.[112] Such a logical approach shifts the basis of atonement from love to justice, which has been the practical and pastoral legacy of the penal theories in the life of the church since the Reformation.

It is apparent, then, that the legal theory differs from the covenant characteristics of the atonement at several critical points. It is motivated by love in Calvin's penal version, although the elements of legal justice remain completely separate from any aspects of love. This seems to be an anomaly in Calvin's view. He clearly emphasizes that God's love initiates the atonement and seems to carry that through in his views on Christ as prophet, king, and priest, and in his views of Christ as the second Adam and the victor. But when he addresses the issue of the cross, he switches to the legal language of justice and penalty to show that although Christ was perfectly righteous in obeying God's Law, he must absorb humanity's penalty by dying under Pilate's law.[113] In conflating the divine and human laws, Calvin brings the legal justice principles into play and thus tends to marginalize the role of God's love in the effecting of atonement. As a result, reconciliation becomes a matter of the payment of the sentence of justice rather than a gracious reconciliation in response to obedience and repentance. Although technical theologians may debate the nuances of this evaluation, the popular interpretation is certainly very often presented along these lines.

For many or all of the above reasons, Wesleyan-Arminian, Friends, Brethren, and many other traditions have tended to avoid the limited atonement and universalism alternatives that often accompany an exclusively penal substitutionary view of the atonement. Even though John Wesley, Richard Watson, and more recent Wesleyan theologians, such as Richard Taylor, have affirmed versions of the penal substitutionary theory of the atonement,[114] many nineteenth, twentieth, and twenty first century Wesleyan-Arminian and Anabaptist theologians, as well as some Lutherans, have raised serious questions about it and have tended to espouse other theories such as the Christus Victor or governmental theories.[115]

Implications for Christian Discipleship. While many in the Protestant tradition have attempted to maintain a balance among the various biblical metaphors to describe the work of Christ, many evangelical Christians have bought into an exclusively penal understanding of salvation. This emphasis has had a serious impact on the meaning of discipleship. Focused only on addressing the removal of guilt and assurance of the goal of getting to heaven, many persons have entirely missed the fullness of life in Christ and both the freedom and discipline of the life of discipleship. Others have completely rejected the reality of Christ's atoning work because they have only heard it presented in this truncated form.

Dallas Willard views this as "sin management" and as a significant reason for the decline of profound behavioral transformation that comes only as a result of the living presence of Christ in one's life. Viewing the atonement exclusively as Christ's work simply to remove the guilt of sin and insure one's ticket to heaven often results in a shallow spirituality represented by the bumper sticker mentality that "Christians aren't perfect, just forgiven." Willard calls this "bar-code faith," in which the store calculator reads only the bar code on an item, regardless of what is actually in the package. He recalls hearing a prominent minister on a radio program spending fifteen minutes expounding the point that "justification" involves only forgiveness of sins, but *no change at all* in the heart or personality of the person. He preached that justification is totally external to the person, and is wholly and objectively related to God himself. This may have been intended to reinforce the Protestant point that salvation is by God's grace alone apart from works righteousness. However, what was actually said, observes Willard, was that "being a Christian has nothing to do with the kind of person you are."[116] The implications of this teaching are stunning.

Is the gospel really only about sin management, and does it really not change one's behavior and character? Is what the Holy Spirit does in a person's life really irrelevant to that person's transformation as a result of being united with Christ in a covenant relationship that seeks to restore the image of God through grace? Willard says:

> [This] is the foundational flaw in the existence of multitudes of pro-
> fessing Christians today. They have been led to believe that God,
> for some unfathomable reason, just thinks it appropriate to transfer
> credit from Christ's merit account to ours, and to wipe out our sin
> debt, upon inspecting our mind and finding that we believe a partic-
> ular theory of the atonement to be true—even if we trust everything
> but God in all other matters that concern us.[117]

In fact, Willard is willing to affirm that the shallowness of large segments of Christianity today is caused by the exclusive teaching of the sin-management emphasis of the penal views of atonement as they are popularly presented and applied in Christianity. To focus exclusively on the avoidance of hell and the guarantee of heaven, rather than on the fellowship and spiritual transformation of life that leads to the enjoyment of the kingdom of God in this life, ignores the heart of the gospel.[118] And lest one accuse Willard of picking on conservatives, he continues with a scathing analysis of more liberal views of Christianity that reduce the faith to the immanence of social ethics that ignore the transcendent transformation of life that provides the motivation for ethical living, often rejecting the atonement altogether as a result of hearing it only in the penal form.[119] The corresponding "disconnection of life from faith" that occurs in both the Christian right and left is, he says, "caused and sustained by the basic message that we constantly hear from Christian pulpits . . . flooded with what I have called 'gospels of sin manage-ment,' . . . while Jesus' invitation to eternal life now—right in the midst of work, business, and profession—remains for the most part ignored and unspoken."[120]

If Willard is correct, then not only must we ask if an exclusive emphasis on penal substitution can adequately express the profound nature of what occurs in the atonement of Jesus Christ; we must also ask how those who emphasize its exclusively objective, imputational, forensic declaration of acquittal of the conse-quences of sin can explain how this view addresses the seriousness of the existential reality of sin itself. As long as the work of the atonement does not address the power of sin itself, Christians who depend upon Christ's work to save them will suffer from an insurmountable moral paralysis in this life.

When a presentation of atonement pictures the removal of guilt without sufficiently dealing with the moral being of sin itself, it fails to provide for the development of spirituality and the sanctification of the believer in a process of discipleship. Wesley's concern that this leads logically to antinomianism is both prophetic and sound. Popular manifestations of the penal view call for little moral change and accountability for behavior and thus constitute an evangelical form of what Bonhoeffer called "cheap grace."[121] Since Christ's merits cover the guilt for all sins the elect can ever commit, there is no pressing need for moral transformation or holiness. Furthermore, the limited atonement version of this view fails to provide a motivation for the need for movement toward sanctification in this life because one's election is perceived to be unrelated to one's faith or works of obedience. And if these are simply popular distortions of a more nuanced forensic view, this indicates serious difficulties in clearly communicating the moral renewal elements of salvation by using exclusively the penal categories in the pastoral context.

The need to find dynamically equivalent theological constructs to communicate the message of salvation in every age is absolutely essential. When the penal view was developed by Anselm and modified by the Reformers, it did speak to an age that was just emerging from medieval feudal darkness and the totalitarianism of despotic lords and monarchs. However, many of its contemporaries saw problems with it even then. Although they were unorthodox, the Socinians saw the logical inconsistencies in Calvin's penal views and vociferously objected to the imputational and moral issues involved. And Hugo Grotius, himself a lawyer, after attempting to modify the penal view because of its association with limited atonement, became an Arminian. Many of the Pietists, Brethren, Quakers, and Anabaptists, as well as the whole of Eastern Orthodoxy with its ancient traditions of spirituality and theology, all saw the penal view as problematic.

It is clear that this forensic penal substitutionary theory has become the default evangelical view on atonement to the neglect of other rich models. Even sophisticated contemporary theologians such as Alister McGrath tend to limit the atonement options to those views with forensic foundations. His discussion of atonement tends to be limited to the work of the cross only. McGrath focuses on the cross as sacrifice, victory, and forgiveness. He understands sacrifice as payment of penalty to turn back God's wrath, which we have shown is at least a debatable interpretation. The incarnation, life, and resurrection of Christ are not fully presented as a part of his saving work.[122]

Vulnerability to Distortion

Finally, the exclusively penal substitutionary explanation of Christ's work is vulnerable to serious misrepresentation and misunderstanding, requiring a sophisticated level of nuanced support that is incomprehensible to many lay persons. As Garry Williams demonstrates in his Evangelical Union address, the defenses against critiques of the penal theory necessitate very involved exegetical and philosophical nuances that scarcely address the profound difficulties that many contemporary persons have with the penal concepts. He certainly makes a strong case, but ultimately states that only the penal view is acceptable as a foundation for Christian community. His conclusion that "I cannot see how we can remain allied together"[123] exemplifies my concerns about the exclusiveness associated with this view, in spite of the fact it has never been identified by any orthodox council or creed as the only acceptable interpretation of Christ's atoning work. And even though the Old Testament sacrificial system is established by the New Testament as the context for interpreting Christ's work, Williams fails to reference the covenant renewal that is the major biblical context for the temple sacrifices and Christ's work as described in Hebrews and the rest of the New Testament. His exclusive use of the Western forensic categories to express the atoning work of Christ is indicative of the predominant influence of the legal views in evangelical theology. The upshot of this is that he seems to equate the penal *theory* with the *fact* of Christ's atoning salvation. No theory is identical to the reality, nor is it biblically or morally legitimate to use issues other than those most central to Christian Scripture and the creeds as tests of orthodoxy or fellowship. The tendency to define orthodox evangelical faith as conformity to our theories of the essential facts of the Christian faith demonstrates exclusivist attitudes that are having seriously negative consequences in evangelism and influence in the broader culture because it is interpreted as disunity rather than legitimate debate about faith issues.

11

A Historical Survey of Atonement Theories: Moral Influence and Other Theories

Classic Moral Influence Theory

Not everyone was convinced that Anselm's satisfaction and debt-oriented views of atonement satisfactorily explained the dynamics of the atoning work of Christ. These alternative views object to the Western forensically-based themes that focus exclusively on the removal of guilt and penalty because they believe these views lack adequate explanation for how the death of Christ results in the moral inspiration for renewed discipleship.[1] Maddox notes that a major criticism of the objective Western forensic views of atonement is that they do not adequately explain how Christ's death inspired sinful humanity to effective discipleship.[2] This pastoral issue is even more sharply focused later after the Reformation with Calvin's emphasis not only on the satisfaction of penalty, but also on substitutionary justification. In this exclusively objective perspective, Christ's passive obedience of suffering the ultimate penalty for sin in death was based on his active obedience of fulfilling God's moral law in his life. This obedience becomes the righteousness that is imputed to the elect to warrant their salvation.[3] The concern of the more subjective "moral influence" approach, on the other hand, has been to show the love of God revealed in the cross as the motivation that draws humanity to moral response.

Abelard

The most well-known advocate of the redemptive power of love that is shown in Christ's death is Peter Abelard (1079–1142). He had extensively studied the life of Jesus but was unsatisfied about why it was necessary for Christ to have spent as long on earth before his death. He found no adequate motivation for

God's requiring Jesus to die in order to bring salvation in either the medieval ransom theories that honored the devil's rights or in Anselm's satisfaction view.[4] Furthermore, he reasoned that if humanity owed a debt to God's honor that had to be satisfied, then Christ's death would have only made matters worse since he was murdered by human beings, and not by God, to whom the debt was owed.[5] The primary divine motivation Abelard can find to explain why the Son of God went through his suffering and death to redeem us is the absolute and pure love of God.[6] Since Christ's sacrifice is an example of God's love and forgiveness, it should remove our fear of divine wrath and motivate us to love God and others.[7] However, he does not, as is often alleged, merely reduce Christ's death to a demonstration of divine love. He also includes traditional concepts such as the cross as a sacrifice for sin.[8]

As McGrath points out, Abelard is restating the classical Augustinian idea that Christ's incarnation is a public demonstration of the extent to which God's love evokes humanity's loving response. Abelard accentuates this affirmation by showing how Christ's uniting himself with human nature joins us and our neighbor through a profound bond of love that frees us from slavery to sin and secures our liberty in Christ. The power of this subjective impact of divine love has often been ignored by his critics.[9] Fiddes notes that Abelard is not simply showing the emotional response one makes to God through one's own efforts, but the much deeper power of God's love "to *create* or generate love within human beings" through the Holy Spirit by renewing the bond of love God had with humanity at creation.[10] While his view lacks the theological foundation to bear the complete explanation of Christ's death, it is certainly true that any other view of atonement that does not include Abelard's subjective emphasis of divine love inadequately expresses what Christ has done.

Moderns

A number of modern approaches to the atonement reflect the moral exemplar emphasis of Abelard. Friedrich Schleiermacher, Hastings Rashdall, and John Hick expanded on this concept in the context of Enlightenment thought.[11] An eloquent articulation of the exemplar view came from the nineteenth-century pastoral theology of McLeod Campbell in *The Nature and Extent of the Atonement*.[12] Although ultimately accused of heresy by the staunchly Calvinistic Church of Scotland, Campbell emphasized that the atonement was grounded in the love of God. The spirit of obedience and love in Christ's sufferings, rather than their penalty nature, form their atoning value. His perfect expression of repentance on behalf of humanity serves to demonstrate God's love and forgiveness.[13]

F.D. Maurice, nineteenth-century Anglican, saw the sufferings of Christ as a sacrificial and sympathetic participation in the pain of humanity, rather than as a penalty for sin. His obedience to God through enduring the painful consequences of sin in humanity serves to demonstrate divine love and call for repentance and obedience from believers.[14]

These theories articulate positive aspects of Christ's identification and sympathy with human suffering and sin. However, they do not adequately reflect the biblical covenant renewal emphasis that creates a covenant community that reflects God's character.[15]

Sacramental or Therapeutic Models

S. J. Gamertsfelder

Another theologian of the Evangelical United Brethren tradition, early twentieth-century scholar S. J. Gamertsfelder, develops a theory that is somewhat sacramental in nature. He notes that there is no schism in the Godhead. Christ does not need to contrive a scheme to make the Father willing to forgive the sinner and receive him/her back into fellowship. Mercy and justice are not divine attributes contending for preeminence. God takes the initiative to seek reconciliation with the sinner. The motive that moved God to give the gift of his Son (John 3:16) was not "a desire to collect a debt from the human race, nor merely a desire to exhibit the rights of a ruler and uphold a government nor yet was it a craving to avenge a wrong; it was pure, everlasting love."[16] Since humanity has fallen into sin and sorrow, the Redeemer must go to the lengths of self-sacrifice in order to get in touch with it. Gamertsfelder says:

> Given the fact of sin, degrading the human race and hurling it into endless misery as a natural consequence, nothing less than a Divine Sacrifice of infinite value can fully demonstrate to human thought the great truth that God is love and that He is seeking to save mankind from sin and all its woe.[17]

Thus the motive that moved God to redeem was love. Christ's example of obedience serves as an act of condemnation on sin. This is a community issue in that the highest expression of God's condemnation of sin is that suffering is allowed to fall on the innocent because of the sin of the guilty. Sin is seen as the repulsive evil it is and condemned, and humanity is compelled by love to turn to God and away from sin. Gamertsfelder thus views the obedient life, death, and resurrection of Christ as a sacrifice that supremely reveals the divine love in a way that fulfills both God's justice and love.[18]

This view is very consistent with the biblical evidence that the atonement was initiated by God's love. It maintains the unity of the Trinity in the atonement, and it acknowledges the community aspects of sin and understands the need for obedience as the foundation of the believer's response to Christ's atonement. It still views the sacrifice as a commodity of such value that the sinner interprets it in terms of its worth. It does not succeed in demonstrating why Christ's sacrifice is effective in restoring the sinner to God, however, other than in viewing the cross as a morally compelling demonstration of God's love that brings transformation through worship and spiritual devotion to Christ.

This position would be strengthened by the integrating motif of the covenant, which would explain the nature of the believer's identification and faith-union with Christ as the basis of spiritual transformation. In the covenant context, the sacrifice of Christ would be seen not just as a demonstration of love, but as a participatory act of obedience that brings moral transformation through union with the death-resurrection of Christ.

P. P. Waldenström

A fascinating position on the atonement as reconciliation rather than payment of penalty is presented by nineteenth-century Covenant scholar and Professor of Theology and Biblical Languages, P. P. Waldenström.[19] Rather than attempting to propound a particular theory of atonement, he asks, "What is written in God's Word?" He asserts that several of the words usually used to describe the work of Christ in atonement are not biblical words, such as "divine justice," "appease," "render satisfaction," "vicarious sacrifice," and "substitution." Indeed, he says, "reconciliation" is the most consistently biblical description of salvation. And this salvation is the reconciliation of man to God, not vice-versa as in traditional Reformation theology.[20] With these perspectives in mind, Waldenström examines the biblical issues. It is the heathen, he says, that image God as a dreadful and wrathful being who is only appeased by the sufferings of those who have offended him. This perception that God is angry with humanity pervades human nature. In this distorted view, Christ is sent so that God may pour out his wrath on him instead of humanity. Thus Christ's chief significance is "that he be a shelter or shield against God, or, so to speak, a lightning-rod for his wrath, in order that they may feel safe before him."[21]

In response to this appeasement view, Waldenström says:

> Contrary to all such perverse imaginations, the Scriptures teach that **no change took place in God's disposition towards man** in consequence of his sin; that, therefore, it was **not God who needed to be reconciled to man,** but that it was **man who needed to be reconciled to God;** and that, consequently, **reconciliation is a work which proceeds from God** and is directed towards man, and aims **not to appease God, but to cleanse man from sin, and to restore him to a right relation with God** (bolding his).[22]

He continues that God's disposition has never been other than love, in spite of the terrible consequences of humanity's sin. God can never be anything else but love (1 John 4:8, 16). He says, "Consequently, the love of God never needed to be restored by any propitiation, because it was never lost; it never needed to be increased, for it was never diminished."[23] This love is illustrated by the stories of the lost sheep, the lost coin, and the prodigal son (Luke 15). Jesus uses these stories to show how God's disposition had always been towards sinners.

To the objection that while God's love may not be diminished by sin, his justice suffered injury and requires satisfaction. Waldenström says this is nowhere written, for "there is not to be found a single passage in the Bible setting forth the atonement as having its cause in this, that the justice of God needed satisfaction."[24] Love and justice are in no way in conflict with each other. Nothing can be more just than to "right-wise" humanity and bring it into correspondence with God's own righteousness. To present Christ as in some way attempting to convince the Father to bend his sense of justice in order to make humanity righteous implies that the Father's love favors a justice that judges and punishes, while Christ's love favors a justice that would rather love than punish is to say that there are two kinds of righteousness and two members of the Trinity are not in agreement. This is not consistent with the biblical witness that depicts them in total agreement about salvation

> Now all *these* things are from God, who reconciled us to Himself through Christ and gave us the ministry of reconciliation, namely, that God was in Christ reconciling the world to Himself, not counting their trespasses against them, and He has committed to us the word of reconciliation. (2 Cor. 5:18–19 NASV)

This emphasis on reconciliation rather than penalty payment does not mean Waldenström denies God's wrath toward sin. Indeed, it is God's work in Christ's justifying sinners by his blood (Rom. 5:8–9) that saves us from divine wrath. However, he asks, does the Bible anywhere state that the wrath of God needs to be appeased, or that this appeasement should come through the death of Christ? He responds confidently in the negative, "No, it is nowhere thus written . . . that the wrath of God was to be appeased through the death of Christ. . . ."[25]

He asks, "But what, then, is the wrath of God? By the wrath of God may be meant **that God hates all sin and unrighteousness** (bold his)."[26] God's wrath toward sin can never be appeased or changed. If God ceased to hate sin, he would no longer be just and righteous. Even humans who do not hate sin are unrighteous people. It is clear that God is displeased with and will punish all who live in sin. And this wrath of God is not quenched or appeased by the death of Christ. Paul says, "For the wrath of God is revealed from heaven against all ungodliness and unrighteousness of men" (Rom. 1:18). Even today, God's wrath still falls on the sinful and disobedient (Luke 21:23; Eph. 2:3 and 5:6; Rom. 3:5 and 12:19; and Col. 3:6). The New Testament never states that this fact is changed by the death of Christ. In fact, this wrath toward sin still continues, and Christ shares this displeasure toward sin. The wrath of the Lamb will still fall on the ungodly at the day of wrath (Rom. 2:5; Rev. 6:16). In fact, as long as sin exists, God will hate it, as should all righteous people.[27] Those who seek to show God's wrath is appeased or propitiated do not take wrath toward sin seriously enough.

Then how does Christ's work save us from God's wrath, if it does not appease God's wrath? For those who live in faith, however, God does not intend for them to suffer wrath (1 Thess. 5:9), but to receive salvation from Christ who rescues those in him from the coming wrath (1 Thess. 1:10). Believers are delivered from God's wrath *when they are restored to the appropriate covenant relationship with God through faith in Christ*. And those who through the justification and reconciliation through faith in Christ have gained access to God's grace shall be "saved from God's wrath through him," because through Christ's death and life they have been reconciled to God (Rom. 5:9–11) and reconnected to the source of life through union with Christ in his death and resurrection (Rom. 6). Salvation from God's wrath is a result of having been justified and reconciled to God through the sacrifice of Christ's death. But nothing in Scripture says that the way this has happened is that God's wrath is satiated by being poured out on Christ.[28] Thus Waldenström bases his view of how reconciliation occurs in the dynamics of covenant renewal to fellowship with God through a faith union with

Jesus Christ. This concept is very consistent with the covenant renewal emphasis of Christ's work.

Mimetic and Incarnational Models

René Girard

Another very interesting recent approach to understanding the atonement is found in the work of René Girard.[29] Daniels and Michelson analyze Girard's development of the ancient ideas of imitation, or mimesis, and scapegoating as a framework for understanding the meaning of atonement in the Judeo/Christian religious tradition.[30]

They point out that fresh readings and critiques of the atonement teaching of the canonical texts understand Christ's work as a victim *of* violence, not as a victim *through* violence. Thus the atonement functions as a victory *over* violence. Daniels and Michelson look to Girard's motif as an opportunity for renewing the theology of worship to reflect victory *over* violence. Girard sees in the ancient religious myths the escalation of violent conflicts between alienated communities through the response of mimetic acting out of each other's violence—each group mimics the violent behavior of the other as the conflicts escalate to murderous proportions. But rather than the groups annihilating each other, they eventually redirect their hostilities toward a victim who is then killed. This violence against the victim falsely accused of wrongdoing results in a catharsis that reconciles the tensions of the communities. This mimetic contagion of violence now subsides as the one scapegoat victim unjustly bears the hostilities of the many. In these cultures, it is finally the illusion of the scapegoat's guilt that breaks the cycle of mimetic violence.[31] This scapegoat sacrifice approach to the resolution of violence can be found in numerous ancient cultures, but in none of these situations is the underlying problem actually resolved.[32] Scapegoating only presents the illusion of resolution, not the realization of it.

The deeper truth of Jesus' death, however, is that rather than being *only a victim* as the scapegoat, he becomes the salvation of the hostile parties *by being the means of* their cessation of violence. He also unmasks the victimizers and becomes the reconciling mediator by participating in the scapegoat mechanism as victim. "He sides with the victim at the hands of the violent victimizers. In so doing, Jesus' willing death at the hands of the angry mob becomes God's identification with the suffering death that brings healing to the violence inherent in all cultures," conclude Daniels and Michelson.[33] Thus Jesus "detoxifies" violence and sets the standard by which it can be cured. By participating in the scapegoat role, Jesus sets humanity free from the necessity to continue these cycles of mimetic violence and thus brings judgment upon these acts of substitutionary violence by revealing their futility as illusory solutions. This judgment that is brought by Christ's cross, then, is not the visiting of God's wrath and condemnation upon a victim, but is the revelation of the illusory nature of unjust human actions of substitution that collapse in upon themselves.[34] The nature of Jesus' death was the unjust execution of a righteous victim, revealing the futility of accomplishing a righteous reconciliation through the unjust scapegoating. Thus the victim's innocence in reality negates the illusory nature of seeking peace through violence by the re-creation of violence.

It is as we understand this significance of the cross and its call for the disciple to participate in bearing it that the highly problematic nature of the substitutionary atonement theories becomes evident. This sets up the dilemma of the penal formula that propitiation depends upon the perfection of Christ as a substitutionary sacrifice and implies that since God's wrath has been appeased in Christ, then it makes no sense for disciples further to take up their cross after Christ's example.[35] Thus the tendency for the focus on praise for Christ's substitutionary payment to satisfy God's wrath against sin tends to preclude the need for sharing in Christ's work of cross-bearing and "radical participation in the world."[36]

The biblical call for discipleship, on the other hand, assumes that the atonement calls the Christian to recapitulate the sacrificial attitude of Christ through participation in living out the consequences of the atoning work of Christ in the world. This involves living intentionally against the violent patterns that characterize this world. Just as the Hebraic tradition calls for God's people to participate in the co-creating work of nurturing creation, the atonement calls for participation in God's atoning activity in Christ (Rom. 6:1–14).

While some might see only a new version of moral influence atonement in this non-violent emphasis, there are strong foundations for a new understanding of the Christus Victor emphasis in the mimesis and participation emphasis of René Girard.[37] Daniels and Christenson affirm, "A non-violent understanding of the cross cannot simply stand in awe of the non-retributive grace of the crucifixion and resurrection, but it logically includes the call for those who are part of the body of Christ to extend that same grace into the world today."[38]

Robin Collins

The work of Robin Collins reflects a more philosophical analysis of Girard's mimetic participation concept of atonement. Collins observes that Western theories of atonement have tended to include violence at the core of divine order. The satisfaction and penal theories of atonement, he says, require God to punish sin, thus rendering violence against the sinner, unless, as in the satisfaction theory, a substitute can be found to pay sin's penalty or debt. While Collins is careful to point out that in the satisfaction theory it is claimed that violent punishment of the sinner may be avoided if someone else pays our debt of obedience to God.[639] However, it could be argued that in both Anselm's satisfaction of debt and the Reformation penal theory, violence directed at either the sinner or the substitute is necessary to meet the demands of moral order. Although Anselm contends that the God-Man paid the debt by obedience unto death, it is difficult to avoid the practical conclusion that the payment of obedience by death is something exactly like violence. The feudal tradition of chivalry that provides the background for Anselm's theory requires that the offender either face the offended party in a duel, or that champions either take their place in the duel or pay a bribe. It can be argued that this is at least psychological and economic violence against a defenseless party.

The nonviolent peace tradition in theology, along with a number of other Christian perspectives, has recognized that the church needs alternative understandings of the atonement. The penal and satisfaction theories raise significant ethical and exegetical issues. Collins says that these views are contrary to Scripture, and they challenge clear concepts of justice with the claim that divine justice is satisfied "by one person accepting the punishment of another."[40]

René Girard's theory of mimetic participation and scapegoating is a creative form of the moral influence theory. Growing out of his mimetic theory of culture that examines culture, religion and violence from the perspective of the nonviolent core of the gospels, Girard's approach has generated significant enthusiasm from those committed to nonviolent understandings of Christianity. However, as Collins notes, Girard does suffer some of the same defects that have aroused criticism of the standard moral influence theory. One of these issues that critics have noted is his unmasking of the scapegoat sacrifice mechanism. Understanding Christ's sacrificial work as simply unmasking the mimetic scapegoat process does not resolve what his sacrificial atonement means for salvation. Collins notes that being justified and given a new life (Rom. 5:9; 8:3) and Christ's blood cleansing us from all sin (1 John 1:7) indicate a much more radical result than just helping develop a more nonviolent society or to provide a "perfect moral example for us to imitate."[41]

Collins sees that the moral influence emphases of both Abelard and Girard need to go further in explaining *how* Christ's work brings atoning reconciliation. He proposes an *incarnational theory* to expand Girard's emphasis on mimesis, or imitation. He says mimesis involves not only the contagion of cultural behavior, but also participation. For example, we may imitate Christ's moral example through the desire of a moral contagion, but we must also share in participation in Christ's attitudes in order to remain connected to his Body. The vine metaphor in John 15 shows that a branch withers when disconnected from the vine. So the participatory connection with Christ can be understood as a "mimetic participation." Salvation is thus "an ongoing participation in the life of God as it exists in Christ." Since Christ's life is human as well as divine, we can participate in it (John 6:53–56; Col. 3:4; 2 Pet. 1:4; Heb. 3:14).[42]

The nature of this sharing in Christ's life involves "mimetically participating in Christ's subjectivity as expressed in his life, death, and resurrection" in which Christ's subjectivity is integrated with our own selves by faith. This occurs by consciously habituating Christ's example, through reading and hearing the biblical and other inspirational texts, and through the supernatural operation of the Holy Spirit and divine grace in the sacraments. The Holy Spirit empowers this transmission of Christ's subjectivity and divine character, thus avoiding the criticism of Pelagianism that often accompanies a moral influence perspective.[43] Thus we are, he says, "saved by mimetically partaking of the incarnated subjectivity of God the Son, hence the name, the incarnational theory."[44]

Sharing in Christ's cross and resurrection (Rom. 6) works to deconstruct the world-system of inappropriate desires with the antidote of appropriate desire to seek the kingdom of God and be transformed by the mind-renewal from participation in Christ (Rom. 12:1–2; Phil. 2:1–11).[45] This opens up the hope of the ultimate fulfillment of God's kingdom of peace and justice, and enables us to act in the faith, hope, and love called for by Christ's example.

Thus the incarnational theory depicts the transformational participation enabled by the Holy Spirit that results in the "new self" and "new creation" in Christ of which Paul speaks (Col. 3:9; Rom. 6:6; Eph. 2:10 and 4:24; Col. 3:9–10; 2 Cor. 5:17; and Gal. 6:15). This incarnational understanding also enables us to see the character of the Jewish sacrificial ritual of participation in the death of the animal by laying the hand on its head. This identification and participation in the life of the animal sacrifice provides the basis for interpreting Christ's offering of his life for others and our identification by faith with his redemptive death (Rom. 6:6–10).[46] Thus Christ's blood cleanses from sin, but not in the compensatory, penal way it is usually interpreted in Western theology. Instead, Christ's blood represents his life given to God and others in perfect trust and self-giving love. We are saved by participation in this life given to others as it re-orients us in obedience and participation with God. This incarnational understanding of atonement finds expression in the Eucharist as eating the bread and drinking the cup vividly re-enact the participation in Christ's divine-human subjectivity.[47] The practice of baptism is also informed by this incarnational understanding. Paul's servant metaphor in Romans 6 develops the theme that baptism—identification—portrays the union with Christ's death and resurrection life so that through identification with his subjectivity we become "crucified" to the world-system of psychic and spiritual bondage. We thus are enabled to share in his death the mastery of the old system and in his resurrection life that overcomes our alienation towards God, ourselves, and others (Rom. 6:5).[48]

In many ways the mimetic, participation, incarnational emphases of the Girardian-influenced understanding of Christ's atonement are significantly compatible with and complementary to the covenant relational understanding. The concern to emphasize the role of the Trinity in salvation, the incarnational and participatory role of Christ, the concern to avoid violent and unbiblical metaphors that introduce impersonal forensic components of justice as vengeance are all helpful. Girard's tendency to see sacrifice as simply violence is overcome by the mimetic understanding of sacrifice as participation, especially in the theology of Marlin Miller, another Girardian,[49] and in Collins' own view. The pastoral implications of the participation and union with Christ emphases of these mimetic expressions of atonement are quite helpful in rethinking the meaning of the atonement for twenty-first century mission. The participatory understanding of the role of the sacraments in worship and discipleship also emphasize the realism of union with Christ, a realism that is often obscured in the symbolic interpretations of Western theology. A closer dialogue between the mimetic understanding and covenant relational thinking would result in an even more effective, biblical, and relevant presentation of the work of Jesus Christ for salvation.

12

Divine Expectations in Christian History: Covenant Interpersonal Perspectives

In seeking an effective approach for retelling the redemption story for the twenty-first century audience, it is imperative that we keep in mind this culture's emphasis on interpersonal and community values. The concern for relational—as opposed to rationalistic, or "modernist"—values and methods in this postmodern age suggests a model for the atonement that focuses on the story of the atonement rather than upon the theoretical and abstract approach that characterizes some of the prevailing presentations today, particularly in the evangelical community. The power of the redemption story of Christ's atonement may effectively draw persons of any culture and age to the Christian faith no matter what theory we use to interpret it, particularly when the effective work of the Holy Spirit is operational in the church and society. Nonetheless, many persons are repelled from responding to Christ's message when it is presented exclusively by means of a judicial, forensic model. The historical precedent of Christian theology for two thousand years has been to consider the cultural and linguistic contexts of the audience for whom it intends the message and to contextualize it in forms meaningful to that community.[1]

One example of an understanding of Christ's atonement that takes seriously this concern for contextualization and also reflects the interpersonal and covenantal character of the ancient sacramental community of Israel is observed in the discussion on the person and work of Christ by Wesleyan theologian H. Ray Dunning.[2] Another example is the position presented in this present study as a covenantal community redemption motif, described as the "divine expectations" of the cross and covenant.

A Wesleyan Interpretation: H. Ray Dunning

Seeking a mediating position that is both biblically and theologically consistent and culturally relevant, H. Ray Dunning analyzes the Christology of John Wesley. Long dissatisfied with the inconsistencies between the penal views and Wesley's teachings on salvation, Wesleyan theologians have sought adequate alternative solutions in the theology of the atonement. Wesley understood that all the benefits of salvation are based on the work of Christ. However, in the absence of a theory that supported what he understood to be the biblical provision of salvation, he developed a somewhat eclectic view that resembled Anselm's satisfaction theory more than any other. He probably held to this view because of its traditional place in Anglican theology, as Wesley was reluctant to separate from its doctrines. He also saw the importance of the objective dimensions of God's initial activity in the atonement process, as represented in this approach. This penal satisfaction doctrine, however, contained implications that created problems with some salvation positions that Wesley believed were biblically based.[3]

Interestingly, although he never developed it into an atonement theology, Wesley's own Christology may provide the key to a view of the atonement that is both orthodox and provides a basis for a non-penal understanding. Dunning presents Wesley's understanding of the work of Christ in terms of his threefold office as prophet, priest, and king. In his sermon at Nazareth (Luke 4:18–19), Jesus described himself as bringing together the prophetic, priestly, and kingly functions in one person. The functions are objective in that they are designated and anointed by God. In terms of our atonement, though, they are subjective, since they respond to the needs present within ourselves. We need the prophet to enlighten us and teach us the will of God. We need the priestly mediation to overcome our alienation from God and reestablish right relationship between ourselves and him. And we need the kingly power of Christ to enable us to break free from our enslavement to sinful appetites and to reign within us.[4]

Wesley relates each of these offices to aspects of justification and sanctification. They are interdependent, even though they address different aspects of Christ's work of salvation. Furthermore, even though they are objectively the finished work of God, subjectively they require the existential faith response of the believer if they are to have value. In this latter sense, God's intentions for salvation through the work of Christ are not finished until we respond in personal faith and obedience. This does not make the reality of the doctrine of salvation dependent upon my response, for it has been completed from God's perspective even before the creation of the world (Eph. 1:4). However, it has not been completed in terms of the actuality of our individual participation in it until we have responded in faith.[5]

Prophet

The prophetic role of Christ is to perfectly reveal divine truth. Because his person and his teaching are grounded in his relation to the Father, Christ proclaims and embodies both gospel and the Law. The Law, Wesley says, is the embodiment of the nature of God. It is the positive elaboration of the image of God. Christ as Prophet embodies God's perfect moral Law and also perfectly fulfills the divine image. As the ideal image of God, Christ incarnates not just the proper behavior but the very ideal toward which the work of sanctification leads.[6]

Priest

In Dunning's presentation, the covenant in God's Old Testament salvation plan plays a central role in the reconciling and mediating work of Christ, particularly in the priestly aspect of the atonement. Basing his interpretation of the atonement ministry of Christ upon the sacrificial cultus of the Old Testament, as much of the New Testament seems to suggest, Dunning proceeds to show that the priestly responsibilities in the Old Testament were broader than just the offering of sacrifice and intercession. The priest served as a mediator, "a bridge-builder who effects the bringing together of two parties," says Dunning. The primary means of accomplishing this reconciliation was through a sacrifice. The two major functions of sacrifice were, first, the establishing of covenant relations between parties and, second, the maintaining and developing of that relationship.[7]

Dunning next considers the issue of exactly *how* the work of Christ in his priestly role effects salvation by noting two key characteristics of priesthood: *identification* and *representation*. Both of these ideas are central to the establishment of covenant through the means of sacrifice. As the atoning sacrifice, Christ identified himself fully with sinful humanity "in such an intimate way that he can now represent humanity before God (he died for me) even to the ultimate degree through his death on the cross." At the same time, Christ is so identified with God in his divinity that he fully represents God to humanity.[8] As people identify in faith with God's divine-human representative, they are reconciled to God. Those who are identified with God through Christ are in fellowship, and thus righteous, in their relationship with the holy and righteous God. This forms the basis of one of Wesley's primary ways of describing sanctification as grounded in the atonement. Furthermore, both the identification and representation motifs appear in the primary sources of the atonement metaphors: the Isaiah 53 Servant of the Lord and the sacrificial Lamb of God concepts.[9]

Christ's identification with us then becomes the ground of his representing us before God as well as in the encounter with evil at the cross. In this work of representation, Christ acts "on behalf of" humanity. Dunning follows Vincent Taylor and others in noting that Paul prefers the preposition *huper,* "on behalf of," to describe the work Christ does "for us," rather than *anti,* "instead of," which Paul never uses of Christ's work of atonement.[10] We can therefore understand the work of Christ as vicarious, but in the sense of representing us rather than as a substitution "instead of" us. In this representational understanding, Dunning reflects the influence of Irenaeus and the recapitulation interpretation of the priestly and mediatorial work of Jesus Christ and his continuing intercessory work on behalf of humanity.[11]

King

Finally, Dunning describes the kingly work of Christ as being grounded in the Trinitarian foundation of the Godhead. While Christ's kingly authority is eternal as far as his divine nature is concerned, his sovereign power must be bestowed on his human nature. Dunning understands Christ's God-bestowed kingly authority as beginning with David's kingship, the basis of the Jewish messianic hope thus fulfilled in Christ's kingship. Christ's kingship is thus foreshadowed by the kingship of David in analogous ways. First, God's covenant promises to the patriarchs concerning the land of Canaan were eventually realized by their descendants in David's reign. Analogously, the promises of God to his people were fulfilled in Jesus Christ (2 Cor. 1:20). Second, as a corollary to the first, Israel's enemies, especially the Philistines, were conquered by David's rule. By analogy, Christ as king has defeated "the powers and authories" (Col. 2:15).[12] This kingship was publicly revealed through Christ's miracles and in the cross, resurrection, and ascension. At the cross the decisive encounter between Christ and Satan occurred to provide the basis for the establishment of the kingdom. Wesley says in this regard, "Satan brought in sin, and sin brought forth death. And Christ when He of old engaged with these enemies, first conquered Satan, then sin, in His death; and lastly, death, in His resurrection."[13]

With this victory over the kingdom of evil, Christ sets in motion the kingdom of God, which Dunning sees as the reign of God both in the present age and the age to come. The divine kingdom entered history with Christ's triumph over the spiritual forces of evil but will be fully established at the second advent. Dunning cites George Ladd's summary: "There is a twofold dualism in the New Testament: God's will is done in heaven; his Kingdom brings it to earth. In the Age to Come, heaven descends to earth and lifts historical existence to a new level of redeemed life."[14] Christ both brings in the kingdom as a present reality and will establish it as a final reality at the end of the age.

Divine Wrath

Another issue related to the atonement is the final destiny of those who do not identify in faith with Christ's covenant salvation. Dunning points out that final salvation is the destiny of those who in faith receive Christ's gift of life, while final separation is the end for those who refuse it. Calvinism addresses the fate of such persons with the doctrines of predestination and limited atonement. In the Wesleyan concept of universal atonement, salvation is not coercive, but is based on a response of faith made available by God's free distribution of prevenient grace. Since God's nature is understood as holy love, there is no sense of an incompatibility between love and justice. Instead, love allows choice to respond to God's gracious invitation. Wrath is not some sort of vengeful decree that consigns humanity to the vindictive judgment of an angry God. It is the "eschatological symbol for the work of love that allows its objects to choose self-destruction," says Dunning.[15]

The judgment of God follows from his wrath. It is determined on the basis of humanity's response to Christ. It is a process in which persons judge themselves by their acceptance or rejection of the gospel (John 3:18–20; Rom. 2; Heb. 4:12). Those who in faith identify with the sacrifice of Christ in the present have already experienced God's verdict of the last day (1 John 4:17). On the other hand, those who do not believe seal their own doom and make their own decision to accept God's judgment in the last day. Those who refuse the choice to identify with Christ in faith will face final separation, or hell. Whatever the imagery used to describe this state, the nature of this separation is to be excluded from the joy and pleasures of the future kingdom of God, and to experience total despair and lostness.[16]

Thus Dunning's conclusions regarding the nature of sacrifice, covenant renewal, and the wrath of God are significantly consistent with the biblical covenant framework developed in the previous chapters in this study. His view addresses all the key issues called for within a covenant understanding of atonement, and his interpretations agree with this study's conclusions regarding the historical theories and their relevance for the twenty-first century.

Covenant Restoration Atonement: "Divine Expectations" as a Missional Model

One faces many challenges in seeking to articulate an understanding of the atonement of Christ that is consistent with biblical emphases, useful for effective communication in a postmodern cultural context, valid for mission in diverse cultural settings without undue projection of Western philosophical categories, and theologically harmonious with the history of the Christian understandings of the work of Christ. A number of approaches to the atonement have been surveyed and their effectiveness analyzed for missional usefulness in the twenty-first-century world. Just as in each previous historical period theologians and preachers have sought the most clear and effective ways to present the gospel message so that it would be heard and understood in their respective times and cultures, so we need this same effort today. To that end, we have examined the implications of the biblical idea of inclusion in God's covenant relationship and the means for renewing and maintaining one's participation in it, designated here as God's "divine expectations."

Christ has effectively completed his mediating work of reconciling humanity to God and restoring the divine covenant between communities and between individuals by identifying with humanity through his incarnation and obedient living and by giving himself as a sacrifice. In all this he recapitulates God's covenantal creation in the divine image and so brings humanity back into its righteous relationship with God, as individuals and communities obediently reaffirm their identity through their faith-union with Christ. The Holy Spirit enabled Christ to suffer, die, and rise from the dead on behalf of humanity to bring them back to God. The Holy Spirit also graciously enables humanity to believe that they are included in Christ's life and death of obedience to God and in his glorious resurrection to newness of life. The alienation of the first Adam is dealt with on the cross, and through the resurrection the firstfruits of the new life are now available for all humankind. This is the meaning of covenant renewal and the participation in it through Christ's work for us and in us. *Because Christ has identified with every person in his incarnation and has represented every person in giving his life as a sacrifice to renew their covenant with God, every person is included in his atoning work.* By the enablement of God's grace, any person who accepts his/her participation with Christ in his obedience to God and who in faith and repentance sacrifices his/her life to be a servant of God is included in Christ's covenant renewal. This obedience meets God's "divine expectations" for eternal life in union with Christ.

The covenant perspective thus overcomes the debate between imputation and impartation of righteousness because the righteousness of God is expressed as covenant relationship, not as a virtue to be transmitted or a metaphor to be interpreted as if it were a reality. Righteousness is the reality of living in the covenant relationship divinely established between God and humanity at creation. The reconciled relationship of sinners being "rightwised" with God is in fact a functioning "righteous" relationship made possible by the mediation of Jesus Christ in bringing two alienated parties together in himself. This is atonement. This is the role of the death of Christ as a sacrifice to reveal both the love of God and the divine participation in the life of humanity through the incarnation. This identification and participation in human experience enables Christ as the representative of both humanity and divinity to bring about a restoration of the covenantal union that God originally intended to be the context of the divine-human relationship. A Christology that does not take seriously this Trinitarian involvement in Christ's incarnation and sacrificial death and glorious resurrection does not adequately express the biblical witness of Christ's work.

An understanding of the meaning of sacrifice as a covenant-restoring gift allows a more consistent understanding of Christ's vicarious work than either the exclusively forensic penalty concept or the governmental choice of a provisory substitute for penalty. In the context of covenant renewal, the death of Christ fills the role of the sacrifice that restores covenant fellowship. Christ's identification with sinful humanity and his obedience to all covenant expectations allow those in him also to share his death to sin. This is the message of Romans 6, in which Christ's union with us calls us to union with him by faith and enables us to share his life, including his death and resurrection. This covenant union forms the basis for the faith community, a covenant body brought together in oneness through the Holy Spirit's witness of Christ's work and through the Spirit's transformation of those in Christ into a spiritual fellowship of faith and worship and hope. Such a community fulfills God's "divine expectations" for creation and for Christ's body, the church.

Holiness consists of living out the reality of this restored covenant relationship. This is characterized by obedience to "law of Christ" (Gal. 6:2), which is love (which is, incidentally, the ultimate relationship of righteousness). Holiness is the obedience of love, not the coercion and guilt motivated obedience of the Law. The latter leads to legalism and externalism. The former leads to relational intimacy and obedience out of love for God. It is motivated by gratitude versus duty, freedom versus bondage, grace versus guilt. Sanctification means radically appropriating the obedient Spirit of Christ as our own through faith, so that our actions are motivated by Christ's Spirit and patterned after Christ's life/death of obedience as the second Adam.

Since the covenant relational concept of the atonement of Christ is not conceived in commercial or transfer-of-merits terms, it does not create the dilemma of avoiding universalism by the particular election of those who will be saved by Christ's merits. In the covenant relationship, individuals always have had the option by grace of leaving behind the covenant community or being restored to the covenant community on the basis of repentant faith and the offering of sacrifice. In the covenant theology of atonement, all humanity is universally invited to identify with Christ through God's covenant promises of faith. Humans in their fallenness are not morally capable of responding unaided to this loving offer.

John Wesley rejected the implications of limited atonement in Calvin's doctrine in his teaching on the "righteousness of faith," in which he presented the doctrine of prevenient grace.[17] Therefore, he says, God in his mercy has offered his prevenient grace to enable fallen humanity to cease its rebellious resistance to his love and to respond to the offer of inclusion in his salvation covenant. This salvation is established through Jesus Christ's mediating work in the gift of his atoning sacrifice on our behalf. This grace can be accepted or rejected, and its action is voluntary rather than coercive. Thus all people are held accountable for obedience to God, but none are inevitably saved or lost apart from their own choices. As a benefit of the atonement of Christ, Wesley says a measure of free grace is restored to all persons; this lays upon humanity the moral responsibility and grace-filled capability to comply with God's will for salvation.[18]

The demonstration of God's love through his offer of a righteous covenant relationship with the Trinity is completed through Christ's work of salvation. This atoning work of Christ establishes the basis for covenant renewal and the restoration of the image of God through the recapitulation work of the second Adam. In his triumph over death through the power of the Spirit, Christ has victoriously confronted the forces of spiritual evil and vanquished them through his power, love, and justice. Those who live in him by faith have participated in this victory over sin and death and may also share in his glorious resurrection life both in this age and the age to come (Rom. 6).

The biblical understanding of Christ's role in his incarnational identification and participation in humanity presents him as a loving sacrifice who restores a real relationship with God.[19] This atoning work not only addresses the management of sin in justification, but also establishes the basis for spiritual formation and sanctification in our participatory union with Christ as we allow the Holy Spirit to transform us into Christ's image. Christ's sacrificial atoning work inaugurates a new covenant that not only forgives sins, but enables humanity to fulfill God's will of covenant relationship.[20] It is based on a righteousness by faith rather than on justice resulting from penalty (Rom. 9:30; Gal. 5:5; Heb. 11:7). This is a positive message that will communicate more effectively to today's world. It focuses on transformation and life, rather than on guilt and death. It emphasizes spiritual formation and maturity of life. It forms community and relational bonds within the context of covenant renewal and relational responsibility. It reflects the reconciliation of love rather than the vindictive nature of penalty. It is consistent with the principles of divine justice based in love that are reflected in the interpersonal covenant Law concepts of Scripture. It transcends cultural and temporal boundaries and will enhance cross-cultural communication of the concept of the atonement in the very diverse global context of the twenty-first century.

Incarnational identification brings a new Head, in Christ, to a humanity that has lost its bearings and gives it a renewed connection with the Creator in Christ. It is given a chance for a moral "do-over." Its new source of life, Christ, restores its focus of direction by obedience to the protocol of repentance and identification with the new life through faith-obedience. Newness of life is not the end of humanity's physical death, but does restore its eschatological hope. It gives humanity a renewed moral directive, a spiritual orientation, and a direction toward wholeness in this present life.

Humanity's dying body has had a new source of life implanted in it. My story as the recipient of a heart transplant from the sacrificial giving of life from another human being provides an analogy, albeit a limited one, for my understanding of how Christ's life was transplanted into humanity through his incarnation. As my own body was given new life through the literal implantation of the life of another, so Christ entered into a body of humanity that suffered from a blockage from its source of life. Christ came as the Word of God made flesh and entered into the human life and death experience—rescuing it from the fate of ultimate death—and brought humanity into new life through the resurrection Spirit, the Life-Giver. This truly has transformed my future and yours from death into life. "Therefore if [anyone] *be* in Christ, *he/she is* a new creature: old things are passed away; behold, all things are become new"(2 Cor. 5:17 KJV, my edit). This is indeed cosmic good news.

Notes

FOREWORD BY LEONARD SWEET

[1] Gabriel Josipovici, "Digging Into Sand," *TLS: Times Literary Supplement*, 21 December 2001, 5.

[2] See the chapter "Fear as Wildfire" in Cass R. Sunstein's *Laws of Fear: Beyond the Precautionary Principle* (Cambridge: Cambridge University Press, 2005).

[3] For example, many people who co-sign Cambridge scholar Aubrey de Grey's papers disagree with him (e.g. University of Chicago's Leonid Gavrilov and S. Jay Olshansky).

[4] As found in the joke collection compiled by John Campbell Gordon, Lord Aberdeen, Viceroy of Ireland from 1906 to 1915, entitled *More Cracks with "We Twa"* (London: Methuen, 1929).

FOREWORD BY TODD HUNTER

[1] James V. Brownson, et al., *StormFront: The Good News of God* (Grand Rapids: Eerdmans, 2003), 51.

[2] Walter Brueggemann, *The Prophetic Imagination* (Minneapolis: Fortress Press, 2001), 39, 59.

[3] Charles Wesley, "O for a Thousand Tongues To Sing," *Hymns for the Living Church,* ed. Donald Hustad (Carol Stream, IL: Hope Publishing Co., 1974), hymn no. 90.

[4] Robert E. Quinn, *Deep Change: Discovering the Leader Within* (San Francisco: Jossey-Bass, 1996), 3.

[5] Elizabeth O'Connor, *Journey Inward, Journey Outward,* (New York: Harper & Row, 1968), 10, 28–30.

[6] Charles H. Kraft, *Christianity in Culture: A Study in Dynamic Biblical Theologizing in Cross-Cultural Perspective* (Maryknoll, NY: Orbis Books, 1979), 12–13.

CHAPTER 1

[1] Graham Ward, *The Blackwell Companion to Postmodern Theology* (Oxford: Blackwell, 2003); Steven Connor, *Postmodernist Culture: An Introduction to Theories of the Contemporary*, 2nd ed. (Oxford: Blackwell, 1996). Regarding the context of

postmodernism for evangelical theology, see Craig Bartholomew, Robin Parry, and Andrew West, eds., *The Futures of Evangelicalism: Issues and Prospects* (Grand Rapids: Kregel, 2004). Regarding implications for biblical theology and hermeneutics, see Craig Bartholomew, Colin Greene, and Karl Moller, eds., *After Pentecost: Language and Biblical Interpretation* (Grand Rapids: Zondervan, 2001). For less recent but cogent works, see Diogenes Allen, *Christian Belief in a Postmodern World* (Louisville: Westminster/John Knox, 1989); David S. Dockery, ed., *The Challenge of Postmodernism: An Evangelical Engagement* (Wheaton: Victor Books, 1995); Stanley Grenz, *A Primer on Postmodernism* (Grand Rapids: Eerdmans, 1996); Dennis McCallum, *The Death of Truth* (Minneapolis: Bethany House, 1996.)

[2] Italics in scripture quotations are used by publishers to indicate words supplied for clarity in translation process.

[3] R. Larry Shelton, "A Covenant Concept of the Atonement," *Wesleyan Theological Journal* 19, no. 1 (Spring 1984), 91–108.

[4] See Charles N. Kraft and Tom N. Wisley, *Readings in Dynamic Indigeneity* (Pasadena, CA: William Carey Library, 1979). These readings illustrate the emphasis on dynamic equivalence in translation and interpretation in the missiological context.

[5] Brian McLaren, "A Radical Rethinking of Our Evangelistic Strategy," *Theology News and Notes* 51, no. 3, (Fall 2004): 4, 5. Also, see the other relevant articles in this same *TNN* issue by Robert Webber, Richard Peace, John and Priscilla Levison, Bill Pannell, and Eddie Gibbs. Todd Hunter is president of Alpha USA, a discipleship development organization.

[6] Leonard Sweet, *SoulTsunami* (Grand Rapids: Zondervan, 1999), 385.

[7] R. Larry Shelton, "A Wesleyan/Holiness Agenda for the Twenty-First Century," *Wesleyan Theological Journal* 33, no. 2 (Fall 1998): 80–97.

[8] Howard Snyder, "The Gospel as Global Good News," *Global Good News: Mission in a New Context*, ed. Howard Snyder (Nashville: Abingdon, 2001), 223.

[9] Michael Gray, "Postmodernism: The Church and Its Response as We Move Toward the Twenty-First Century" (M.Div. research paper, Western Evangelical Seminary/GFU, 1997), 36–44.

[10] Leonard Sweet, *Postmodern Pilgrims* (Nashville: Broadman & Holman Publishers, 2000), xvi–xxi.

[11] See Robert Webber, *Ancient-Future Faith: Rethinking Evangelicalism for a Postmodern World* (Grand Rapids: Baker, 1999).

CHAPTER 2

[1] Isaac Watts, "When I Survey the Wondrous Cross"; public domain.

CHAPTER 3

[1] David Noel Freedman, "Divine Commitment and Human Obligation: The Covenant Theme," *Interpretation* 18 (1964): 419–31.

[2] Michael Lodahl, *The Story of God: Wesleyan Theology and Biblical Narrative* (Kansas City, MO: Beacon Hill Press, 1994), 91. This is an excellent survey of the biblical narrative. It is directed toward the college student audience and is an excellent blend of very good scholarly content and very relevant communication styles.

[3] For clarity, Law will be used to denote references to the interpersonal covenant-related concepts of the Hebrew scriptures. References to the more forensic concepts related to impersonal civil code understandings of judicial elements in the Western contextualizations will be designated by lower case (law).

[4] Lodahl, *The Story of God*, 91.

[5] Charles M. Sheldon, *What Would Jesus Do?* (Philadelphia: H. Altemus, 1899). The concern of evangelical theology is that, without the regenerating and empowering of the Holy Spirit in the transformed life, one is morally incapable of acting out what Jesus would do in life situations. Sheldon's minimizing of the enslaving power of sin gives rise to a naïve optimism.

[6] Steven L. McKenzie, *Covenant* (St. Louis: Chalice Press, 2000), 120. Also see David Noel Freedman, "Divine Commitment and Human Obligation, The Covenant Theme," Interpretations 18 (1964): 419–31.

[7] The biblical emphasis on salvation and covenant-renewal on the basis of faith is pervasive. Examples are seen in Hab. 2:4; Rom. 1:17; 3:27–30; 5:1; Gal. 3:2; Heb. 11:6.

[8] Henry Spaulding II, "Milbank's Trinitarian Ontology and a Re-Narration of Wesleyan-Holiness Theology," *Wesleyan Theological Journal* 36, no. 1 (Spring 2001): 146–59.

[9] Spaulding, "Milbank's Trinitarian Ontology," 149.

[10] Stanley J. Grenz, *Created for Community: Connecting Christian Belief with Christian Living* (Grand Rapids: Baker Books, 1998), 42–52, 80.

[11] Joel B. Green and Mark D. Baker, *Recovering the Scandal of the Cross: Atonement in New Testament and Contemporary Contexts* (Downer's Grove, IL: Intervarsity, 2000), 89–97, 194–97.

[12] Rita N. Brock, "And a Little Child Will Lead Us: Christology and Child Abuse," *Christianity, Patriarchy, and Abuse: A Feminist Critique,* Joanne Carlson Brown and Carole R. Bohn, eds. (New York: Pilgrim, 1989), 52–53. Cited by Green and Baker in *Recovering the Scandal of the Cross*, 91. While one may disagree with their interpretation, these authors and numerous others from this perspective object to what they see as the implied authoritarian model in the penal models, which, they say, has contributed to domestic abuse and social inequity toward women.

[13] J. Denny Weaver, *The Nonviolent Atonement* (Grand Rapids: Eerdmans, 2001). While disagreeing with the rejection of atonement altogether by feminist authors, he takes their concerns seriously and responds to them with the "narrative Christus Victor" approach in his chapter, "Feminist Theology on Atonement," 122–56.

[14] While I recognize and strongly affirm the inclusive nature of God that is reflected in the divine image in both genders, I will use masculine pronouns to refer to the first and second persons of the Trinity. Also, although it is often customary in scholarly contexts to refer to the divine name with the use of the Tetragrammaton, YHWH, the complete spelling (Yahweh) will be retained for the sake of the general reader.

[15] Th. C. Vriezen, *An Outline of Old Testament Theology* (Newton Centre, MA: Charles T. Branford Co., 1966), 162–165.

[16] Ibid., 166–169.

[17] Ibid., 171.

[18] Lodahl, *The Story of God*, 68–69. Also see Grenz on the "social Trinity," *Created for Community,* 42–52.

[19] Ibid., 71.

[20] Clark H. Pinnock and Robert C. Brow, *Unbounded Love* (Downers Grove, IL: InterVarsity, 1994), 71.

[21] William T. Kirwan, *Biblical Concepts for Christian Counseling: A Case for Integrating Psychology and Theology* (Grand Rapids: Baker, 1984), 73–76. Kirwan provides a good analysis from the perspective of psychology on the implications of the image of God in personality and of the loss of a positive self-identity resulting from the brokenness of a lost relationship with God.

[22] Vriezen, *Old Testament Theology*, 215–218. Also see 1 Chron. 28:4–5, where David says, "Yet the LORD, the God of Israel, chose me from my whole family to be king over Israel forever. He chose Judah as leader, and from the house of Judah he chose my family, and from my father's sons he was pleased to make me king over all Israel. Of all my sons . . . he has chosen my son Solomon. . . ."

[23] Ibid., 72.

[24] Ibid., 82–90.

[25] Glenn Barker, William Lane, and Ramsey Michaels, *The New Testament Speaks* (New York: Harper & Row, 1969), 78.

[26] Vriezen, *Old Testament Theology*, 162–65, 326–27.

[27] For example, the use of sacrifices in Israel was to express obedience to God's law by offering thanks, worship, or repentance at the temple. As the early Christian theologians and preachers sought to interpret the gospel to the Western cultures in Europe and North Africa, they tended to reinterpret "sacrifice" in terms of payment of legal penalty. To those who did not know much about God's interpersonal love and covenant law, the death of Christ as a sacrifice was understood more in terms of payment of a judicial penalty for breaking of a law.

[28] Calvin's full statement: "For who is so devoid of intellect as not to understand that God, in so speaking, lisps with us as nurses are wont to do with little children?" John Calvin, *Institutes of the Christian Religion, The Library of Christian Classics*, vol. XX–XXI, ed. John T. McNeil, trans. Ford Lewis Battles (Philadelphia: Westminster, 1960), I, 13, 1.

[29] Robert A. Traina, *Methodical Bible Study* (Grand Rapids: Francis Asbury Press, 1985), 93–200. Traina's approach to inductive Bible study is a foundational text which is compatible with other forms of exegetical and historical study. This is a valuable practical guide for studying the biblical text with a minimum of dogmatic and methodological bias. Such principles include:

Inductive: A thorough, inductive, and critical analysis of the biblical text is essential to sound theological understanding. This requires that theological interpretations not be derived from dogmatic doctrinal requirements or critical presuppositions, but vice versa. An inductive approach recognizes that the Bible is an objective body of literature that exists because people need to know certain truths that they themselves cannot know and which must come to them from without. This requires a correspondingly objective approach to the biblical text that allows it to speak without undue distortion from external dogmatic and deductive conclusions. Doctrine should grow out of the biblical text, and one should not bring subjective, preconceived points of view to the text for proof.

Holistic: A holistic approach to the treatment of salvation in the biblical canon is also needed. The incarnation, cross, and resurrection of Christ are not separable—all are related to salvation and are necessary expressions of covenant love toward humanity's redemption. Approaches that ignore or marginalize any of these aspects of Christ's mission in interpreting the atonement are inadequate for gaining a clear perspective on the focus of the divine expectations and promises expressed in the covenant.

Contextual: The context, both biblical and cultural, of the materials related to covenant atonement must also be considered. The tendency to read our own cultural perspectives back into other historical periods leads to a misunderstanding of the original use and meaning of concepts. While it is tempting to focus only on the reader's response to a text, one may risk falling into complete subjectivism in interpretation without taking the historical situation into consideration in understanding its meaning. Using dogmatic theological presuppositions as criteria for interpreting biblical concepts, on the other hand, also leads to distortion in interpretation, as often happens in attempting to understand concepts such as sacrifice, which are not a formal part of our own culture in any literal sort of way. Before we can accurately understand the relevance of sacrifice for understanding the atonement of Christ in the New Testament, for example, we must first understand what it meant for the community of Israel and its faith.

Relational: Relational models and metaphors must take precedence over nonbiblical concepts drawn from external culture in understanding divine expectations. The very nature of the creation of humanity was interpersonal—God breathed the "breath of life" into the human creature (Gen. 2:7). The image of God into which humanity was formed expressed the ability to communicate with Yahweh. A case in point is the role of sacrifice in biblical materials as opposed to its use in the pagan world or in religious rituals today. In the Old Testament the sacrificial system dealt not only with the removal of the guilt and consequences of sin, but it provided the foundation for worship, discipleship, and growth in sanctification. Thus an adequate and biblical atonement motif must address not only the removal of the guilt of sin but freedom from its enslavement—as well as the issue of the restoration of the image of God, since this is the core of what was lost by humanity in the fall. If the atonement of Christ fully addresses the problem of human sin, it must address the core of that problem, as well, for sin is not fully confronted if it is only punished and not cured.

Proportional: The amount of attention given to a concept in proportion to other ideas is a significant indicator of emphasis in Scripture, as in other literature. This raises concerns about the evangelical tendency to give exclusive attention to penal expressions of atonement while ignoring other more prominent themes. For example, the words *penalty*, *substitute*, and *vicarious* seldom occur in Scripture. But covenant-related words defy enumeration—the word *covenant* itself occurs nearly 300 times in the Old Testament, while ideas related to covenant are ubiquitous. *Obey* and its cognate words occur literally hundreds of times in the Old Testament. Furthermore, relational metaphors abound, such as husband-wife, parent-child, shepherd-sheep. How do the proportionate emphases of these various atonement motifs affect our theological expressions of salvation activity?

Linguistic: One of the difficulties of language translation is finding dynamic cultural equivalents for words and concepts. This is particularly problematic when the word concepts being translated are metaphorical, as in much of religious language. For example, the phrase "shedding of blood" has one nuance of meaning in a hospital emergency room, another in a homicide investigation, and still another in a religious ceremony. The concept "to hold harmless" has decidedly different meanings in a legal document than in a petting zoo. The problem becomes quite acute when issues of eternal significance are at stake.

[30] Stanley J. Grenz, *Revisioning Evangelical Theology* (Downer's Grove, IL: InterVarsity, 1993), 11.

[31] Ibid., 153–155.

[32] Ibid., 74.

[33] Ibid., 22–35.

[34] Ibid., 156–80.

[35] Ibid., 187–89.

[36] Pinnock and Brow, *Unbounded Love*, 7–12.

[37] Ibid., 29–30.

[38] Ibid., 99 (my italics).

[39] Ibid., 100–103.

[40] Green and Baker, *Recovering the Scandal of the Cross*, 20–23.

[41] Ibid., 13.

[42] Ibid., 211–12.

[43] Martin Buber, *Moses* (New York: Harper, 1958), 103; he affirms the Jewish perception of this relationship: "YHVH and Israel enter into a new relation to one another by making the covenant, a relation which had previously been in existence." Cited by Jakob Jocz, *The Covenant: A Theology of Human Destiny* (Grand Rapids: Eerdmans, 1968), 31.

[44] McKenzie, *Covenant*, 8.

[45] Ronald Youngblood, *The Heart of the Old Testament,* 2nd ed. (Grand Rapids: Baker, 1998), 40.

[46] David R. Wilson, M.Div. student, George Fox Evangelical Seminary.

[47] See Robert G. Tuttle Jr., "Cross-Cultural Common Denominators: Tools for a More User-Friendly Evangelism," *Global Good News: Mission in a New Context*, ed. Howard Snyder (Nashville: Abingdon, 2001), 176–89.

CHAPTER 4

[1] See Steven L. McKenzie, *Covenant* (St. Louis: Chalice Press, 2000), chapters 2, 3, 4. McKenzie deals at length with the canonical sources of the various covenant literature. He provides thorough surveys of the Deuteronomistic history, the priestly backgrounds, and the prophetic materials in analyzing the origins of the covenant ideas in the Hebrew Bible.

[2] Brevard Childs, *Biblical Theology of the Old and New Testaments: Theological Reflection on the Christian Bible* (Minneapolis: Fortress, 1993), 504.

[3] Bruce Birch, Walter Brueggemann, Terence Fretheim, and David Petersen, *A Theological Introduction to the Old Testament* (Nashville: Abingdon, 1999), 42. These writers emphasize the relational and covenantal character of God throughout their thorough analysis of Old Testament theology.

[4] Martin Buber, *Moses* (New York: Harper, 1958), 103; Buber reflects this concept in showing, "YHVH and Israel enter into a new relation to one another by making the covenant, a relation which had previously been in existence." Cited by Jakob Jocz, *The Covenant: A Theology of Human Destiny* (Grand Rapids: Eerdmans, 1968), 31.

[5] Birch et al., *Introduction to the Old Testament*, 42–51.

[6] Paul D. Hanson, *The People Called: The Growth of Community in the Bible* (Louisville: Westminster John Knox, 2001), 11–13.

[7] McKenzie, *Covenant*, 37. Also see David Noel Freedman, "Divine Commitment and Human Obligation: The Covenant Theme," *Interpretation* 18 (1964): 419–31.

[8] Ibid., 38.

[9] Although the origin of the covenant concept is actively debated, its canonical function in the text of the Old Testament is certainly central.

[10] G. Ernest Wright and Reginald Fuller, *The Book of the Acts of God* (Garden City, NJ: Doubleday and Co., 1960), 93.

[11] Carl E. Braaten, *New Directions in Theology Today: Volume II, History and Hermeneutics* (Philadelphia: Westminster Press, 1966), 108.

[12] The discussion continues on whether the covenant, particularly the Abrahamic application, was conditional or unconditional. The continual patience of God in view of the unfaithfulness of Israel and its leaders such as David, Solomon, and the later kings would argue for the unconditional nature, while the conditionality of the covenant expectations seems to be the burden of the messages of the prophets. Beyond the Old Testament context, the thrust of the New Testament role of the church as the "new Israel" and the message of Paul in Romans that Israel is in need of the gospel quite as much as the Gentiles (Rom. 1:18–3:9) and is under the obligation to return to the vine under the same conditions of faith in Christ as is laid upon the Gentiles (Rom. 9–11, especially 10:12–21 and 11:23) indicates the broader canonical emphasis to be nuanced in favor of the conditionality of Israel's final salvation only as it is grafted back into Christ the vine.

[13] A debate grows out of the thesis that the concept of covenant does not reflect the traditional connotation of pact or mutual agreement, but rather an obligation imposed upon one party by another. Primary contributions to this discussion are: Ernst Kutsch, *Verheissung und Gesetz; Untersuchungen zum sogenannten Bund im Alten Testament* (Berlin, New York: Walter de Gruyter, 1973), 131; M. Weinfeld, "*Berit*-Covenant vs. Obligation," *Biblica* 56 (1975): 120–28; James Barr, "Some Semantic Notes on the Covenant," *Beiträge zur alttestamentlichen Theologie: Festschrift für Walther Zimmerli zum 70. Geburtstag*, H. Donnor, R. Hanhart, and R. Smend, eds. (Gottingen, Germany: Vandenhoeck and Ruprecht, 1977), 23–38.

[14] A. B. Davidson, "Covenant," *A Dictionary of the Bible*, vol. 1 (Edinburgh: T. & T. Clark, 1898), 509; G. E. Mendenhall, "Covenant," *The Interpreter's Dictionary of the Bible*, vol. 1 (Nashville: Abingdon, 1962), 715.

[15] Francis Brown, S. R. Driver, and C. A. Briggs, *Hebrew and English Lexicon of the Old Testament* (Oxford: Clarendon Press, 1952), 136; Mendenhall, "Covenant," 715; J. A. Thompson, "Covenant," *International Standard Bible Encyclopedia*, vol. 1 (Grand Rapids: Eerdmans, 1979), 790; Davidson, *Covenant*, 509.

[16] James Barr, "Semantic Notes on the Covenant," 23–36.

[17] Mendenhall, "Covenant." Also see G. E. Mendenhall, *Law and Covenant in Israel and the Ancient Near East* (Pittsburgh: The Biblical Colloquium, 1955); Klaus Balzer, *The Covenant Formulary in Old Testament, Jewish, and Early Christian Writings* (Philadelphia: Fortress Press, 1978). For further discussion of interpersonal nature of covenant, see R. Larry Shelton, "Initial Salvation," in *A Contemporary Wesleyan Theology*, ed. Charles W. Carter (Grand Rapids: Zondervan, 1983), 476–82.

[18] William J. Dumbrell, *Covenant and Creation: A Theology of Old Testament Covenants* (New York: Thomas Nelson, 1984), 16–17. Also see D. J. McCarthy, *Old Testament Covenant: A Survey of Current Opinions* (Atlanta: John Knox Press, 1972), 19.

[19] Dwight Van Winkle, "Christianity and Zionism," *Journal of the Irish Christian Study Centre*, vol. 2 (1984): 38–46. The Wesleyan tradition has consistently interpreted the covenantal language in conditional and interpersonal terms rather than in juristic and unconditional terms. As Van Winkle's exegesis shows, the covenant with Abraham in

Gen. 15 and 17 and with Moses in Lev. 18:24–28 is conditioned upon Israel's obedient response to its conditions. In Ex. 19:5–6, the declaration is "*If* (emphasis mine) you obey me fully and keep my covenant, then out of all nations you will be my treasured possession. Although the whole earth is mine, you will be for me a kingdom of priests and a holy nation." Obedience is the condition of covenant maintenance (see Van Winkle, "Christianity and Zionism," 42–43).

[20] Birch et al., *Introduction to the Old Testament*, 151.

[21] D. J. McCarthy, *Treaty and Covenant* (Rome: Biblical Institute Press, 1978), 175–176.

[22] John Peterson Milton, *God's Covenant of Blessing* (Rock Island, IL: Augustana Press, 1961), 5–8.

[23] Walther Eichrodt, *Theology of the Old Testament*, 2 vols. (Philadelphia: Westminster, 1967), 1:75.

[24] E. P. Sanders, *Paul and Palestinian Judaism* (Philadelphia: Fortress Press, 1987), 92–97.

[25] Ibid., 154, 157.

[26] Eichrodt, *Theology of the Old Testament*, 1:43–44.

[27] McKenzie, *Covenant*, 106–7.

[28] Ronald Youngblood, *The Heart of the Old Testament*, 2nd ed. (Grand Rapids: Baker, 1998), 44, 52–53.

[29] *The New Oxford Annotated Bible with the Apocryphal/Deuterocanonical Books, New Revised Standard Version,* Bruce M. Metzger and Roland E. Murphy, eds. (New York: Oxford University Press, 1991), 1197.

[30] Howard Snaith, *Mercy and Sacrifice: A Study of the Book of Hosea* (London: SCM Press, 1957), 55.

[31] McKenzie, *Covenant*, 133.

[32] J. Barton Payne, T*he Theology of the Older Testament* (Grand Rapids: Zondervan, 1962), 296.

[33] Sanders, *Paul and Palestinian Judaism*, 83–84, 106. Sanders' description of the attitudes of later Judaism as "covenant nomism" has sparked an extensive debate. While not the purview of this study, his point is the recognition that Judaism is not a religion of self-righteousness whereby humankind seeks to merit salvation before God. See ThePaulPage.com, a website devoted to this "new perspective" debate, with links to extensive resources.

[34] Walter Brueggemann, *Theology of the Old Testament: Testimony, Dispute, Advocacy* (Minneapolis: Augsburg Fortress, 1997), 669.

[35] Eichrodt, *Theology of the Old Testament*, 2:39.

[36] Walter Brueggemann, *A Social Reading of the Old Testament* (Minneapolis: Fortress Press, 1994), 61.

[37] Brueggemann, *Theology of the Old Testament*, 559.

[38] Brueggemann, *Social Reading*, 48–49.

[39] Eichrodt, *Theology of the Old Testament*, 2:296.

[40] John E. Hartley, *Word Biblical Commentary: Leviticus*, vol. 4, ed. David Hubbard and Glenn Barker (Dallas: Word, 1992), lxv.

[41] W. Gutbrod, "Law in the Old Testament," *Bible Key Words,* vol. 4, ed. Gerhard Kittel (New York: Harper and Row, 1962), 27–30; Eichrodt, *Theology of the Old Testament,* 2:296, 298.

[42] Eichrodt, *Theology of the Old Testament,* 1:291.

[43] Hanson, *The People Called,* 41–43.

[44] McKenzie, *Covenant,* 134–135. McKenzie presents an exhaustive and perceptive analysis of the concept of "covenant" and shows convincingly the predominance of interpersonal characteristics that distinguish Israel's covenant and Law from the forensic and judicial models of civil jurisprudence.

[45] John Bright, *A History of Israel* (Philadelphia: Westminster, 2000), 149–51.

[46] Sanders, *Paul and Palestinian Judaism,* 82–94.

[47] Ibid. For more on the "new Paul research" surrounding this debate, see the website at: http://www.thepaulpage.com/.

[48] Dennis Bratscher, *"Torah* as Holiness: Old Testament 'Law' as Response to Divine Grace" (paper presented at the annual meeting of the Wesleyan Theological Society, Hobe Sound, FL (March 2, 2001).

[49] Hartmut Gese, *Essays on Biblical Theology,* trans. Keith Crim (Minneapolis: Augsburg, 1981), 65.

[50] Ibid., 71, 80.

[51] Birch et al., *Introduction to the Old Testament,* 103.

[52] Eichrodt, *Theology of the Old Testament,* 1:74–82.

[53] G. Ernest Wright and Reginald Fuller, *The Book of the Acts of God* (Garden City, NJ: Doubleday and Co., 1960), 93.

[54] Eichrodt, *Theology of the Old Testament,* 2:381.

[55] G. Ernest Wright, *The Challenge of Israel's Faith* (Chicago: University of Chicago Press, 1944), 76.

[56] Gerhard von Rad, *Old Testament Theology* (Edinburgh: Oliver and Boyd, 1962), 264, 266.

[57] Otfried Hofius, "Atonement and Reconciliation: On the Pauline Understanding of Jesus' Death on the Cross," unpublished translation of Daniel P. Bailey from Hofius, "Sühne und Versöhnung: Zum paulinischen Verständnis des Kreuztodes Jesu" (1983), 5–21, in idem, *Paulusstudien,* Wissenschaftliche Untersuchungen zum Neuen Testament 51 (Tübingen: Mohr Siebeck, 1989), 33–49.

CHAPTER 5

[1] Paul D. Hanson, *The People Called: The Growth of Community in the Bible* (Louisville: Westminster John Knox, 2001), 73–75. Hanson's work in this monograph is an encyclopedic and nuanced treatment of the entire heritage of Israel's development as a covenant community and its legacy for the Christian communities of faith.

[2] Walter Brueggemann, *Theology of the Old Testament: Testimony, Dispute, Advocacy* (Minneapolis: Augsburg Fortress, 1997), 669.

[3] Th. C. Vriezen, *An Outline of Old Testament Theology* (Newton Centre, MA: Charles T. Branford Co., 1966), 284–286.

[4] H. Wheeler Robinson, *The Religious Ideas of the Old Testament* (Manchester: John Rylands Library, 1950), 133–141.

[5] Vriezen, *Old Testament Theology*, 224–227; Walther Eichrodt, *Theology of the Old Testament*, 2 vols. (Philadelphia: Westminster, 1967), 1:121, 130–34. Eichrodt shows the extensive involvement of the surrounding culture in the practices of many diverse aspects of mystery religions, the occult, divinations, magic, etc., under the category of "Magic" in the index to vol. 1.

[6] Bruce Birch, Walter Brueggemann, Terence Fretheim, and David Petersen, *A Theological Introduction to the Old Testament* (Nashville: Abingdon, 1999), 254–55.

[7] John Bright, *A History of Israel* (Louisville: Westminster John Knox, 2000), 150.

[8] John E. Hartley, *Word Biblical Commentary: Leviticus*, vol. 4, ed. David Hubbard and Glenn Barker (Dallas: Word, 1992), 5.

[9] H. H. Rowley, *The Meaning of Sacrifice in the Old Testament* (Manchester: John Rylands Library, 1950), 87–88.

[10] Hartley, *Leviticus*, 20.

[11] Ibid.

[12] Hartmut Gese, *Essays on Biblical Theology*, trans. Keith Crim (Minneapolis: Augsburg, 1981), 104–6; Hartley, *Leviticus*, 53.

[13] Hartley, *Leviticus*, 241, 244.

[14] Ibid., 238.

[15] Ibid., 236.

[16] Ibid., 241.

[17] Gese, *Essays on Biblical Theology*, 104–6; see Hartley, *Leviticus,* 53.

[18] Hartley, *Leviticus,* 20–21.

[19] Rowley, *Sacrifice in the Old Testament*, 88.

[20] The issue here is not a compensatory offering as penalty, but the sacramental offering of the animal in participation in the covenant bond of life with God.

[21] Hartmut Gese, *Essays on Biblical Theology,* tran. Keith Crim (Minneapolis: Augsburg, 1981),106; also see 106–9.

[22] It was only the male who participated in the Jewish ritual, although the consecration is inclusive of all.

[23] Howard Snaith. *Mercy and Sacrifice: A Study of the Book of Hosea* (London: SCM Press, 1957), 118.

[24] Steven L. McKenzie, *Covenant* (St. Louis: Chalice Press, 2000), 106.

[25] Ronald Youngblood, *The Heart of the Old Testament,* 2nd ed. (Grand Rapids: Baker, 1998), 81–83.

[26] Birch et al., *Introduction to the Old Testament*, 160 (italics in the original).

[27] Douglas Davies, "An Interpretation of Sacrifice in Leviticus," *Zeitschrift für die alttestamentliche Wissenschaft* 89 (Berlin, New York: Walter de Gruyter, 1977), 396; reprinted in *Anthropological Approaches to the Old Testament*, 151–62, ed. Bernhard Lang, Issues in Religion and Theology, 8 (Philadelphia: Fortress, 1985), 158.

[28] Bright, *A History of Israel*, 149.

[29] Vriezen, *Old Testament Theology,* 51–52.

[30] Brueggemann, *Theology of the Old Testament,* 666 (my italics).

[31] R. Larry Shelton, "Initial Salvation," in *A Contemporary Wesleyan Theology*, ed. Charles W. Carter (Grand Rapids: Zondervan, 1983), 488–89. The substitutionary emphasis of Christ's work should not be seen apart from the subjective balance of appropriating his work by faith. His death benefits humanity as it is experienced in faith union, not in an exclusively substitutionary and objective way.

[32] Hartley, *Leviticus*, lxvii; Hartley summarizes the descriptions of the various sacrifices in lxvii–lxxii.

[33] Ibid., lxviii, 42, 99–101.

[34] Ibid., lxviii, 100.

[35] Ibid., lxviii, 101.

[36] Ibid., lxviii–lxxii, 55–63.

[37] Ibid., lxvii–lxix.

[38] Ibid., 77.

[39] NIV Study Bible

[40] Hartley, *Leviticus*, 75–77, 85.

[41] See previous discussion of this point in section on "The Transference Theory" above.

[42] Ibid., 241, 244–245 (my italics).

[43] James Denney, *The Death of Christ* (London: Hodder and Stoughton, 1902), 9. See the further discussion of Denney's reinterpreting propitiation in terms of expiation in H. Ray Dunning, "Toward a Personal Paradigm for the Atonement," *Wesleyan Theological Journal* 40, no. 2 (Fall 2005): 163.

[44] This phrase means "out of the working of the work." It is used to describe the "automatic" implementation of a ritual as a result of applying the appropriate formula or code words.

[45] Hartley, *Leviticus*, lxix.

[46] Bernhard W. Anderson, *Contours of Old Testament Theology* (Philadelphia: Fortress Press, 1999), 120–21.

[47] P. P. Waldenström, *Reconciliation,* trans. J. G. Princell (Chicago: John Martenson Publishers, 1888), 11–12.

[48] Jakob Jocz, *The Covenant: A Theology of Human Destiny* (Grand Rapids: Eerdmans, 1968), 120.

[49] Hartley, *Leviticus,* lxx.

[50] Davies, "An Interpretation of Sacrifice in Leviticus," 157.

[51] I. Howard Marshall, "The Theology of the Atonement" (paper presented at the Evangelical Alliance Symposium on the Atonement, London, July 6–8, 2005; available at: http://www.eauk.org/contentmanager/content/acute/acute.cfm), 13. Even though Marshall understands the need for penitence and obedience in the offering of the sacrifice and of the participatory nature of the believer's identification with Christ, he still insists on interpreting Christ's work as "penal substitution," although he admits that the term may lend itself to misunderstanding.

[52] Robert A. Peterson, *Calvin's Doctrine of the Atonement* (Phillipsburg, NJ: Presbyterian and Reformed Publishing Company, 1983), 66. Peterson cites Calvin's commentary on Rom. 3:25. Similar functions are seen in two related figures of speech:

Metonymy: A figure of speech in which one word or phrase is substituted for another with which it is closely associated, as in the use of *Washington* for *the United States government* or of *the sword* for *military power.*

Synecdoche: A figure of speech in which a part is used for the whole (as *hand* for *sailor*), the whole for a part (as *the law* for *police officer*), the specific for the general (as *cutthroat* for *assassin*), the general for the specific (as *thief* for *pickpocket*), or the material for the thing from which it is made (as *steel* for *sword*). Excerpted from *The American Heritage Dictionary of the English Language, Third Edition* (Boston: Houghton Mifflin Company, 1992).

[53] E. P. Sanders, *Paul and Palestinian Judaism* (Philadelphia: Fortress, 1977), 178–80.

[54] Walther Eichrodt, *Theology of the Old Testament*, 2 vols. (Philadelphia: Westminster, 1961), 1:52.

[55] Hartley, *Leviticus,* 65.

[56] Birch et al., *Introduction to the Old Testament*, 151, (italics in the original).

[57] Thomas White, medal ceremony at Fort Meyer, Virginia; reported by NBC News, October 25, 2001.

[58] E. P. Sanders, *Paul and Palestinian Judaism* (Philadelphia: Fortress Press, 1977), 166–70.

[59] Hartley, *Leviticus,* 64–65.

[60] John E. Hartley, "Expiate; Expiation," *International Standard Bible Encyclopedia*, vol. 2 (Grand Rapids: Eerdmans, 1982), 246–47; C. L. Mitton, "Atonement," *The Interpreter's Dictionary of the Bible* (Nashville: Abingdon, 1962), 310; Shelton, "Initial Salvation," 486–90.

[61] C. H. Dodd, *The Bible and the Greeks* (London: Hodder and Stoughton, 1935), 88–93.

[62] Hartley, "Expiate, Expiation," 247.

[63] Leon Morris, *The Apostolic Preaching of the Cross* (Grand Rapids: Eerdmans, 1965), 149–154.

[64] Birch et al., *Introduction to the Old Testament*, 159–60.

[65] Anderson, *Contours of Old Testament Theology*, 120.

[66] Ibid., 121.

[67] Jacob Milgrom, "The Priestly Doctrine of Repentance," *Revue Biblique* 82 (1975), 198–99. See also Birch et al., *Introduction to the Old Testament*, 160.

[68] Rowley, *Sacrifice in the Old Testament*, 87.

[69] R. Larry Shelton, "Sanctification in Romans Chapter 6," (Th.M. thesis, Asbury Theological Seminary, 1968), 15–17.

[70] Walther Eichrodt, *Theology of the Old Testament,* 2 vols. (Philadelphia: Westminster, 1967), 2:309.

[71] Ibid., 1:256.

[72] See Megory Anderson and Philip Culbertson, "The Inadequacy of the Christian Doctrine of Atonement in Light of Levitical Sin Offering," *Anglican Theological Review* 68, no. 4 (October 1986): 308.

[73] Hartley, *Leviticus,* lxx–lxxi.

[74] Otfried Hofius, "Atonement and Reconciliation: On the Pauline Understanding of Jesus' Death on the Cross," unpublished translation of Daniel P. Bailey from Hofius, "Sühne und Versöhnung: Zum paulinischen Verständnis des Kreuztodes Jesu" (1983), 5–21, in idem, *Paulusstudien*, Wissenschaftliche Untersuchungen zum Neuen Testament 51 (Tübingen: Mohr Siebeck, 1989), 33–49. See Gese, *Essays on Biblical Theology*, "The Atonement," 93–116.

[75] Hofius, "Atonement and Reconciliation," 14–15 (my italics). See Gese, *Essays on Biblical Theology*, 106.

[76] Rowley, *Sacrifice in the Old Testament*, 87–88.

[77] Hofius, "Atonement and Reconciliation," 14–16. See Gese, *Essays on Biblical Theology*, 106–7, 114.

[78] Birch et al., *Introduction to the Old Testament*, 160.

[79] Hartley, *Leviticus,* lxxii.

[80] H. Wheeler Robinson, *Inspiration and Revelation in the Old Testament* (Oxford: The Clarendon Press, 1946), 227.

[81] Birch et al., *Introduction to the Old Testament*, 159–60.

[82] Davies, "An Interpretation of Sacrifice in Leviticus," 154.

[83] Eichrodt, *Theology of the Old Testament*, 2:58–59, footnote 5.

[84] Ibid., 2:310.

[85] Ibid., 2:295.

[86] Randy Maddox, *Responsible Grace* (Nashville: Abingdon, 1994), 144–45.

[87] Daniel Clendenin, *Eastern Orthodox Christianity: A Western Perspective* (Grand Rapids: Baker, 1994), 147.

[88] Ibid., 134–37.

[89] Vincent Taylor, *Jesus and His Sacrifice* (London: Macmillan and Co., 1959), 88.

[90] H. Ray Dunning, *Grace, Faith, and Holiness* (Kansas City, MO: Beacon Hill Press, 1988), 375–76.

[91] Taylor, *Jesus and His Sacrifice,* 88, 131. Alan Richardson, *An Introduction to the Theology of the New Testament* (Grand Rapids: Eerdmans, 1958), 231.

[92] Sue Groom, "Why Did Christ Die?" European Union Symposium, 2005, 8–11, 22–23, accessed www.eauk.org/contentmanager/content/acute/acute.cfm; 9/28/2005. Sue Groom, "Why Did Christ Die?" (paper presented at the Evangelical Alliance Symposium on the Atonement, London, July 6–8, 2005; available at http://www.eauk.org/contentmanager/content/acute/acute.cfm), 8–11, 22–23.

[93] Morna Hooker, "Did the Use of Isaiah 53 to Interpret His Mission Begin with Jesus?" in *Jesus and the Suffering Servant: Isaiah 53 and Christian Origins*, ed. William H. Bellinger Jr. and William R. Farmer (Harrisburg, PA: Trinity Press International, 1998), 98. Also, Gese, *Essays on Biblical Theology*, 106.

[94] Bruce Reichenbach, "By His Stripes We Are Healed," *Journal of the Evangelical Theological Society* 41, no. 4 (December 1998): 551–53.

[95] Bernd Janowski, "He Bore Our Sins: Isaiah 53 and the Drama of Taking Another's Place," in *The Suffering Servant: Isaiah 53 in Jewish and Christian Sources*, ed. Bernd Janowski and Peter Stuhlmacher, trans. Daniel P. Bailey (Grand Rapids: Eerdmans, 2004), 73–74.

[96] Groom, "Why Did Christ Die?" 10–11; also seeDaniel P. Bailey, "Concepts of *Stellvertretung* in the Interpretation of Isaiah 53," in *Jesus and the Suffering Servant*, 240.

[97] *Star Trek II: The Wrath of Khan* (Paramount Home Video, 1998).

CHAPTER 6

[1] Hartmut Gese, *Essays on Biblical Theology*, trans. Keith Crim (Minneapolis: Augsburg, 1981), 94–95.

[2] Steve Chalke, *The Lost Message of Jesus* (Grand Rapids: Zondervan, 2003).

[3] See Donald M. Lewis, ed., *Christianity Reborn: The Global Expansion of Evangelicalism in the Twentieth Century* (Grand Rapids: Eerdmans, 2004).

[4] Jakob Jocz, *The Covenant: A Theology of Human Destiny* (Grand Rapids: Eerdmans, 1968), 10; see "Introduction," 9–15.

[5] Steven L. McKenzie, *Covenant* (St. Louis: Chalice Press, 2000), 120.

[6] Vincent Taylor, *The Atonement in New Testament Teaching* (London: Epworth Press, 1953), 51–52.

[7] See Caleb F. Heppner, "A Covenantal View of Atonement," The Paul Page website, http://www.thepaulpage.com/Atonement.htm.

[8] H. Ray Dunning, *Grace, Faith and Holiness* (Kansas City, MO: Beacon Hill Press, 1988), 377.

[9] Ibid., 377–78.

[10] Vincent Taylor, *Forgiveness and Reconciliation* (London: Macmillan and Co., 1977), 39; H. A. A. Kennedy, *The Theology of the Epistles* (London: Gerald Duckworth and Co., 1959), 135.

[11] Jocz, *The Covenant*, 115–28.

[12] Ibid., 127–28.

[13] Karl Barth, *Church Dogmatics,* trans. G. W. Bromiley, ed. G. W. Bromiley and T. F. Torrance, vol. IV/1 (Edinburgh: T. and T. Clark, 1958), 22–66; see his extended discussion of Christ's work.

[14] R. Larry Shelton, "Initial Salvation," in *A Contemporary Wesleyan Theology*, ed. Charles Carter (Grand Rapids: Zondervan, 1983), 497–98.

[15] C. L. Mitton, "Atonement," in *The Interpreter's Dictionary of the Bible* (Nashville: Abingdon, 1962), 312.

[16] Glenn Barker, William Lane, and Ramsey Michaels, *The New Testament Speaks* (New York: Harper and Row, 1969), 77–79.

[17] Irenaeus, *Against Heresies, The Ante-Nicene Fathers*, vol. 1, Library of Christian Classics, ed. Alexander Roberts and James Donaldson (Grand Rapids: Eerdmans, 1956), Book V, 526. The entire quotation is: ". . . but following the only true and steadfast

teacher, the Word of God, our Lord Jesus Christ, who did, through His transcendent love, become what we are, that He might bring us to be even what He is Himself."

[18] Ibid.

[19] Thomas Edward McComiskey, *Covenants of Promise* (Grand Rapids: Baker, 1985), 80–88.

[20] Ibid., 89–90.

[21] Ibid.

[22] The covenant is "new" in the sense that its function and efficacy as the foundation for the divine-human relationship is restored, not in the sense that it is a "different" covenant. The "old" and "new" covenants have the same basis and the same goal, the maintenance and renewal of the relationship between God and the community of faith.

[23] C. E. B. Cranfield, "St. Paul and the Law," *Scottish Journal of Theology* 17 (1964): 57.

[24] McComiskey, *Covenants of Promise*, 129–30.

[25] McKenzie, *Covenant*, 83–84.

[26] Leon Morris, *The Apostolic Preaching of the Cross* (Grand Rapids: Eerdmans, 1965), 103 (see 90–109).

[27] McKenzie, *Covenant*, 94–95.

[28] Ibid., 85–86.

[29] Ibid., 86–88.

[30] Ibid., 87–89. Also see John E. Hartley, *Word Biblical Commentary: Leviticus*, vol. 4, ed. David Hubbard and Glenn Barker (Dallas: Word, 1992), extended comments on Lev. 17:11: "The life of a creature is in the blood . . . to make atonement for yourselves on the altar," 273–77.

[31] Ibid., 90–91.

[32] Ibid., 92–95.

[33] The word covenant (*diathekē*) appears seventeen times in the book of Hebrews, more than any other New Testament book. The terms "new covenant" and "better covenant" appear six times in NAU and four times in NIV, showing that Christ's covenant provision is "better than" that of the Old Testament version (e.g., Heb. 7:19, 22; 8:6; 9:23).

[34] Steve Motyer, "The Atonement in Hebrews" (paper presented at the Evangelical Alliance Symposium on the Atonement, London, July 6–8, 2005; available at http://www.eauk.org/contentmanager/content/acute/acute.cfm).

[35] McKenzie, *Covenant*, 118; here he follows Raymond Brown, *Christ Above All: The Message of Hebrews* (Downers Grove, IL: InterVarsity, 1982), 148.

[36] Ibid., 117. McKenzie cites here the work of Susanne Lehne, "The New Covenant in Hebrews," *Journal for the Study of the New Testament*, Supplement 44 (Sheffield: JSOT Press, 1990).

[37] Ibid.

[38] Ibid., 115–18; McKenzie also refers to William L. Lane, *Hebrews 1–8*, Word Biblical Commentary 47A, (Dallas: Word, 1991); Barnabas Lindars, *The Theology of the Letter to the Hebrews* (Cambridge: Cambridge University Press, 1991).

[39] Oscar Cullmann, *The Christology of the New Testament*, trans. Shirley Guthrie and Charles Hall (Philadelphia: Westminster, 1959), 83–107.

[40] Again, "blood" is used as a synecdoche, representing the totality of the sacrificial work Christ did. There is no forgiveness of sin apart from Christ's work because it is in his life that brings the new covenant that we can be restored to covenant fellowship with God.

[41] Ibid., 102–5.

[42] Motyer, "Atonement in Hebrews" (italics in original).

[43] Wayne McCown, "Such a Great Salvation," in *An Inquiry Into Biblical Soteriology*, ed. John Hartley and R. Larry Shelton (Anderson, IN: Warner Press, 1980), 171; McCown's translation.

[44] Ibid., 169–77; McCown's translation.

[45] Motyer, "Atonement in Hebrews."

[46] McKenzie, *Covenant*, 102–4.

[47] Ibid., 107.

[48] Ibid., 106.

[49] Ibid., 88–89.

[50] While "justification" is a legal term, Paul's Hebrew context uses it primarily in reference to covenant "Law" and less as "law" in the purely civil law forensic sense of "acquittal."

[51] Robert W. Wall, "Community (New Testament)," in *Anchor Bible Dictionary*, vol. 1, ed. David Noel Freedman (Garden City, NJ: Doubleday and Co., 1992), 1106.

[52] Robert Wuthnow observes changes in the American evangelical church since World War II: "What the fellowship [community of Christians] was like, what it would do, what would hold it together, were matters left unaddressed. Fellowship was seen mainly as a byproduct of individual devotion." *The Restructuring of American Religion* (Princeton: Princeton University Press, 1988), 56. Robert Bellah et al., in the seminal work *Habits of the Heart*, present a thorough and cogent evaluation from a sociological perspective of the American church's move toward such an individualistic faith; Robert Bellah, et al., *Habits of the Heart: Individualism and Commitment in American Life* (Berkeley: University of California Press, 1985).

[53] McKenzie, *Covenant*, 132–33.

[54] Stanley J. Grenz, *Theology for the Community of God* (Nashville: Broadman and Holman Publishers, 1994), 605–14. Grenz notes that the New Testament people of God are not "based on membership within a specific ethnic group. Now people from the entire world are called together to belong to God" (p. 607). Hans Küng has offered the same taxonomy of metaphors, using church as the "creation of the Spirit" where Grenz uses "temple of the Spirit." Hans Küng , *The Church*, trans. Ray Ockenden and Rosaleen Ockenden (New York: Sheed and Ward, 1967), 162–179.

[55] Küng, *The Church*, 388.

[56] Willard M. Swartley, *Slavery, Sabbath, War, and Women* (Scottdale, PA: Herald Press, 1983), 189.

[57] The idea of a community ecology is not new. The intrinsic interrelatedness of humans with creation has been noted by Robert Bellah et al., *Habits of the Heart*, 283–84.

[58] Grenz, *Theology for the Community of God*, 269.

[59] Howard Snyder, *Liberating the Church: The Ecology of Church and Kingdom* (Downers Grove, IL: InterVarsity, 1983), 114.

[60] Walter Brueggemann, *Texts That Linger, Words That Explode: Listening to Prophetic Voices* (Minneapolis: Fortress Press, 2000), 12.

[61] Regarding Jer. 31:33, Brueggemann offers this translation of Jer. 31:33: "I will put my torah in their midst," thus expressing the corporate message (opposed to "excessive personalizing") and conveying the synecdoche of *Torah*, which represents more than legalistic codes, enabling God's people "to see things through the eyes of God's passion and anguish . . . a reminder that God's will focuses on large human questions and that we may also focus on weighty matters of justice, mercy, and righteousness." Brueggemann points out that the translation of the Old Testament word *Torah* as "law" is inadequate for understanding the synecdoche of the word, as also is the rendering "within them" (NAU). Walter Brueggemann, "Covenant as a Subversive Paradigm," in *A Social Reading of the Old Testament* (Minneapolis: Fortress Press, 1994), 48. Note that his point addresses why we are using "Law" instead of "law" to refer to the entire covenantal context of the Hebrew faith. In this sense, our use of "Law" functions also as a synecdoche to connote this entire interpersonal context of faith in Yahweh.

[62] There is some debate over the identity of the original readers of this epistle (whether Jewish, Gentile-Christian, or other). Despite such debate, there is internal evidence and scholarly agreement that the book was intended for a corporate audience identified by a subscript, "To the Hebrews." See Werner Georg Kümmel, *Introduction to the New Testament*, trans. Howard Clark Kee (Nashville: Abingdon, 1975), 398–401.

[63] The use of the plural "laws . . . on their hearts" in Heb. 8:10, expresses the interpersonal covenantal emphasis we are denoting by "Law."

[64] Dietrich Bonhoeffer has explored the theological-sociological foundations of the Christian community. He writes, "The church is organized towards a certain aim, namely the achieving of the will of God. But the will of God is aimed at the church itself, as a community of spirit, so that it is both a purposive society and an end in itself. . . . God, as he seeks to make his will prevail, gives himself to the hearts of men and creates community, that is, he provides himself as the means to his own end. . . . This mutual co-inherence must neither be distorted into a picture in which there is a community which has in addition an aim, nor into the idea that there is a society with an aim which becomes a community—both of which cases would be possible sociologically. But in the idea of the church the one element does in fact mingle with the other in such a way that every attempt to separate them genetically completely destroys the sense." Dietrich Bonhoeffer, *The Communion of Saints: A Dogmatic Inquiry Into the Sociology of the Church*, trans. Eberhard Bethge (New York: Harper and Row, 1960), 180–81.

[65] Karl Barth, *Evangelical Theology: An Introduction*, trans. Grover Foley (New York: Holt, Rinehart and Winston, 1963), 202–3. Also see Howard Snyder, *Radical Renewal: The Problem of Wineskins Today* (Houston: Touch Publications, 1996), 96.

[66] Ibid.

[67] G. E. Mendenhall, "Covenant," in *The Interpreter's Dictionary of the Bible* (Nashville: Abingdon, 1962), 722–23; J. A. Thompson, "Covenant," 792, D. F. Estes, "Covenants (New Testament)," 793, in *International Standard Bible Encyclopedia*, vol. 1 (Grand Rapids: Eerdmans, 1979).

[68] Alan Richardson, *An Introduction to the Theology of the New Testament* (New York: Harper & Row, 1958), 370–371.

[69] G. E. Mendenhall, *Law and Covenant in Israel and the Ancient Near East* (Pittsburgh: The Biblical Colloquium, 1955), 36.

[70] J. Barton Payne, *The Theology of the Older Testament* (Grand Rapids: Zondervan, 1962), 392–93.

[71] Jocz, *The Covenant*, 125–27.

[72] Morna Hooker, "Did the Use of Isaiah 53 to Interpret His Mission Begin with Jesus?" in *Jesus and the Suffering Servant: Isaiah 53 and Christian Origins*, ed. William H. Bellinger Jr. and William R. Farmer (Harrisburg, PA: Trinity Press International, 1998), 102; R. Larry Shelton, "Sanctification in Romans Chapter 6" (Th.M. thesis, Asbury Theological Seminary, 1968), 54.

[73] Hartmut Gese, *Essays on Biblical Theology*, trans. Keith Crim (Minneapolis: Augsburg, 1981), 90.

[74] Ibid., 88.

[75] Ibid.

[76] Ibid., 80.

[77] Ibid.

[78] Ibid., 92. While it is clear that Christ participates in humanity's death resulting from Adam's sin, Gese does not view this as a substitute penalty but as an incarnational participation of Christ in the consequences of humanity's plight, even as humanity participates in his own victory over death. This is "inclusive substitution."

[79] N. T. Wright, *The Climax of the Covenant: Christ and the Law in Pauline Theology* (Minneapolis: Fortress Press, 1993), 244–45. This is a definitive exegetical study of Paul and the Law. Wright reviews the relevant scholarship and moves beyond the traditional Patristic, Reformation, and post-Enlightenment historical scholarship answers to examine Paul's teaching in the context of his Jewish worldview. He views Paul as examining the two key Jewish themes of God and Israel's election in terms of Christology and pneumatology, particularly as they are developed in the covenant context.

[80] Ibid., 251.

[81] McKenzie, *Covenant*, 94.

[82] Cranfield, "St. Paul and the Law," 57; McComiskey, *Covenants of Promise*, 128–129.

CHAPTER 7

[1] C. L. Mitton, "Atonement," in *The Interpreter's Dictionary of the Bible* (Nashville: Abingdon, 1962), 312; R. Larry Shelton, "Initial Salvation," in *A Contemporary Wesleyan Theology*, ed. Charles Carter (Grand Rapids: Zondervan, 1983), 491–96.

[2] James Barr, "Some Semantic Notes on the Covenant," in *Beiträge zur Alttestamentlichen Theologie: Festschrift für Walther Zimmerli zum 70, Geburtstag*, ed. H. Donnor, R. Hanhart, and R. Smend. (Gottingen, Germany: Vandenhoeck and Ruprecht, 1977), 23–26.

[3] Jakob Jocz, *The Covenant: A Theology of Human Destiny* (Grand Rapids: Eerdmans, 1968), 169.

[4] The exclusively forensic understanding of God's integrity and salvation work as based on justice rather than love portrays the extensively Greek-oriented influences upon Western theology. D. M. Baillie, for one, asserts that the atonement issues are understood adequately only in the context of relationships. See D. M. Baillie, *God Was in Christ* (London: Faber and Faber, Ltd., 1961). See also H. Ray Dunning, "Toward a Personal

Paradigm for the Atonement," *Wesleyan Theological Journal* 40, no. 2 (Fall 2005), 157–68.

[5] Jocz, *The Covenant*, 168, 126–28.

[6] Alan Richardson, *An Introduction to the Theology of the New Testament* (New York: Harper and Row, 1958,) 77.

[7] P. P. Waldenström, *Reconciliation,* trans. J. G. Princell (Chicago: John Martenson Publishers, 1888), 20–27. The NIV and some other translations render *hilasterion* in Rom. 3:25 as "propitiation," or appeasing God's wrath. As will be shown in the section "Christ as the Mercy Seat" below, linguistic issues raise serious questions about this interpretation.

[8] I. Howard Marshall, "The Theology of the Atonement" (paper presented at the Evangelical Alliance Symposium on the Atonement, London, July 6–8, 2005; available at http://www.eauk.org/theology/atonement), 8–12. Marshall notes that divine retribution is justly directed toward the "impenitent sinner." Agreed, but he does not demonstrate in his excellent survey of wrath and punishment the inevitability of God's punishment of anyone who has ever sinned. It is clearly biblical that God exacts retribution against evil and unrepentant sinners, but the sacrificial system exemplifies that other means of repentance and obedience, such as sacrifice, are available to avoid the wrath of God if one expresses faith and obedience to the covenant expectations. It is this alternative to inevitable punishment that the penal theory does not adequately express. Sin can be justly expiated if one is repentant and acts obediently to covenant expectations. This is in fact what Jesus is doing by including humanity in his sacrificial offering of himself to bring humanity to incorporation in his own acceptance of the consequences of human sin so that he could bring reconciliation to humanity in his resurrection. Thus the covenant perspective bases the act of salvation in Christ but presents it as *covenant sacrificial obedience*, rather than *forensic propitiatory penalty*.

[9] Gustaf Aulén, *Christus Victor,* trans. A. G. Hebert (New York: Macmillan Co., 1972), 131; Waldenström, *Reconciliation*, 20–27.

[10] Christ's incarnation extends to identification with all the consequences of humanity's sinful alienation from God (Phil. 2:5–11). His cry, "My God, my God, why have you forsaken me?" (Mark 15:34) is out of his fully experiencing humanity's alienation from the Creator.

[11] This addresses Marshall's concern that if "penal" concepts are not used, it is necessary to find alternative ways of expressing divine justice and holiness; Marshall, "Theology of the Atonement," 10.

[12] James D.G. Dunn, *Word Biblical Commentary: Romans 1–8,* vol. 38, ed. David Hubbard and Glenn Barker (Dallas: Word Books, 1988), 40.

[13] David Hill, *Greek Words and Hebrew Meanings* (New York: Cambridge University Press, 1967), 82. See J.A. Ziesler, *The Meaning of Righteousness in Paul* (Cambridge: University Press, 1972), 17–45, for a definitive and exhaustive treatment of the Old Testament usage of *tsedeq* and its cognates.

[14] Edmond Jacob, *Theology of the Old Testament* (New York: Harper and Row, 1958), 94.

[15] Brown, Driver, and Briggs, *A Hebrew and English Lexicon of the Old Testament* (London: Oxford Press, 1952), 841; Jacob, *Theology of the Old Testament*, 95.

[16] Hill, *Greek Words and Hebrew Meanings*, 84.

[17] Ibid. See also R. Larry Shelton, "Initial Salvation," *A Contemporary Wesleyan Theology,* ed. Charles W. Carter (Zondervan Publishing House, 1983), 493.

[18] Ibid., 85.

[19] Hermann Cremer, *Die paulinische Rechtfertigungslehre im Zusammenhange ihrer geschichtlichen Voraussetzungen, (*1899); cited by Eichrodt, *Theology of the Old Testament,* 1, 240; cited by E.P. Sanders, *Paul and Palestinian Judaism*, (Philadelphia: Fortress Press, 1977), 525.

[20] Dunn, *Romans 1–8*, 41.

[21] Hill, *Greek Words and Hebrew Meanings*, 88–89.

[22] Hunter, *Church for the Unchurched.* (Nashville: Abingdon, 1996), 27; Dunn, *Romans 1–8*.

[23] Walther Eichrodt, *Theology of the Old Testament,* 2 vols.(Philadelphia: Westminster, 1967), 1, 246.

[24] Hill, *Greek Words and Hebrew Meanings*, 90.

[25] The gospel is the "power of God for salvation" *because* it reveals God's righteous fulfillment of covenant salvation promises.

[26] E.P. Sanders, *Paul and Palestinian Judaism*, 175–180, 514.

[27] See Shelton, "Initial Salvation," 492–494, for additional discussion on "Righteousness of God." See Sanders' discussion on the atoning nature of repentance in the Rabbinic traditions, 175–182.

[28] Richardson, *Theology of the New Testament,* 81–83; Joachim Jeremias, *Rediscovering Parables* (New York: Charles Scribner's Sons, 1966), 97–116.

[29] Ibid., Also see Matt. 5:6,10,20; 6:1,33; Luke 1:75; Acts 10:35; 24:25; James 1:20; 3:18; 1 Pet. 3:14; 1 John 3:7,10; Rev. 22:11.

[30] A.M. Hunter, *Interpreting Paul's Gospel* (Philadelphia: The Westminster Press, 1954), 27. See section on "The Righteousness of God" in R. Larry Shelton, "Justification by Faith in the Pauline Corpus," in *An Inquiry into Soteriology from a Biblical Theological Perspective* 1, Wesleyan Theological Perspectives Series (Anderson, Ind.; Warner Press, 1981), 104–114.

[31] For a more extensive treatment of this discussion on whether 3:26 refers to forgiveness or penalty payment, see Simon Gathercole,"Romans 3:25–26: An Exegetical Study," Evangelical Union Atonement Symposium, July 2005, 1–6; and Douglas Moo, *The NIV Application Commentary:Romans* (Grand Rapids: Zondervan, 2000), 128–130; and advocating the forgiveness interpretation in J.A. Ziesler, *Paul's Letter to the Romans* (London: SCM Press, 1989), 115–116.

[32] Hunter, 140; also, Vincent Taylor, *Forgiveness and Reconciliation* (London: Macmillan and Co., 1952), 39.

[33] Jocz, *The Covenant*, 125–26.

[34] Hunter, 140; Taylor, *Forgiveness and Reconciliation,* 39; Vincent Taylor, *The Atonement in New Testament Teaching* (London: Epworth Press, 1953), 57–74.

[35] Robert Brinsmead, "The Scandal of God's Justice-Part 1," *The Christian Verdict, Essay 3,* 1983, 8; cited by Caleb Heppner, "A Covenantal View of Atonement," *The Paul Page*, accessed 10/9/2005, http://www.thepaulpage.com/#Articles.

[36] Hill, *Greek Words and Hebrew Meanings*, 141.

[37] See Don Garlington, "Imputation or Union with Christ? A Response to John Piper," Evangelical Union Symposium on Atonement,2005,1;http://www.eauk.org/contentmanager/content/acute/acute.cfm, Accessed 9/30/2005 (no longer available).

[38] Richardson, *Theology of the New Testament*, 82.

[39] Gottfried Quell and Gottlob Schrenk, "Righteousness," *TDNT* 1, ed. Gerhard Kittell; trans. and ed. by Geoffrey W. Bromiley (Grand Rapids: Wm. B. Eerdmans Publishing Co., 1964), 1:207.

[40] George E. Ladd, *A Theology of the New Testament*(Grand Rapids: Wm. B. Eerdmans, 1974), 438; see Wilhelm Wrede, *Paul* (London: P. Green, 1907; American Theological Library Association, 1962), 123; also, Albert Schweitzer, *The Mysticism of Paul the Apostle* (New York: The Seabury Press, 1968), 225, 226; and W.D. Davies, *Paul and Rabbinic Judaism* (London: S.P.C.K., 1962), 222.

[41] James S. Stewart, *A Man in Christ* (London: Hodder and Stoughton, 1964), 204–272.

[42] C. A. A. Scott, *Christianity According to St. Paul* (Cambridge: University Press, 1961), 16; A.M. Hunter, *The Gospel According to St. Paul* (Philadelphia: The Westminster Press,1966), 14.

[43] Ladd, *Theology of the New Testament*, 438.

[44] Ralph P. Martin, *Reconciliation: A Study of Paul's Theology* (Grand Rapids: Academie Books, 1989), 36–37.

[45] E. P. Sanders, *Paul and Palestinian Judaism* (Philadelphia: Fortr ess Press, 1987), 434, 508; see pages 431–523 for an extensive review of scholarship related to justification and righteousness studies to his publication date and a very helpful discussion of the participatory emphasis.

[46] Ibid., 525.

[47] Quell and Schrenk, "Righteousness," *TDNT* 1, 1:207–209.

[48] James Denney, *The Christian Doctrine of Reconciliation* (New York: Doran, 1918), 164.

[49] Sanders, *Paul and Palestinian Judaism*, 544; Ziesler, *Meaning of Righteousness*, 208, 209.

[50] Quell and Schrenk,"Righteousness," *TDNT* 1:207–209.

[51] Paul Fiddes, *Past Event and Present Salvation: The Christian Idea of Atonement* (Louisville: Westminster, John Knox Press, 1989), 86–87; see Quell and Schrenck, "Righteousness," 1:202–207. In the Old Testament, acquittal of the wicked is forbidden (Ex. 23:7; Prov. 17:15; Isa. 5:23).

[52] See Ladd, *Theology of the New Testament*, 440.

[53] Jocz, *The Covenant*, 122, 170. See Karl Barth, "Jesus, Man for Other Men," *Church Dogmatics*, vol, III/2, 45, 1, ed. G.W. Bromiley and T.F. Torrance (Edinburgh: T. & T. Clark, 1960), 203, 204; also, Dietrich Bonhoeffer, *Chrst the Center*, intro. Edwin H. Robertson and trans. John Bowden (New York: Harper and Row, 1966), 114–116.

[54] Hartmut Gese, *Essays on Biblical Theology*, trans. Keith Crim (Minneapolis: Augsburg, 1981), 106.

[55] E. P. Sanders, *Paul and Palestinian Judaism* (Philadelphia: Fortress Press, 1987), 467–469.

[56] Sanders, *Paul and Palestinian Judaism*, 503, 507, 508.

[57] Gese, *Essays on Biblical Theology*, 97, 98.

[58] See Chapter Five on sacrificial identification vs. transference.

[59] Otfried Hofius, "Atonement and Reconciliation: On the Pauline Understanding of Jesus' Death on the Cross," unpublished translation of Daniel P. Bailey from Hofius, "Sühne und Versöhnung: Zum paulinischen Verständnis des Kreuztodes Jesu" (1983), 5–21, in idem, *Paulusstudien*, Wissenschaftliche Untersuchungen zum Neuen Testament 51 (Tübingen: Mohr Siebeck, 1989), 33–49.

[60] Jocz, *The Covenant*, 126.

[61] Hofius, "Atonement and Reconciliation," 19 (my italics).

[62] Paul Fiddes, *Past Event and Present Salvation* (Louisville: Westminster/John Knox, 1989), 91.

[63] Ibid.

[64] Morna Hooker, "Did the Use of Isaiah 53 to Interpret His Mission Begin with Jesus?" in *Jesus and the Suffering Servant: Isaiah 53 and Christian Origins*, ed. William H. Bellinger Jr. and William R. Farmer (Harrisburg, PA: Trinity Press International, 1998), 96–98.

[65] Ibid., 102; she emphasizes Rom. 4:25 and 5:12–21 where Paul shows that as the trespass of Adam led many to sin and die, so the grace of God in Christ made them *righteous.*

[66] *Metonymy*: A figure of speech in which one word or phrase is substituted for another with which it is closely associated, as in the use of *Washington* for *the United States government* or of *the sword* for *military power.* Excerpted from *The American Heritage Dictionary of the English Language, Third Edition* (Boston: Houghton Mifflin Company, 1992).

[67] Hooker, "Use of Isaiah 53," 102.

[68] Gese, *Essays on Biblical Theology*, 106. Otfried Hofius, "The Fourth Servant Song in the New Testament Letters," in *The Suffering Servant:Isaiah 53 in Jewish and Christian Sources,* ed. Bernd Janowski and Peter Stuhlmacher, trans. Daniel P. Bailey (Grand Rapids: Eerdmans, 2004, 164–174.

[69] Richard H. Bell, "Sacrifice and Christology in Paul," *Journal of Theological Studies* vol. 53, (1, 2002), 14–17.

[70] Fiddes, 108.

[71] Shelton, "Justification in the Pauline Corpus," 1, 117; in footnote no. 80, p. 131 of this chapter I note that "the distinction between the believer and Christ is maintained. The 'union with Christ' terms are metaphorical and not ontological. Further, the use of the term *mystical* to describe this relationship is totally misleading and unacceptable. Its connotations of ontological and metaphysical union and loss of identity are not appropriate for describing the Christian's relationship to Christ."

[72] Hofius, "Atonement and Reconciliation," 20–22. See Gese, *Essays on Biblical Theology*, 114–116. Hofius also notes that this metonymy is recognized by Martin Luther in his exposition of Gal. 3:13 where he describes the identification of the crucified Christ with the *person* of the sinner. See the American edition of *Luther's Works*, vol. 26, *Lectures on Galatians 1535*, ed. J. Pelikan (St. Louis: Concordia, 1963), 287–289.

[73] P. P. Waldenström, *The Reconciliation*, trans. J. G. Princell (New York: John Martenson, Publisher, 1888), 8, 10–12.

[74] James Dunn, *The Theology of Paul the Apostle* (Grand Rapids: Eerdmans, 1998), 228–229.

[75] T.W. Manson, *On Paul and John*, ed. M. Black (Naperville, IL: A.R. Allenson, 1963), 50 (italics his); cited by Ralph P. Martin, *Reconciliation: A Study of Paul's Theology* (Grand Rapids: Academie Books, 1989), 4.

[76] Robin Collins, "Girard and Atonement: An Incarnational Theory of Mimetic Participation," *Violence Renounced*, ed. Willard Swartley (Telford, PA: Pandora Press, 2000), 145–146.

[77] Martin, *Reconciliation*, 12, 70–72.

[78] Ibid., 97.

[79] Ibid., 5, 9–31.

[80] Waldenström, *Reconciliation,* 70–85; Waldenström's classic exposition of reconciliation shows the centrality of this biblical concept for salvation. His careful reading of the text opens areas of theological reflection that are most fruitful for understanding the covenant interpersonal relationship as a key for interpreting the atonement.

[81] James S. Stewart, *A Man in Christ: The Vital Elements of St. Paul's Religion* (London: Hodder and Stoughton, 1964), 147. His extensive development of the theme of union with Christ is among the most thorough treatments of the implications of the atonement of Christ for the life of the believing community, particularly in the chapter on "Mysticism and Morality."

[82] Ibid., 151.

[83] Ibid., 152.

[84] Ibid.

[85] Ibid., 153, 154.

[86] Sanders, *Paul and Palestinian Judaism*, 434–514. Sanders presents an extended exposition of the participation/union with Christ idea and a discussion of relevant passages in this section on Paul's theology. See also Shelton, "Sanctification in Romans Chapter 6." This union with Christ concept is exegeted and developed extensively in this unpublished thesis (available through the library of Asbury Theological Seminary, Wilmore, KY.)

[87] Zeisler, J. A. *The Meaning of Righteousness in Paul* (Cambridge: University Press, 1972), 164–168; Shelton, *Sanctification in Romans Chaper 6,* 46–66.

[88] Sanders, *Paul and Palestinian Judaism*, 502 (my italics).

[89] Ibid., 434–435, 514. Sanders' extensive review of Paul's participation emphasis in comparison with the more traditional forensic views is extremely helpful. His argument that the incorporation into the body of Christ is a more central theme than the German scholars have been willing to admit is convincingly and thoroughly presented. See the very important discussion in pages 434–514.

[90] Of the major Bible translations, only the New International Version uses the word "penalty"as the description of the sin offerings (*chattath*) in Lev. 5:6, 7, and 15. At no other place in the Bible is the term "penalty" used in relation to the issue of atonement, nor is *chattath* used to mean penalty in the Bible. A sacrifice is *not* a penalty, it is an obedient gift of faith.

[91] Hartmut Gese, *Essays on Biblical Theology,* trans. by Keith Crim (Minneapolis, 1981), 116.

[92] Waldenström, *Reconciliation,* 76.

[93] Alan Richardson, *An Introduction to the Theology of the New Testament* (New York: Harper and Row, 1958), 34–36.

[94] See Shelton, "Initial Salvation," 492, for a more extensive discussion on reconciliation as a cessation of hostilities between humanity and God and a restoration to fellowship.

[95] Richardson, *Theology of New Testament,* 34–36.

[96] Ibid.

[97] Shelton, 496; for further development of this topic, see also, Bert H. Hall, "The Pauline Doctrine of Sanctification," in *An Inquiry into Soteriology from a Biblical Theological Perspective,* 5 vols., ed. R. Larry Shelton and John E. Hartley (Anderson, IN: Warner Press, 1981), 133–154; also see R. Larry Shelton, "Sanctification in Romans Chapter Six," Th.M. thesis, Asbury Theological Seminary, Wilmore, KY, 1968.

[98] William M. Greathouse, "Sanctification and the Christus Victor Motif in Wesleyan Theology," *Wesleyan Theological Journal* 7, No. 1, Spring 1972, 47–59.

[99] Bernhard W. Anderson, *Contours of Old Testament Theology* (Minneapolis: Fortress, 1999), 120–121.

[100] Dan P. Bailey, "Jesus as the Mercy Seat: The Semantics and Theology of Paul's Use of *Hilasterion* in Romans 3:25" (Ph.D. dissertation, Cambridge University, 2001), 216.

[101] Joseph A Fitzmyer, *Romans,* in *The Anchor Bible* 33 (New York: Doubleday, 1992), 349; Ziesler, *Paul's Letter to the Romans,* 115–116. Others disagree: Simon Gathercole,"Romans 3:25–26: An Exegetical Study," Evangelical Union Atonement Symposium, July 2005, 1–6. Available at http//:www.eauk.org/theology/atonement/. Also, the text note on 3:25 in the NIV lists "propitiation" as an alternate reading.

[102] Fitzmyer, *Romans,* 343–54. In contrast, Gathercole, and others, such as Douglas Moo, contend that Rom. 3:26 provides a context of God's rendering justice for past sins that were "passed over" by including the penalty for those sins in the penalty now visited upon Christ. Douglas Moo, *The NIV Application Commentary:Romans* (Grand Rapids: Zondervan, 2000), 128–130.

[103] Bailey, 214.

[104] Ibid. In the entire dissertation Bailey exhibits a thorough study of the literature and critically analyzes a variety of interpretations before reaching his conclusions.

[105] Dan Bailey, personal correspondence, Jan. 25, 2001.

[106] John E. Hartley, *Word Biblical Commentary: Leviticus,* vol. 4, ed. David Hubbard and Glenn Barker (Dallas: Word, 1992), 245.

[107] Ibid.

[108] Ibid., 221.

[109] Gathercole, "Romans 3.25–26."

[110] Fitzmyer, *Romans,* 353.

[111] Gathercole, "Romans 3:25–26."

[112] Gese, *Essays on Biblical Theology,* 115.

[113] See chapter five of the present book for development of this idea.

[114] Hartley, *Leviticus,* 245. Hartley summarizes in detail how Jesus fulfills each of the particular Old Testament sacrifices, including the role of the scapegoat.

[115] Shelton, "Sanctification in Romans Chapter 6." This study analyzes the servant and baptism metaphors in Romans 6 in order to show the interpersonal aspects of union with Christ in faith and the ethical expectations growing out of this faith-union.

[116] Waldenström, *Reconciliation,* 59–65.

[117] Larry McShane, (Associated Press), "People Push For Sainthood For Priest Who Died Sept. 11," *The Oregonian,* December 26, 2002, A4. It should be noted, however, the technical meaning of "sacrifice" involves a great deal more than self-giving for others.

[118] George Smeaton, *The Doctrine of the Atonement* (Edinburgh: T. & T. Clark, 1868), 200–203, 207.

[119] Dwight Van Winkle, "Christianity and Zionism," *Journal of the Irish Christian Study Centre* 2 (1984): 44.

[120] For a more thorough development of the concept of justification, see Shelton, "Justification in the Pauline Corpus," 97–132.

[121] On the issue of salvation in Hebrews, see Wayne McCown, "Such a Great Salvation," in *An Inquiry into Soteriology from a Biblical Theological Perspective* , vol. 1, Wesleyan Theological Perspectives (Anderson, IN: Warner Press, 1980),169–194.

[122] Shelton, "Sanctification in Romans Chapter Six," 46–66. Salvation, in turn, is little more than humanity's gaining a new attitude toward the world: harmony, peace of mind, and self-realization

CHAPTER 8

[1] H. D. McDonald, *The Atonement of the Death of Christ: In Faith, Revelation, and History* (Grand Rapids: Baker, 1985), 6–7 (Contents).

[2] Ibid., 27–31. McDonald begins with the penal theory as his presupposition and critiques all the other historical theories from the perspective of how they measure up (or fail to measure up) to the penal theory in various ways. While other views may have benefits, he sees the penal view as the determinative criterion for an adequate Christian theology.

[3] John Driver, *Understanding the Atonement for the Mission of the Church* (Scottdale, PA: Herald Press, 1986), 31–35.

[4] Bernhard Lohse, *A Short History of Christian Doctrine,* trans. F. Ernest Stoeffler (Philadelphia: Fortress Press, 1966), 41.

[5] Michael Frost and Alan Hirsch, *The Shaping of Things to Come: Innovation and Mission for the 21st-Century Church* (Peabody, MA: Hendrickson Publishers, 2003), 6. Frost and Hirsch note, "The cultures that resulted in Europe and later in North America are called Constantinian, or Christendom, or technically the *corpus Christianum.*"

[6] Ibid., 29–30. See also R. W. Southern, *Western Society and the Church in the Middle Ages* (Harmondsworth, England: Penguin Books, Ltd., 1970), 91–202.

[7] Ibid. See also Gustaf Aulén, *Christus Victor,* trans. A. G. Hebert (New York: Macmillan, 1969), chapters 2, 3, and 5. Aulén's historical survey of atonement theories identifies the origins of the legal, Latin, Western penal theories in the penitential theology of Tertullian, Cyprian, and Gregory. His extremely valuable historical analysis of the doctrine is important for evaluating the penal theories, particularly in their Protestant forms.

[8] Driver, *Understanding the Atonement*, 191–192.

[9] See section on "Covenant Law" in Chapter Four.

[10] Ibid., 191.

[11] Ibid., 33.

[12] William P. Le Saint, "Tertullian, On Penitence," 2, *Tertullian: Treatises on Penance: On Penitence and On Purity,* in *Ancient Christian Writers: The Works of the Fathers in Translation,* ed. Johannes Quasten and Walter J. Burhardt (Westminster, MD: The Newman Press, and London: Longmans, Green and Co., 1959), 16–17.

[13] Ibid., 142, footnote 29.

[14] Ibid., 24 (my italics).

[15] Ibid.

[16] At this point, Tertullian is moving away from the covenantal understanding of the Law, and beginning to conceive it in terms of judicial, civil law categories that require specific legal sanctions for lawbreaking. He has begun to quantify the virtue, or "merit," attached to obedience of specific divine laws.

[17] Aulén, *Christus Victor*, 82.

[18] Ibid., 81–83.

[19] Ibid., 33–34.

[20] Kenneth Collins, *A Real Christian: The Life of John Wesley* (Nashville: Abingdon, 1999); Roland Bainton, *Here I Stand: A Life of Martin Luther* (New York: Abingdon-Cokesbury, 1950); James Atkinson, *Martin Luther and the Birth of Protestantism* (Atlanta: John Knox Press, 1981).

[21] Bruce Shelley, *Church History in Plain Language* (Waco: Word, 1982), 450.

[22] Leonard Sweet, *Postmodern Pilgrims* (Nashville: Broadman and Holman Publishers, 2000), 85–108. See also George Hunter III, *To Spread the Power* (Nashville: Abingdon, 1987), 91–108.

[23] Driver, *Understanding the Atonement*, 192–93. This statement in no way denies the importance of sound doctrine, appropriate ecclesiastical organization, or the reality of divine retribution for sinful rebellion. It is stating that a loving image of God is more effective for evangelism in the twenty-first century than are dogmatic methods of guilt manipulation, fear, and threats of impersonal judgment.

[24] Ibid., 37.

CHAPTER 9

[1] H. F. Davis, "The Atonement," in *The Theology of the Atonement: Readings in Soteriology,* ed. John R. Sheets (Englewood Cliffs, NJ: Prentice-Hall, 1967), 11.

[2] John Driver, *Understanding the Atonement for the Mission of the Church* (Scottdale, PA: Herald Press, 1986), 40.

[3] Gustav Aulén, *Christus Victor* (New York: Macmillan, 1969), 5–6.

[4] "Athanasius," in *The Theology of the Atonement*, 56; citing *De Incarnatione*. This anthology edited by Sheets, a Catholic priest, provides an excellent perspective in understanding the modern Roman Catholic analysis of the historical development of the doctrine of atonement.

[5] Aulén, 6. See also R. Larry Shelton, "Martin Luther's Concept of Scripture in Historical Perspective" (unpublished Th.D. dissertation, Fuller Theological Seminary, 1974), 108–17; this section on the "Rise and Fall of the Medieval Synthesis" documents the characteristics of medieval Scholasticism.

[6] Aulén, 9–14.

[7] Ibid., 18–19, Irenaeus cited by Aulén.

[8] Roger Olson, *The Story of Christian Theology* (Downers Grove, IL: InterVarsity, 1999), 74.

[9] Irenaeus, *Against Heresies,* in *The Ante-Nicene Fathers*, vol. 1, ed. Alexander Roberts and James Donaldson (Grand Rapids: Eerdmans, 1956), Book V, Preface, 526.

[10] Davis, 10–13. See Irenaeus, Books II, III, and V.

[11] Aulén, 21–22.

[12] Stefan Zankov, *The Eastern Orthodox Church*, trans. Donald A. Lowrie (Milwaukee, WI: Morehouse Publishing Co., 1929), 49–50; cited by Aulen, 22–23.

[13] Irenaeus, 526–27.

[14] Olson, 76–77. This should not be interpreted in a literal sense of ontologically becoming divine.

[15] Aulén, 33; see Irenaeus, *Against Heresies*, Book III, 18, 6.

[16] Ibid., 34–35.

[17] Ibid., 36–38.

[18] Ibid., 40–41, 83.

[19] Ibid., 49–51. See also George Park Fisher, *History of Christian Doctrine* (New York: Scribner, 1902), 86, 111, 162–63, 180.

[20] In the New Testament, Matt. 20:28; Mark 10:45; 1 Tim. 2:6; Heb. 9:15 refer to "ransom."

[21] Aulén, 58–59; he cites Augustine, *De Trinitate,* in *The Nicene and Post-Nicene Fathers*, ed. Philip Schaff (Grand Rapids: Wm. B. Eerdmans Publishing Co., 1989), Book IV.

[22] R. Larry Shelton, "Initial Salvation," in *A Contemporary Wesleyan Theology*, ed. Charles W. Carter (Grand Rapids: Zondervan, 1983), 500; Fisher, *History of Christian Doctrine*, 86, 111, 162–63, 180.

[23] Aulén, 59–60.

[24] Ibid., preface by Jaroslav Pelikan, xiv–xvii.

[25] Ibid., translator's preface, A. G. Herbert, xxi–xxv.

[26] Gustaf Aulén, *The Faith of the Christian Church* (Philadelphia: The Muhlenberg Press, 1948), 228.

[27] William M. Greathouse, "Sanctification and the Christus Victor Motif in Wesleyan Theology," *Wesleyan Theological Journal* 7, no. 1 (Spring 1972): 47–59.

[28] Aulén, *Christus*, 154–56.

[29] Ibid., 156–58.

[30] Ibid., 156–157.

[31] Ibid., 145–59.

[32] H. Orton Wiley, *Christian Theology* (Kansas City, MO: Beacon Hill Press, 1952), 2:150.

[33] Aulén, *Christus*, 156–57.

[34] David Wells, *The Search for Salvation* (Downers Grove, IL: InterVarsity, 1978), 13, 18.

[35] Aulén, *Christus,* 58–60.

CHAPTER 10

[1] Paul Fiddes, *Past Event and Present Salvation: The Christian Idea of Atonement* (Louisville: Westminster/John Knox Press, 1989), 83–86.

[2] See chapter 7, notes on the "Justification" section.

[3] Gustaf Aulén, *Christus Victor,* trans. A. G. Hebert (New York: Macmillan, 1972), 78, 81–100. See Colin Gunton, *The Actuality of the Atonement: A Study of Metaphor, Rationality and the Christian Tradition* (Edinburgh: T. & T. Clark, 1988), 84–87.

[4] John Driver, *Understanding the Atonement for the Mission of the Church* (Scottdale, PA: Herald Press, 1986), 61–62.

[5] Ibid., 61.

[6] While many Protestants who do not accept a limited atonement view do believe in a penal substitution understanding of atonement, the point here is that it is logically difficult to hold the two together. This is the reason for Wesley's ambivalence about the penal view. See section below, "Analysis of Wesley."

[7] Vincent Taylor, *Jesus and His Sacrifice* (London: The Macmillan Co., 1959), 50.

[8] Fiddes, *Past Event,* 96; H. D. McDonald, *The Atonement of the Death of Christ: In Faith, Revelation, and History* (Grand Rapids: Baker, 1985), 163–164.

[9] McDonald, 154–55.

[10] Eugene R. Fairweather, trans. and ed., *A Scholastic Miscellany: Anselm to Ockham,* The Library of Christian Classics, vol. X (Philadelphia: Westminster Press, 1956), 47–48.

[11] Anselm, "Why God Became Man," in Fairweather, *Scholastic Miscellany,* 119.

[12] Arthur Pollard, "Anselm's Doctrine of the Atonement: An Exegesis and Critique of *Cur Deus Homo,*" in *Churchman,* Vol. 109, no. 4, (1995), 305–307.

[13] Ibid., 312.

[14] Anselm, "Why God Became Man," in Fairweather, *Scholastic Miscellany,* 178–181.

[15] Anselm, *Cur Deus Homo,* I, 12, *Saint Anselm: Basic Writings,* trans. S. N. Deane (La Salle, IL: Open Court Publishing Co., 1962), 203.

[16] Ibid., I, 12, 204.

[17] Ibid., I, 12 , 206.

[18] Ibid., I, 12, 206–7. See also R. Larry Shelton, "Initial Salvation," in *A Contemporary Wesleyan Theology,* ed. Charles Carter (Grand Rapids: Zondervan, 1983), 500.

[19] Ibid., II, 4, 6.

[20] R. W. Southern, *Saint Anselm: A Portrait in a Landscape* (New York: Cambridge University Press, 1990), 225–26.

[21] Colin Gunton, *The Actuality of the Atonement* (Grand Rapids: Eerdmans, 1989), 90–93.

[22] Gunton, 124–25.

[23] Ibid., 92; see Anselm, *Cur Deus Homo,* (I, 21; II, 4 and 16).

[24] Driver, *Understanding the Atonement,* 58–59.

[25] Gunton, 93.

[26] Anselm, II, 18.

[27] Fiddes, *Past Event,* 99.

[28] James Denney, *The Christian Doctrine of Reconciliation* (New York: Doran, 1918), 75; see Pollard, "Anselm's Doctrine of Atonement," 307.

[29] H. F. Davis, "The Atonement," in *The Theology of the Atonement: Readings in Soteriology,* ed. John R. Sheets (Englewood Cliffs, NJ: Prentice-Hall, 1967), 20.

[30] Fiddes, 96–111. Note Fiddes' comparative analysis of the weaknesses of the forensic categories of Anselm and Calvin, 96–111.

[31] See the extensive treatment of the Satisfaction concept in McDonald, *The Atonement,* 163–73. Also, an excellent exegesis of Anselm's theory is provided by Pollard, "Anselm's Doctrine of the Atonement."

[32] McDonald, *The Atonement,* 184.

[33] Paul Althaus, *The Theology of Martin Luther* (Philadelphia: Fortress Press, 1966), 202–4. Althaus cites numerous passages from the German Weimar edition of Luther's *Works* (*WA*) in which the term is used. Luther felt that "satisfaction" was not adequate to carry the full significance of Christ's work, but it is an essential part of it (see Althaus' footnotes).

[34] McDonald, *The Atonement,* 184.

[35] Althaus, *Theology of Martin Luther,* 202, citing *WA* 10 (III), 49 and *Luther's Works,* 51, 92.

[36] Ibid., 204–7.

[37] Gerhard O. Forde, *Where God Meets Man* (Minneapolis: Augsburg, 1972), 32–44.

[38] Althaus, *Theology of Martin Luther,* 210–11.

[39] Ibid., 214.

[40] John Drury, "Luther and Wesley on Union and Impartation in Light of Recent Finnish Luther Research," *Wesleyan Theological Journal* 40, no. 1 (Spring 2005): 58–68.

[41] Alister McGrath, *Christian Theology: An Introduction* (Oxford: Blackwell, 1997), 442.

[42] L. W. Grensted, *A Short History of the Doctrine of the Atonement* (Manchester: Manchester University Press, repr. ed., 1962), 191–207.

[43] Robert Peterson, *Calvin's Doctrine of the Atonement* (Phillipsburg, NJ: Presbyterian and Reformed Publishing Co., 1983), 1.

[44] Ibid., 2–3; Peterson cites Calvin's commentary on Eph. 3:18. Calvin's *Commentaries* are available online through *Christian Classics Ethereal Library*: http://www.ccel.org/c/calvin/.

[45] Ibid., 2; Peterson cites Calvin's commentary on 1 John 4:9.

[46] John Calvin, *Institutes of the Christian Religion, The Library of Christian Classics*, vol. XX ,ed. John T. McNeill, trans. Ford Lewis Battles (Philadelphia: Westminster, 1960), II, 12, 2.

[47] Ibid., III, 21, 5–7; see Peterson, *Calvin's Doctrine*, 6, footnote 24.

[48] Peterson, *Calvin's Doctrine*, 11–23; Calvin, *Institutes*, II, 12–17.

[49] Peterson, C*alvin's Doctrine*, 19; see Calvin's commentaries on Luke 1:35; Luke 2:40; Matt. 8:3; John 11:33; Rom. 8:3; and Heb. 4:15.

[50] Ibid., 30–31; see Calvin, *Institutes*, II 15, 2, and commentaries on Luke 24:32; Rom. 8:15; Matt. 15:23; Luke 24:17; and John 5:25.

[51] Ibid., 32–33; see Calvin, *Institutes*, II, 15, 3, and 5.

[52] Ibid., 34, footnote 38; the citation shows how the uniqueness of Christ compares to the Old Testament priesthood.

[53] Calvin, *Institutes*, I, 15, 6.

[54] Ibid.

[55] Peterson, *Calvin's Doctrine*, 36–39.

[56] Ibid., 55.

[57] Ibid., 40–45.

[58] Ibid., 46–47. Peterson cites Calvin's commentaries on John 13:31 and Eph. 4:8. See also Calvin's commentaries on John 19:30 and Mark 1:21.

[59] Calvin, *Institutes*, II, 12, 3.

[60] Ibid., II, 7, 13.

[61] Peterson, *Calvin's Doctrine*, 55–56; see Calvin, *Institutes*, II, 7, 3, and commentary on Gal. 3:10.

[62] Calvin, *Institutes*, II, 16, 1.

[63] Peterson, *Calvin's Doctrine*, 56–57; see Calvin's commentaries on Rom. 6:14 and Gal. 4:4.

[64] Calvin, *Institutes*, II, 17, 5.

[65] Ibid., II, 16, 5.

[66] Peterson, *Calvin's Doctrine*, 72–73; see Calvin, *Institutes*, II, 17, 1.

[67] Calvin, *Institutes*, II, 17, 3.

[68] Ibid., II, 17, 4–5.

[69] Carl Mosser, "The Greatest Possible Blessing: Calvin and Deification," *Scottish Journal of Theology* 55, no. 1 (2002): 36–57. See Calvin, *Institutes*, I, 15, 4; II, 2, 1; II, 15, 5; IV, 15, 6.

[70] Grensted, *Short History of the Atonement*, 284–85; Shelton, "Initial Salvation," 502.

[71] Randy Maddox, *Responsible Grace* (Nashville: Abingdon, 1994), 108.

[72] James Arminius (1560–1609) was a Dutch theologian who rejected the Calvinist doctrine of predestination in favor of a view of a free will enabled by grace. His position was widely declared heretical and his positions condemned by the Synod of Dort in 1619. These criticisms were often grossly distorted and overstated. A more objective explanation of his views is presented by Roger Olson, *The Story of Christianity: Twenty*

Centuries of Tradition and Reform (Downers Grove, IL.: InterVarsity Press, 1999), 454–472. A useful website entry is by Vic Reasoner, "James Arminius the Scapegoat of Calvinism," at: http://www.imarc.cc/esecurity/arminius.html.

[73] Grensted, *Short History of the Atonement*, 291–97; Shelton, "Initial Salvation," 502–3; H. Ray Dunning, *Grace, Faith, and Holiness* (Kansas City, MO: Beacon Hill Press, 1988), 337.

[74] Maddox, *Responsible Grace,* 108.

[75] Frank H. Foster, "A Brief Introductory Sketch of the History of the Grotian Theory of the Atonement," in the preface to Hugo Grotius, *A Defence of the Catholic Faith Concerning the Satisfaction of Christ, Against Faustus Socinus*, trans. Frank H. Foster (Andover, England: W. F. Draper, 1889).

[76] Cited by Grensted, *Short History of the Atonement*, 300; Grensted quotes from Stephanus Curcellaeus' *Institutes*, V, 19.15.

[77] Shelton, "Initial Salvation," 503.

[78] Richard Watson, *Theological Institutes*, 2 vols. (New York: Carlton & Phillips, 1856), 2:139; see also 2:87–102, 113, 149–51. William Burt Pope, *A Compendium of Christian Theology*, 2 vols. (London: Wesleyan Conference Office, 1880), 2:265, 313–14; Wilbur F. Tillett, *Personal Salvation* (Nashville: Cokesbury Press, 1930), 98–109. See the discussion in Shelton, "Initial Salvation," 504.

[79] H. Orton Wiley, *Christian Theology*, 3 vols. (Kansas City, MO: Beacon Hill Press, 1952), 2:221, 225.

[80] Ibid., 226.

[81] Wiley is referring to "penal substitution" here.

[82] Ibid., 245–49.

[83] Ibid., 258.

[84] Ibid., 275.

[85] Dunning, *Grace, Faith, and Holiness*, 336–37. See also Foster, "Introductory Sketch of the Grotian Theory."

[86] Kenneth J. Collins, *The Scripture Way of Salvation* (Nashville: Abingdon, 1997), 80; Collins here cites Wesley, *Letters*, ed. John Telford, 8 vols. (London: Epworth Press, 1931), 6:297–98. See also Dunning, *Grace, Faith and Holiness*, 332.

[87] John Wesley, *Explanatory Notes upon the New Testament* (London: Epworth Press, repr. ed., 1966), 837 (Heb. 9:8) and 879 (1 Peter 2:24).

[88] Dunning, *Grace, Faith, and Holiness,* 333; see notes 4 and 5.

[89] John Wesley, "Salvation By Faith," *The Works of John Wesley, Sermons*, vol. 1, ed. Albert C. Outler (Nashville: Abingdon, 1984), 121. See also the sermons "The Righteousness of Faith" and "The Lord Our Righteousness" in the same volume. For a very useful treatment of Wesley's doctrine of salvation, see Kenneth Collins, "A Hermeneutical Model for the Wesleyan *Ordo Salutis ,*" *The Wesleyan Theological Journal* 19, no. 2 (Fall 1984).

[90] Collins, *Scripture Way*, 81–83; in notes 64 and 65 on p. 81, Collins cites Wesley's use of the language of the Book of Common Prayer in his liturgical and preaching resources.

[91] Ibid., 84–85.

[92] John Wesley, *Works of John Wesley,, Letters,* vol. XIII, (Grand Rapids: Baker, 1978), 34–35.

[93] Collins, *Scripture Way*, 85; he cites Wesley's "The Principles of a Methodist," see footnote 83. In this section on "The Atonement," Collins has usefully cited numerous relevant quotations on the topic from Wesley's works.

[94] For an extensive analysis of Wesley's concept of "prophet, priest, and king" as an atonement model, see John Deschner, *Wesley's Christology* (Dallas: Southern Methodist University Press, 1960), 74, 165; Maddox, *Responsible Grace,* 110–14; Collins, *Scripture Way*, 44–44; Dunning, *Grace, Faith, and Holiness*, 367–90.

[95] Wesley, *Works of John Wesley, Sermons,* vol. VII, (Grand Rapids: Baker, 1978), 513, 554. See Leon Hynson, *To Reform the Nation: Theological Foundations of Wesley's Ethics* (Grand Rapids: Francis Asbury Press, 1984), 75. While Wesley held the Reformation theology view of original sin and loss of the divine image, his view of "a pessimism of nature, but an optimism of grace" affirmed the restoration of the image of God in sanctification.

[96] Hynson, *To Reform the Nation*, 75.

[97] A. S. Wood, *The Burning Heart* (Grand Rapids: Eerdmans, 1967), 237–239. See also William R. Cannon, *The Theology of John Wesley* (Nashville: Abingdon, 1956), 209–11; and Albert Outler, *John Wesley* (New York: Oxford University Press, 1964), 273, 276, 287–88. Such a position is inherently contradictory. The penal theory is *based* on an unalterable order of justice. Wesley's view is eclectic and more governmental than penal. It involves elements of Anselmic, penal, and governmental views, and he does not consistently develop his views theoretically. He stresses why the death of Christ was needed to achieve the salvation of humanity, not how the atonement functions.

[98] Maddox, *Responsible Grace,* 104, see footnote 63. Maddox notes that Wesley rejected the imputation of Christ's active righteousness or obedience to believers because it discouraged the seeking of holiness. He speaks to this in his sermon "The Lord Our Righteousness," *Works of John Wesley,* I:449–65.

[99] Dunning, *Grace, Faith, and Holiness*, 333–34. Dunning cites extensive resources listed in John Rutherford Renshaw, "The Atonement in the Theology of John and Charles Wesley," (unpublished Ph.D. dissertation, Boston University, 1965).

[100] God desires intimacy of relationship with humanity as was expressed through the *imago Dei* at creation. The loving, meaningful relationships of family and redemptive community grow out of the intimacy of our experience of God's redemptive love expressed through the empowerment and holiness of the Holy Spirit's ministry.

[101] Calvin, *Institutes,* II, 12, 3. See also his commentaries on John 19:17, Rom. 8:3, and Matt. 16, noted in Peterson, *Calvin's Doctrine*, 66–67. In the commentary on 1 John 2:1, Calvin describes Christ as "the price of satisfaction," thus using commercial or legal terminology to describe the sacrifice. He also defines Christ's sacrificial work in terms of appeasement, rather than as obedience and reconciliation. He notes that in the sacrifice of Christ God was reconciled to humanity by the appeasement of his wrath, contrary to the biblical emphasis that humanity is reconciled to God.

[102] Replacing covenant-interpersonal understandings of the Law with exclusively civil categories, the scholars of Protestant orthodoxy, such as Melanchthon, Quenstedt, and Turretin, who followed the Reformers, expanded the legal penal view and largely ignored the balancing perspectives of interpersonal covenant relationships, cosmic victory, recapitulation, and moral example that Calvin himself observed. Justice came to be seen

as exclusively retributive and transactional, with its demands being met only on penal terms.

[103] Peterson, *Calvin's Doctrine,* 57; see Calvin's commentary on Matthew 3:15.

[104] Calvin, *Institutes,* III, 11, 2.

[105] Ibid., II, 16, 11 (brackets by editor).

[106] Grensted, *Short History of the Atonement,* 216–17.

[107] Calvin, *Institutes,* II, 17, 5.

[108] Grensted, *Short History of the Atonement,* 210–19. See also the discussion of these theories in Shelton, "Initial Salvation," 54–66.

[109] Calvin, *Institutes,* II, 17, 3; see Peterson, *Calvin's Doctrine*, 73–75.

[110] McDonald, *The Atonement,* 163–68, 183. See the American edition of *Luther's Works,* vol. 26, *Lectures on Galatians 1535,* ed. J. Pelikan (St. Louis: Concordia, 1963), 323.

[111] McDonald, Ibid., 192–93.

[112] Ibid. An example of a Reformed defense of this limited atonement position is the rather scholastic apologetic of McDonald in the appendix to his very extensive treatment of this doctrine. As is often the case, he consigns those who do not accept a penal and predestinarian conclusion to what he considers to be the pejorative categories of "Arminian" or "Amyraldian" theology. His epistemological structure is so inflexibly established in the logic of the Aristotelian, Augustinian, and forensic categories that he cannot conceive of the legitimacy of a mediating position. The pastoral concern here is that the postmodern audience has no interest in his epistemology, nor in his apologetic nuances. They do not consider it impious to question the justice of a divine Being who can capriciously (from their perspective) consign some persons to salvation and others to damnation without their having any choice in the matter. Such logic is, for them, injustice by definition.

[113] In the Mel Gibson film, *The Passion of the Christ,* the observant viewer sees this anomaly vividly displayed. While the Jewish charge against Christ seems to be based on blasphemy (theological), the actual charge applied to Christ is sedition (political). The general injustice of the entire situation of his crucifixion is diametrically opposed to the ordered and faith-based actions of the offering of sacrifices in Israel (Lev. 1–7; 16–17). If Christ's death is intended by God to be analogous to a sacrificial sin offering expiating or propitiating humanity's sin by payment of a just penalty, as Gibson seems to affirm, then how is an unjust death of the righteous God-man to be understood as a repentant and faith-based sacrifice that pays a just penalty when it is not carried out liturgically in the context of a righteous covenant ceremony, but in a manifestly unjust sham trial and crucifixion under secular Roman law? A covenant understanding, on the other hand, that sees this death as a voluntary participation in the human experience of suffering and brokenness can see it as an ultimate manifestation of love.

[114] Collins, *Scripture Way,* 80–86; Richard S. Taylor, *God's Integrity and the Cross* (Nappanee, IN: Evangel Press, 1999). Taylor apparently intends to answer Wesleyan theologians who have raised critical questions regarding the penal theories. However, his approach is primarily rational rather than providing a sound exegetical basis, and he tends to interpret sacrifice as forensic penalty rather than in the biblical sense of an obedient gift of worship. He also attempts to tie a doctrine of sanctification to penal substitution, which requires an interesting exegetical linking of substitionary dying with Spirit-baptism, all the while neglecting to mention the resurrection at all in his treatment of atonement.

[115] For example, Willard Swartley, ed., *Violence Renounced* (Telford, PA: Pandora Press, 2000); J. Denny Weaver, *Non-Violent Atonement* (Grand Rapids: Eerdmans, 2001); Joel Green and Mark Baker, *Recovering the Scandal of the Cross* (Downers Grove, IL: InterVarsity, 2000); Hartmut Gese, *Essays on Biblical Theology*, trans. Keith Crim (Minneapolis: Augsburg, 1981); Gerhard O. Forde, *Where God Meets Man: Luther's Down-to-Earth Approach to the Gospel* (Minneapolis: Augsburg, 1972); and Dunning, *Grace, Faith, and Holiness.*

[116] Dallas Willard, *The Divine Conspiracy* (San Francisco: Harper, 1998), 36–37.

[117] Willard, *The Divine Conspiracy*, 49; Willard extensively analyzes the implications for discipleship of the exclusively penal substitutionary view of atonement in contemporary Christianity in chapters 2, 8, and 9.

[118] Ibid., 40–49.

[119] Ibid., 50–55.

[120] Ibid., 57.

[121] One of my students listened to a radio message by a proponent of the penal substitutionary view of atonement who insisted that justification is an act of God that requires "absolutely no change in the character of the person." SooYong Song, seminary student, December, 2002.

[122] McGrath, *Christian Theology,* 390–412.

[123] Garry Williams, "Justice, Law, and Guilt?" (paper presented at the Evangelical Alliance Symposium on the Atonement, London, July 6–8, 2005; available at http://www.eauk.org/theology/atonement/).

CHAPTER 11

[1] Randy Maddox, *Responsible Grace* (Nashville: Abingdon, 1994), 106.

[2] Ibid., 106; Paul Fiddes, *Past Event and Present Salvation: The Christian Idea of Atonement* (Louisville: Westminster/John Knox Press, 1989), 139.

[3] Maddox, 103.

[4] Ibid., 142.

[5] Ibid.; see Peter Abelard, "Commentary on the Epistle to the Romans (An Excerpt from the Second Book,")," in *A Scholastic Miscellany: Anselm to Ockham,* trans. and ed. Eugene R. Fairweather, The Library of Christian Classics, vol. X (Philadelphia: Westminster Press, 1956), II, 282–283.

[6] Fiddes, *Past Event,* 143.

[7] Abelard, "Commentary on Romans," 276–84.

[8] Alister McGrath, *Christian Theology: An Introduction* (Oxford: Blackwell, 1997), 407; see critical treatment by H. D. McDonald, *The Atonement of the Death of Christ: In Faith, Revelation, and History* (Grand Rapids: Baker, 1985), 174–180.

[9] Ibid., 407–408.

[10] Fiddes, *Past Event,* 141, 153. Fiddes provides one of the most thorough and perceptive treatments of the depth of Abelard's view that is available. His entire chapter, "The Act of Love," pages 140–168, profoundly explicates the role of divine love in the entire process of salvation. This is an insight that is not adequately dealt with in most forensic understandings, and certainly not in the popular penal presentations of Christ's work.

This inadequacy of perception is exemplified in Letham's peremptory dismissal of Abelard. See Robert Letham, *The Work of Christ*, Contours of Christian Theology series, ed. Gerald Bray (Downer's Grove,IL: InterVarsity, 1993), 166–167.

[11] McGrath, *Christian Theology*, 408–412.

[12] John McLeod Campbell, *The Nature of the Atonement* (Grand Rapids: Eerdmans, 1996 reprint).

[13] H. D. McDonald, *The Atonement of the Death of Christ: In Faith, Revelation, and History* (Grand Rapids: Baker, 1985), 221–230.

[14] Ibid., 232–239.

[15] John Driver, *Understanding the Atonement for the Mission of the Church* (Scottdale, PA: Herald Press, 1986), 44–49.

[16] S. J. Gamertsfelder, *Systematic Theology* (Harrisburg, PA: Evangelical Publishing House, 1921), 305– 306.

[17] Ibid., 277.

[18] Ibid., 310, 335.

[19] P. P. Waldenström, *The Reconciliation,* trans. J. G. Princell (Chicago: John Martenson Publishers, 1888).

[20] Ibid., 5–6.

[21] Ibid., 9–11.

[22] Ibid., 11–12.

[23] Ibid., 12.

[24] Ibid., 15.

[25] Ibid., 20–21.

[26] Ibid., 21.

[27] Ibid., 22–25.

[28] Ibid., 20–27.

[29] See René Girard, *Things Hidden Since the Foundation of the World* (Stanford: Stanford University Press, 1978); Willard M. Swartley, ed., *Violence Renounced* (Telford, PA: Pandora Press, 2000).

[30] T. Scott Daniels and Marty Michelson, "Passing the Peace: Worship that Shapes Non-Substitutionary Convictions" (paper presented at the annual meeting of the Wesleyan Theological Society, Seattle, WA, (March 3–5, 2005).

[31] René Girard, "Violence and Religion: Cause or Effect," in *The Hedgehog Review* 6, No. 1 (Spring 2004), 9–12.

[32] Daniels and Michelson, 10.

[33] Ibid., 11.

[34] Ibid.

[35] Ibid., 3–4.

[36] Ibid., 5.

[37] Ibid., 16. Girard rejects the ancient mimetic-scapegoat view of sacrifice and sees in Christ's work our need to participate by mimesis in Christ's death which transforms the substitutionary scapegoat model into one of participation.

[38] Ibid., 18.

[39] Robin Collins, "Girard and Atonement: An Incarnational Theory of Mimetic Participation," in *Violence Renounced*, ed. Willard Swartley (Telford, PA: Pandora Press, 2000), 132.

[40] Ibid., 133, see footnote #2.

[41] Ibid., 137, see footnote #13.

[42] Ibid., 139–40.

[43] Ibid., 141, see footnote #31, 153.

[44] Ibid.

[45] Ibid., 142–143.

[46] Ibid., 144–145; also, on the meaning of the laying on of one hand as opposed to laying on two hands which is done only on the Day of Atonement, see the Excursus by John E. Hartley, *Word Biblical Commentary: Leviticus*, vol. 4, ed. David Hubbard and Glenn Barker (Dallas: Word, 1992), 20.

[47] Ibid., 145–146.

[48] Ibid., 146.

[49] Marlin Miller, "Girardian Perspectives and Christian Atonement," *Violence Renounced*, ed. Willard Swartley (Telford, PA: Pandora Press, 2000), 31–48.

CHAPTER 12

[1] Charles H. Kraft and Thomas N. Wisley, *Readings in Dynamic Indigeneity* (Pasadena, CA: William Carey Library, 1979); Charles H. Kraft, *Christianity in Culture: A Study in Dynamic Biblical Theologizing in Cross-Cultural Perspective* (Maryknoll, NY: Orbis Books, 1979).

[2] H. Ray Dunning, *Grace, Faith, and Holiness* (Kansas City, MO: Beacon Hill Press, 1988).

[3] Dunning, *Grace, Faith, and Holiness*, 333–34; note Dunning's references to the extensive resources listed in John Rutherford Renshaw, "The Atonement in the Theology of John and Charles Wesley" (unpublished Ph.D. dissertation, Boston University, 1965). See critical summary by H. Orton Wiley, *Christian Theology* (Kansas City, MO: Beacon Hill Press, 1964), 2:248–49: First, the basic premise of penal views is that God's primary nature is justice, which binds him to legal principles. This leads to a separation of sin from the sinner and to putting the guilt of the sinner by imputation on an innocent substitute, which is immoral. Second, the penal views see the innocent victim as taking all the punishment that is required by justice, rather than understanding Christ as our representative in the sense of his priestly work. Third, the penal theory logically leads to either universalism or limited atonement. The suffering of Christ is interpreted as *punishment*, although the biblical terminology is "suffered." Therefore, if the penalty for sin is satisfied in Christ's punishment, those for whom he died must go free. So either Christ died for all humanity universally or he died only for the elect, and thus limited atonement is the outcome. Fourth, the limited atonement option leads logically to a view of irresistible grace, which ignores the gracious work of God that is preparatory

to faith. And fifth, the penal theory eliminates the practical necessity of the doctrine of sanctification, which Wesley believed the Bible required.

[4] Ibid., 366.

[5] Ibid., 367.

[6] Ibid., 368–69.

[7] Ibid., 371.

[8] Ibid., 373.

[9] Ibid., 374.

[10] Ibid., 379. Dunning notes that even in rare cases where Paul does use *anti,* its usage carries the meaning of *huper.* He cites Vincent Taylor who notes the one exception in Paul's usage is 1 Thess. 5:10, where he uses *peri,* "on account of." See Vincent Taylor, *The Atonement in New Testament Teaching* (London: Epworth Press, 1953), 59. However, this term is essentially synonymous with *huper,* and is translated as such in more recent Greek texts. See *Bible Works Greek Text,* UBS4/Nestle-Aland 27th ed. Greek New Testament and Rahlfs' LXX (LXT), Bible Works LLC software, 1998–1999.

[11] Ibid.

[12] Ibid., 386.

[13] John Wesley, *Explanatory Notes upon the New Testament* (London: Epworth Press, repr. ed., 1966), 635 (1 Cor. 15:26).

[14] George Eldon Ladd, *Theology of the New Testament* (Grand Rapids: Eerdmans, 1974), 69.

[15] Dunning, *Grace, Faith, and Holiness,* 391–92.

[16] Ibid., 392–94; Dunning cites Ladd, *Theology of the New Testament,* 77, 205, 307–8. See also H. Ray Dunning, "Toward a Personal Paradigm for the Atonement," *Wesleyan Theological Journal* 40, no. 2 (Fall 2005), 157–68.

[17] John Wesley, "The Righteousness of Faith," *The Works of John Wesley, Sermons,* vol. 1, ed. Albert C. Outler (Nashville: Abingdon, 1984), 1.

[18] See Randy Maddox, *Responsible Grace* (Nashville: Abingdon, 1994), 119–40. Maddox thoroughly examines the free grace and transformational and therapeutic work of Wesley's understanding of the Holy Spirit's ministry. The healing of human brokenness and restoration of the divine image through grace is central to Wesley's theology.

[19] Fiddes notes the clarity of this covenant understanding: "The love of God is demonstrated finally in the death of Christ: it is because God himself undergoes the bitter depths of human experience in the cross. God . . . shows his love by enduring to the uttermost the estrangement of his own creation. This is the depth of God's identification with us." Paul Fiddes, *Past Event and Present Salvation: The Christian Idea of Atonement* (Louisville: Westminster/John Knox Press, 1989), 157.

[20] Peter Stuhlmacher, "Isaiah 53 in the Gospels and Acts," in *The Suffering Servant: Isaiah 53 in Jewish and Christian Sources,* ed. Bernd Janowski and Peter Stuhlmacher, trans. Daniel P. Bailey (Grand Rapids: Eerdmans, 2004), 152–53.

Index

265